THE **BLEAKS**

A MEMOIR **PAUL ILLIDGE**

ECW PRESS

PUBLISHED BY **ECW PRESS**
2120 Queen Street East, Suite 200
Toronto, Ontario, Canada M4E 1E2
416-694-3348 | info@ecwpress.com

Cover design: Gordon Robertson
Author photo: Michael E. Milosh
Printing: Marquis   5   4   3   2   1
PRINTED AND BOUND IN CANADA

To the best of his abilities, the author has
related experiences, places, people, and
organizations from his memories of them.
In order to protect the privacy of others,
he has, in some instances, changed the
names of certain people and details of
events and places.

**LIBRARY AND ARCHIVES CANADA
CATALOGUING IN PUBLICATION**

Illidge, Paul, author
The bleaks : a memoir / Paul Illidge.

ISBN 978-1-55022-985-1 (bound)
also issued as: 978-1-77090-574-0 (pdf);
978-1-77090-575-7 (epub)

1. Illidge, Paul. 2. Illidge, Paul
—Trials, litigation, etc.
3. Marijuana—Law and legislation
—Canada. 4. Authors,
Canadian (English)—20th century
—Biography. I. Title.

PS8567.L54Z465 2014
C813'.54   C2014-902534-3

The publication of *The Bleaks* has been generously supported by the Canada Council for
the Arts which last year invested $157 million to bring the arts to Canadians throughout
the country, and by the Ontario Arts Council (OAC), an agency of the Government of Ontario,
which last year funded 1,793 individual artists and 1,076 organizations in 232 communities
across Ontario, for a total of $52.1 million. We also acknowledge the financial support of the
Government of Canada through the Canada Book Fund for our publishing activities, and the
contribution of the Government of Ontario through the Ontario Book Publishing Tax Credit and
the Ontario Media Development Corporation.

We're all running a wild race.
— Bob Dylan, *Chronicles I*

CHAPTER ONE

LIKE A HURRICANE

"Step away from the tree! Drop the garden shears and put your hands where I can see them!"

This is the barked command of the short, paunchy man with a brown handlebar moustache, wraparound shades and a blue baseball cap who was charging across my front lawn with a Glock pistol pointed at my head. It was shortly before 7 p.m. on a warm July evening in 2007.

In beige cargo shorts, a tight-fitting white T-shirt, ankle socks and running shoes, he came to an abrupt halt about six feet away from me, the Glock now leveled at my chest, even though I'd done what he'd told me to and dropped the garden shears I'd been using to trim the drooping branches of the weeping mulberry tree in my front garden.

Though shears were not my idea of a dangerous weapon, I was reluctant to argue the point with him — not with a dozen or so other cops spilling out of the SUVs that had squealed to a stop in front of the house. Guns on their hips, wearing the same wraparound shades, blue baseball caps, white T-shirts, cargo shorts and running shoes as the guy pointing his gun at me, they snapped to it, racing over and joining two women who had positioned themselves at the foot of my driveway. In navy blue jumpsuits, black boots, shades and blue ball caps — guns on their hips as well — one of the women, whose manner suggested she was in charge, had the team fall in behind her then move up to the house.

Marching quickly, the officer in charge shouted another order and two of the male officers broke away from the group. Drawing their weapons, they rushed forward and converged on my eighteen-year-old son Nicky, who'd been busy in front of the garage vacuuming the inside of the beater Plymouth Voyager van he used for his summer landscaping business. He was listening, as I had been, to Neil Young's rock classic "Like a Hurricane," which his older brother Carson, twenty, was playing on his electric guitar in his bedroom above the garage, the window open, the amplifier on medium volume. My daughter Hannah, fifteen at the time, had gone over to her friend Holly's house several blocks away.

At first unaware of the gun-toting pair over the noise of the guitar and the vacuum, Nicky leapt back when a third officer, who had just joined the others, leaned into the van and wrestled the vacuum hose out of his hand. Standing him up, he held Nicky by the front of his T-shirt while a fourth and a fifth officer ran up, yanked Nicky's arms behind his back and handcuffed him, shouting something to the guy with his gun on me, who promptly gave the order to turn around and head for the front porch. I did so, but the second I started walking, a couple of other officers swooped in, pinned my arms behind my back in a wrist-up stress-position, and slapped the cuffs on me.

Because of the way the handcuffs had been put on, the pain in my upper arms and shoulders was sudden and excruciating, and I shifted my weight from one leg to the other, contorting my body to alleviate it, only to have the officer with his gun on me shout, "Stand still!" I did, but turned, in spite of his menacing tone and the rapidly worsening shoulder pain, so I could see what was happening to Nicky over in the driveway.

The rest of the stern-faced squad hovered behind the officer in charge, who said something to her female counterpart — a woman whom I judged to be in her mid- to late-thirties, a brunette ponytail sticking out of the back of her blue ball cap — then broke away from the three officers holding Nicky and marched up the front walk to where I was standing.

"Paul David Illidge?"

"That's right."

"I have a warrant to search your house, Mr. Illidge."

"And why would you be doing that?"

"Is there marijuana in your house, Mr. Illidge?"

"You want to search my house for marijuana . . ."

"We do."

"Can I ask for some identification?"

"I think you know who we are."

"Right," I said. "I guess the running shoes, shorts and T-shirts should have given it away."

Not appreciating the humour, the woman threw me a sarcastic smirk, casually reached behind her, plucked a folded piece of paper out of her back pocket — what I assumed was a search warrant — and held it up, standing about five feet away from me and making no effort to move closer.

"That doesn't do me much good," I said.

The smirk giving way to a peeved scowl, she flicked her wrist so the paper unfolded: a faxed copy of an official-looking document, too far away for me to read the fine print, though I could just make out a signature, presumably a judge's, scrawled in black pen in the bottom right-hand corner of the page. Below it were the only words I was able to distinguish clearly: *Newmarket, Ontario*. Why a judge from a town thirty miles to the north would be signing a search warrant on a house in Toronto was beyond me, but I wasn't in a position to quibble.

Legalities taken care of, the officer refolded her warrant, slipped it in her back pocket and turned quickly to the squad, calling out a couple of names. Two of the male cops scooted forward and, pulling their guns out of their holsters, scampered quickly up the stoop onto the porch and posted themselves on either side of the front door. Their faces tense and wary, one officer two-handed his gun to cover his partner, who crouched down fast, put his hand on the brass door-handle and yelled, "Go!" as he threw it open. He shot to his feet and two-handed his gun while the other guy raised his. Nodding to each other, the two of them disappeared inside.

The cop in charge immediately ordered everyone else to head in. The raiding party streamed forward on the double, hustled across the porch and raced into the house. Two guys with black steel battering rams about the size of bazookas leaned them against the wall beside the mailbox before scooting inside after the others.

"Okay!" said the guy covering me. He jabbed the barrel

in my back and told me to get moving. Up the stoop, onto the porch and into the front hall we went, just in time for me to call to the two cops who'd gone in first, who were just reaching the top of the curving staircase, crouched down, intent looks on their faces as they signaled to one another and trained their weapons on Carson's bedroom door.

"My other son's playing guitar in there!" I shouted up to them, though I knew there wasn't a chance they'd hear me with "Like a Hurricane" wailing from Carson's amplifier and the police on the main floor deploying noisily around the house, shouting their location and tactical details to the female cop in charge, standing a few feet away from me in the front hall now, hollering confirmations and shouting back further instructions.

The guy with his gun on me poked it in my back again, directing me into the living room. He yelled something I couldn't quite hear and, with the gun barrel still firmly in my back, finally screamed into my ear that I should take a seat on the couch — at which point another cop brought Nicky into the living room at gunpoint and made him sit down beside me.

The two cops holstered their Glocks and stood together off to the side of the couch with their legs spread apart, their arms crossed, their eyes zeroing in on Nicky and me.

Nicky gave me a frantic look, wondering what was going on with Carson. He had his answer a second later when, after a high-pitched burst of feedback, the guitar went silent. "That'll be the cops that went upstairs to get him —"

"Oh, shit!" Nicky said.

"— with their guns out."

Maybe it was a defence against the anger, or shock due to the nightmare-quality terror of what was happening, but a sense of detachment came over me as I sat there. I remember feeling like I was perched on the wall near the ceiling, looking at what was going on down below — like a spectator watching actors in a performance — only in this one, my sons and I were playing ourselves.

There was no sign of Carson for the next few minutes. A late-arriving officer drifted into the front hall and made his way through the pandemonium. He wasn't dressed in leisure-wear like the others. I imagined he was a cop too, but he moved in a casual, almost relaxed manner and had the viewfinder of a video camera pressed to his right eye, a broad smile on his face as he glided past the living room, slowing long enough to glance in and shout at Nicky and me: "You'll never live in *this* house again, boys!" sounding almost gleeful at the prospect. "No *sir*. This house is *gone*, baby!" And with the camera rolling, he strolled off down the hall toward the kitchen. One of the cargo shorts officers, leaning against the door of the computer room with his hands in his pockets, watched him go. "No *sir*, baby," he said, echoing his colleague. "*This* little grow-show is *over*." Whereupon he laughed, looked over and made eye contact with the officer in charge.

A cellphone to her ear, her wraparound shades propped up on the bill of her blue ball cap now, she snickered at the "grow-show" comment. From the way the other cops had been addressing her, I gathered her name was Val.

The female officer with the blond ponytail stepped up behind Val and took over shouting out instructions to the search squad while Val waited for her call to go through. On hold and not liking it, Val kept the cell against her ear but shifted her gaze when she noticed Carson being brought down to the front hall in handcuffs, at gunpoint and from the looks of it more confused than frightened. He threw Nicky and me a puzzled glance before the officer guarding him told him to face front.

Val eyed him up and down. At six-foot-four he towered over her, his head of curly blond hair making him look even taller. Val cast a sneer up at him, made a dismissive "Puh!" sound and signaled with her eyes toward the living room. The other cop shoved him forward, his gun up until Carson had come over and taken a seat on the couch with Nicky and me. The cop holstered his weapon and motioned for the other two cops to join him in the hall. They talked with Val for a moment before heading off, presumably to join the search party. And from where we sat, with the general mayhem upstairs and down, it certainly sounded like they were having one. With all the whooping, shouting, slamming, thudding and crashing going on, the police seemed to be having a ball looking for our marijuana.

Irritated that her call had yet to go through, Val turned and shot us a look. Carson, Nicky and I had been talking amongst ourselves. "Zip it in there!" she snapped, taking her finger and punching a button on the cellphone to cancel her call. She put it away and stood for a few seconds contemplating the hall floor.

Wheeling around suddenly, with a now-we'll-get-to-the-bottom-of-things look on her face, she walked toward us and stationed herself directly in front of the couch, arms crossed, feet shoulder-width apart, her eyes moving in a hostile way from Nicky to me and then to Carson, who was returning Val's sneer with one of his own . . . and she wasn't liking it.

The shouts and commotion continued throughout the

house, and Val warned us that things would go a whole lot better for us if we just told her the truth right off the bat.

"The truth about what?"

"The marijuana grow-op you're running."

"We have some plants growing for personal use, so what?"

"They're illegal."

"From some points of view."

"You're producing for the purposes of trafficking."

"It's not a commercial operation. We have a few plants. That's all."

"So you *know* about commercial operations, then."

"Of course I do. But ours isn't one."

I nodded at Nicky, explained that it was his hobby cultivating marijuana plants, something that he became interested in a few years ago and liked doing. "He also has four kinds of vegetables growing," I added. "I hope your people find those, too . . ."

Without the requisite smirk for my sarcasm, Val waited for me to continue.

"He likes growing," I said, "and he does it with my approval." I told her I was in the process of applying for a medicinal licence and was just waiting to get a doctor's signature, which I pointed out wasn't the easiest thing to do. "In fact, the forms for Health Canada are all filled out and in a file folder on the dining-room table, if you want to have a look."

"Makes no difference," Val came back. "You're trafficking in controlled substances here. Which means you're looking at jail time, thousands of dollars in fines, and the federal government will seize your house as the proceeds of crime."

"We're not traffickers," I said.

"You're breaking the law."

"So are you."

This seemed to be the cue for one of the T-shirt and cargo shorts gang, who must have been listening from the hall, to let us know, as his colleagues had a little earlier, that we'd never be living in *this* house again. "No *sir*!" he hollered with relish, "this place is *gone*, baby!"

Val, making no comment about the interruption, continued her interrogation for the next twenty minutes or so, maintaining the same pose and shifting her suspicious gaze between the boys and me — until out of the blue she turned her head and shouted over her shoulder to one of the cops milling about in the front hall: "Woz, get in here!"

In cargo shorts, T-shirt, ankle socks and running shoes, Woz looked to be in his mid-forties. He had a florid, round face, his hair was thinning on top and there was a thick brown moustache on his upper lip. A belly of considerable girth under his white T-shirt, he hurried into the living room, a flustered and somewhat hapless look on his face, a new-looking burgundy leather attaché case in his one hand.

Surveying the situation, he planned his strategy carefully before sitting down, shifting his holster around on his waist then slowly lowering himself into the armchair next to the couch, taking a few moments to adjust position, as the holster was making for an awkward fit. In the end, he removed his gun belt and set it down on the carpet beside the armchair, made himself comfortable in the chair and then rested the attaché case on his knees. He unfastened the latches, opened it and took out a handful of empty file folders and a legal-size pad of printed forms, which he explained to the boys and me that he'd be using to take down our personal information.

For some reason, whether it was police procedure or because he was having trouble hearing over the noise the search team was making, Woz made a point of asking us to repeat our answers to each of his questions two or three times. Spelling seemed to be the issue, but at the same time the cramped and awkward way he held his pen had me wondering if handwriting was part of the problem as well. His Methuselah-slow, hard-to-take-seriously performance left Val unfazed, however, and she continued with her probing stare, a coolness in her eyes that suggested we could go on three-peating for Woz all night long for all she cared. He kept up a steady banter as he worked, affable despite the official nature of his business. He stopped writing twice, glanced up from his forms and shook the pen in the air, warning us with a troubled frown that it might be running out of ink. On both occasions I offered him one of mine, telling him there were a couple of pens on the dining-room table he was welcome to use. But Woz declined politely each time and pressed on — until the ballpoint finally did run dry and, with a disgruntled grumble, he had to hold the information forms down on top of his attaché, open it a crack and feel around inside until he eventually retrieved another pen. After testing it on the back of one of his file folders, he announced that we could carry on.

The spelling of our street, Friendship Avenue, proved to be a conundrum, Woz chuckling to himself as I reminded him of the old rhyme about I before E, except after C, which he readily admitted was a rule he'd always had a problem with. It threw him for a loop, too, that my daughter Hannah, "the other occupant of the house," spelled her name with an 'H' on the end. He stared at it on the form where he'd written it down and asked if I was sure about the spelling.

"It's a palindrome," I said, which drew a stiff glare from Val.

"A what?" asked a puzzled Woz.

"When a word is spelled the same way forwards and backwards," I explained. "You know, like Otto on *The Simpsons*?"

He looked at the name again. "Hey," he smiled, "how 'bout that? H-A-N-N-A-H."

Our last name, of course, proved even more elusive. Woz went through numerous spellings — *Elledge, Idleridge, Illrich, Illigdee* — before he managed to get it down correctly, running into further difficulty when he discovered he'd made "too many damn changes" on Nicky's information form. He tore the page off his pad in frustration, crumpled it up and stuffed the ball of paper into one of the half-dozen pockets in his cargo shorts, then asked Nicky to give him his personal information again, starting at the beginning.

Val continued to look on, still unmoved by Woz's bumbling antics, shooting a glare at Carson when he used the word "doofus" under his breath after Woz, shifting in his chair, lost control of the file folders and they slipped off the attaché case and scattered on the carpet around his feet, prompting smiles from Nicky and me. Val gave all three of us a steely look before she bent down and picked them up for Woz so he wouldn't have to extricate himself from the chair and retrieve them himself.

When it came out, on further questioning from Woz, that the children's mother and I were separated, Val interrupted to ask if I had custody.

"De facto custody."

"Day what?"

"Their mother has some personal problems and can't look after them right now," I said. "They've been living with me for the last four years."

"What kind of personal problems?"

"Health problems."

"Like what?"

"It's not relevant to this conversation."

"I'm the one who decides that, not you."

I turned my head away to let her know she was wasting her time. I was certain that she wanted to press the issue further and would happily have done so had there not been a sudden commotion and some shouting in the basement, a cop bounding noisily up the stairs a few seconds after. He charged into the living room carrying a small aluminum saucepan. Out of breath, an intent look on his face, he showed it to Val, pointing out the white powdery residue on the sides and bottom of the pot. She took it from him, gave it a frown and asked him what he thought.

"Looks like crystal meth to me."

Val confirmed the analysis with a nod, glanced over at me like she was disgusted. "You're making crystal *meth*?" she exploded. "Crystal *meth*?" she repeated even louder.

Carson chuckled, amused.

Val shot him a glare.

"It's a saucepan we use under the sink in the basement bathroom," he said, "to catch drips from the leaky faucet."

"It's just mineral build-up from the dried water," Nicky explained.

"I know what it is!" Val snapped indignantly, handing the pot back to the officer and telling him to enter it into evidence.

Woz, moving ahead with his questioning, chose that moment to ask for some details about what I'd put down as my occupation, "Professional writer."

"What do you write?" Val cut in.

"Books."

"Yeah?" she asked belligerently. "What kind of books?"

"I'm rewriting some of Shakespeare's plays as novels at the moment."

"What're you doing that for?"

"To make it easier for students to understand them."

"And exactly how are *you* able to do that?"

"I taught high-school English for twenty-six years."

"Where 'bouts?"

"Upper Canada College, a private school here in Toronto."

"I've heard of it."

"And Thornlea Secondary, a public high school in Thornhill. There are some copies of the Shakespeare novels I've published so far on the dining-room table, if you want to have a look."

"Why wouldn't you write your own books?"

"I do write my own books. I just happen to be working on this Shakespeare series right now."

She gave me a blank stare, moved into the dining room, spotted the Shakespeare books (easy to do with his face prominent on the cover) and picked up a copy. Appropriately enough, considering the hurly-burly that was going on, it was *Macbeth*. Lips pressed together, she studied the portrait of Shakespeare, opened the book and riffled through the pages. Not impressed, she tossed it back on the table. "So that's what you do besides growing dope?"

"Excuse me?"

"The way you make your living."

"It is," I told her, smiling thinly to show I wasn't rising to the bait.

She snickered. "Some teacher you must've been. What'd you teach?"

"I told you, English."

"Where'd you teach?"

Carson and Nicky turned their heads away, their turn to snicker.

"I just told you, Officer. Upper Canada College. Then a public high school in Thornhill."

"Huh," is all she said, and stepped back into the living room, bringing one of the dining-room chairs with her, which she turned around, threw a leg over and sat down on. Her eyes on us all this time, she drummed her fingernails impatiently on the back of the chair, poked her tongue reflectively in her left cheek and, narrowing her eyes, continued the interrogation with a series of lingering, pointedly accusing stares that Carson, Nicky and I did our best to ignore, our attention, at that point, on the noises emanating from the kitchen. Sounds of glass and china breaking on the ceramic-tile floor, with cops blurting, "Oops, what a shame . . ." or "That's the way the cookie crumbles!" Nicky wondered out loud what they were doing in there. "Having fun, it sounds like," I offered, my sarcasm winning me yet another searing look from Val.

"You're really something, aren't you?" she said, rhetorically, and started in, once again, on what kind of a father I must be. Using my own children to front a criminal operation? Exposing them to mould, toxic fumes and who knows what else, with no concern at all about damage to their *health*? Especially my daughter's — who might have contracted breast cancer for all I knew: that and lung cancer, according to Val, the biggest dangers of indoor marijuana grow-ops. "We *know* that now," she declared fervently, "and about all sorts of other diseases as well. What were you thinking," she wanted to know, "risking your daughter's health so her chances of getting breast cancer are now going to be increased ten times? Are you de*lib*erately trying to give your daughter breast cancer?"

Warming to her topic, she jumped up from the chair, stepped in front of it and leaned down in front of me so her face was only a couple of inches from mine. So I could smell the tinge of coffee and cigarettes on her breath; see the pores on her rough, tanned skin. "Is *that* what you're trying to do here?" she shouted in my face. "Give your own daughter *breast* cancer? What kind of *father* would do that to his own daughter?"

"Any idiot knows that's not how you get cancer," Carson blurted out in my defence.

"Shut it!" Val snapped at him, her right hand, as if by instinct, settling on the butt of her holstered gun. Agitated, she turned and paced a few steps, swung around quickly and, with an accusing scowl, asked me the *real* reason that the children weren't living with their mother. "What's that all about, anyway?"

"It's not *all about* anything. It's just a health problem."

As she threw me a truculent you-don't-fool-me-for-a-minute look, baiting me to say something that would only make things worse than they already were, I just glared back at her and kept my mouth shut. Though even that proved the wrong thing to do: Val sneered at my continuing silence in disgust, gave a disdainful shake of her head, then turned and stormed from the room, leaving us to answer a few more questions from the hapless Woz, who at that point was desperately searching in his attaché case for yet another pen, the one he'd started using only about ten minutes earlier having apparently also run out of ink.

A shout from upstairs in Nicky's bedroom had Val rushing for the bottom of the stairs. She called up and asked what was going on.

"We got cash in a wall safe, Val!"

"Really? How much?"

"Least a thousand by the looks of it — I'm just counting it now!" News that brought a steaming-mad Val back to the living room, flinging the dining-room chair she'd been sitting on out of her way so that it crashed against the dining-room table with such force that the crystal flower vase tipped over, the bouquet I had in it went flying and water spilled over the mahogany table, dripping onto the Oriental rug below.

"I thought you weren't trafficking!" Val shrieked in a fury, thrusting her face directly in front of mine, though thankfully not quite as close as before.

"That's my son's money," I said calmly, motioning with my head toward Nicky.

"My birthday was in June," Nicky explained. "I got around $200 as gifts. The rest is from my businesses. I cut lawns and recycle scrap metal in the summer."

"What're you doing with it in a wall safe?"

"My grandfather puts them in people's houses to store their valuables," Nicky replied. "He gave me one for my birthday two years ago."

"Come on," Val said with a mocking smirk. "You can do better than that."

"It's the truth," Nicky said.

"It's his money, and it's all legitimate," I said, backing him up. "It's got nothing to do with drugs."

"Right . . ." said Val with a sarcastic smile, shaking her head. "Tell you what," she said. "I'm gonna do you a favour and give you a few minutes to get your story straight. I need to know the truth about what's really going on here. One of you is gonna end up taking the rap. I want to know who it's gonna be," she said, directing what I'm sure she thought was a guilt-inducing frown at me — no mistaking who *she* figured should take the rap — before she turned and left the room. The second female officer entered the living room in her place as the beleaguered Woz scrambled out behind Val, his file folders, information forms and attaché case in one hand. Remembering his gun belt, however, he ran back in and, with some noisy huffing and puffing, stooped and picked it up off the floor not far from Nicky's right foot.

Better looking than Val, with a pale complexion, smooth skin and light-blue eyes, the blond officer stepped over to the dining room, picked up the chair Val had tossed and brought it back to the living room. She turned it backwards as Val had done, set it about six feet across from the couch and sat down. With a kind of half-sneer no doubt meant to be intimidating, she set one of her hands on the back of the chair and rested the other on the handle of her holstered pistol.

"Would you mind giving us a moment alone, Officer?" I asked her.

Without breaking her stare, she shook her head. "No can do."

"Val said she was giving us time to get our story straight."

"Val's not here now," she said.

"True enough," I said, catching her drift, and let the matter go.

We passed the next half hour just sitting there, the second female officer's gaze trained on us the whole time, her stare not letting up even when her radio went off and she had to update someone on the status of the situation. While she gave a person named Hector the gist of what was going on, I told Nicky and Carson we should just stand by the truth and not be scared by the way we were being treated.

"She's a wacko," Carson said under his breath, meaning Val.

The blond cop, now off the phone, must have heard him because she leaned forward in her chair, frowned and rested her elbows on the back of the chair.

"What was that?" she said, directing her question at Carson.

"Nothing," he said, an insolent tone to his voice, but the officer seemed content to let it go, at least for the time being.

The search — which Officer Val had escalated into a full-blown interrogation that, legally, should have taken place in a video-monitored interview room at a police station — had lasted for more than an hour at this point. With most of the activity around the house having subsided, a half-dozen of the T-shirt and cargo-shorts crew gathered around Val in the front hall for a powwow, the main issue now apparently being how long it would take to get some patrol cars over here for our ride to the station. "We've got another one to deal with in the west end," Val said into her cellphone. Things were wrapping up here, she said, so they needed to be motoring ASAP. Plus it would be getting dark soon and she wanted to be out of this place while it was still daylight.

After a word with the cluster of officers, she returned to the living room, fetched a second chair from the dining room and placed it beside her partner's. She turned it around, sat down and rested her forearms on the back as the blond officer had.

"So," she said to the three of us, "what's it gonna be?"

Nicky spoke up. "Like my dad told you, I'm the one doing the growing. My brother isn't involved at all."

Obviously not what she wanted to hear, Val stared at him a moment, tapped her fingers calmly on the back of her chair but didn't say anything. Just pursed her lips and put her tongue in her cheek reflectively, like she was mulling things over.

"How old are you?" she asked, turning to Nicky.

"I turned eighteen in June."

She snickered, but made no comment. She turned to her blond partner. "Give Kozak a call and find out what he wants us to do."

The blond officer nodded, got to her feet, moved to the front hall and spoke to one of the other officers, who glanced into the living room, nodded and started to make a call on his cellphone.

We sat for another fifteen minutes or so, during which time Carson began throwing me increasingly panicked glances.

"I have to go to the bathroom," he finally said to Val, but with her eyes on Nicky and me at the time, she acted like she hadn't heard him. "It's a bowel movement," he added. Val continued to ignore him, even though it was perfectly clear, from the distressed look on his face, that he wasn't making things up and he badly needed to go.

"Would you let him use the bathroom, please," I appealed to her. No response after three or four minutes, I tried again.

"He needs to use the bathroom, Officer, or he'll have to go here on the couch."

Continued silence, her eyes remaining on Nicky and me in a vacant stare, I spotted Woz moving about in the front hall and called to him. "Can somebody take my son to the bathroom, please?"

On his way into the living room anyway, Woz handed our files over to Val, who took her time opening them so she could inspect the contents.

Carson was groaning beside me, wincing with the cramps in his stomach. Not normally given to crying, it looked as though that's what he was about to do if he was forced to shit his pants in front of the cops.

I caught Woz's eye. "Would you *please* take my son to the bathroom, Officer?"

Woz glanced at Val, who waited a moment before she looked up from the file folders and, after a casual glance at me, shook her head.

"You're one disgusting human being," I said.

"Huh," she chuckled. "Not gonna get too far with an attitude like that," Val came back indifferently.

"Probably not," I said, meeting her eyes, and on a guess added, "not with someone who's never had kids."

Carson closed his eyes, moaned and gritted his teeth in agony, trying to hold off what seemed inevitable now: that she had every intention of letting him shit himself there on the couch.

"I think we better do something, Val," Woz piped up, concerned.

Val and I exchanged mutually hateful looks for a moment. "Make it fast," she said to Woz after a moment, holding her expressionless look for a second before she went back to perusing our files.

Carson already on his feet, he shifted about from one foot to the other until Woz took him by the arm, walked him quickly out of the room and down the hall to the powder room.

"What about the cuffs, Val?" he called back a moment later.

"Leave them on."

"For *fuck's* sake!" I erupted.

"Could be tense, Val!" Woz shouted in alarm.

Cool as ever, Val glanced over but she didn't say anything, not until Carson appealed to her from the powder room, "For *Christ's sake*, lady! How am I supposed to pull my pants down?"

She paused a moment, deliberating some more. "All right," she finally said, in a level tone. "But the door stays open."

"What?" called Woz, who obviously hadn't heard.

"The door stays open."

I forced my eyes shut, took a slow breath and in a supreme act of self-control kept from throwing myself at her and head-butting her in the face. Hard as it was, restraint was key. With a dozen armed police surrounding me, one wrong move on my part and chances were good that I'd end up with a bullet or two somewhere in my body. The pain in my shoulders, especially in my left — which was held together by a titanium staple inserted to repair an athletic injury as a teenager — had become unbearable, like a hot steel chisel was being hammered into the bone. Above the din, I could hear several cops laughing in the upstairs hall as the search continued.

A look of strained relief on his ashen face, Carson returned from the bathroom about five minutes later, the cuffs back on, Woz waiting for him to sit down before he turned to Val, accepted the file folders from her and hurried out of the room.

"Everything okay, Carson?" Nicky asked under his breath when he sat down.

"Just barely," Carson said, casting Val a not very pleasant look.

"So what happens now?" I asked.

She gave a casual shrug. "We'll take the three of you to the station. You and Curly here," she said, nodding at Carson, "can make statements and come home. This one," she glanced at Nicky, "stays in jail."

Nicky let out a nervous breath, his face and neck turning red, as they always did when he was scared or under stress, but he held his chin up, kept his eyes squarely on Val and let her see his undeterred look.

"Don't worry, Nick," I said to him under my breath, "you won't be going alone." I knew that on the off chance Val might agree to let Carson walk, there was no way she'd be letting *me* out of her clutches any time soon.

"I'd like to phone my daughter before we go, Officer," I said to Val. "She's over at a friend's, and I don't want her coming home later to find the house trashed and her father and brothers missing."

"Not my problem, mister," said Val.

"I need to call my daughter, Officer."

"You need to keep your mouth shut, is what you need," she said, turning her head and shouting to an officer in the front hall. "Tommy, what's going on, for cryin' out loud?"

"We're good to go any time, Val," he said, mobilizing the T-shirt and cargo-shorts crew, who were awaiting further instructions.

Val assigned two officers to Nicky, who led him into the front hall first. Two more took Carson by the arms and stepped up behind Nicky, while another pair kept me back on Val's orders, emptying my pockets for me and putting the contents on the hall table: about $80 in cash, some loose change, the leather billfold in which I kept my driver's licence, birth certificate, health and social insurance IDs and my credit and ATM cards.

I told them, when they were finished, that I'd lost all feeling in my left arm; that I had a metal staple in my shoulder from an operation when I was young and it was digging straight into the bone. I asked them to let me have the handcuffs moved from their position up-behind to down in front, otherwise I was probably going to pass out from the pain.

"The guy wants his cuffs switched to the front," one cop called to Val who, surrounded by five or six of the cargo-shorts crew, was in the process of dialing a number on her cell.

"Too bad," she replied as she finished dialing and held the phone up to her ear.

No surprise, I asked the cop anyway if he could let me use the phone in the computer room (we were standing right beside it) to call my daughter and let her know what had happened.

"You'll get your call later," was all he said.

"Time?" Val asked the group.

"Eight forty-five!" somebody answered.

"Okay, let's roll!" she announced, walked over to the front door and yanked it open. "Go!" she barked at the officers with Nicky, closing the door immediately after they'd led him out. She motioned the officers holding Carson to bring him forward, waited a minute or so and, after a glance at her watch, pulled the door open, gave the order to "Go!" and shut it the moment they'd stepped onto the front porch.

The cops holding my arms brought me forward so I was standing maybe five feet away from Val. I repeated my request to call my daughter, adding that as she and her crew had violated just about every other right my sons and I were supposed to have, why couldn't she do the decent thing and let me warn my daughter what to expect when she came home?

Pretending like she hadn't heard me, Val stared absently at the mirror on the wall next to the front door, spent about ten seconds looking at herself before she turned away, glanced at the cops holding me and shouted the order to *Go!* "Time's a-wasting," she said, her smile the first I'd seen on her face all night.

Though the sun was starting to go down, there was still plenty of light along Friendship Avenue, a quiet, upper-middle-class street in the Rouge Valley area of Scarborough. But it was alive with action that night, a scene right out of a movie: five or six police cruisers, with their red-and-blue roof-lights flashing, were lining the middle of the road between the drug squad SUVs. Two uniformed police officers in their black bulletproof vests were standing beside each vehicle; and more officers, at either end of the line of patrol cars, were blocking traffic, most of the drivers with their engines off, standing at the yellow police tape that had been strung across the road.

The neighbours up and down both sides of the street were out front of their houses, taking in the excitement. A good-sized crowd of onlookers had gathered on the sidewalk across the street, maybe a hundred people or so by the looks of it, with more still arriving — kids on their bikes, people who'd been walking their dogs, several women with strollers and carriages — all watching in stunned silence as the two cops brought me across the front lawn to a patrol car at the curb, where an officer in uniform and bulletproof vest was opening the rear door.

"Wait!" a voice rang out.

The police on either side of me froze, their grip tightening on my arms, both of them turning their eyes, as everyone else on the street was, toward my next-door neighbour's house. Mary-Ellen McCluskey, a notorious gossip and known community busybody in her late forties, wearing gold aviator-frame glasses, a sleeveless yellow blouse and a pair of pale-blue jeans too tight for her large hips, was rushing across her front lawn toward me.

Pulling her mild-mannered husband, Wes, by the hand after her, Mary-Ellen stopped just short of the waiting patrol car and, though she was only about ten feet away from me, called out in a voice that was loud enough for everyone in the vicinity to hear, "It wasn't *us*, Paul! I *swear*, it wasn't us!!"

CHAPTER **TWO**
WISE GUYS

Though 43 Division was only about ten minutes from our house, the ride in the back of the patrol car was torturous. Because of Officer Val's refusal to let my handcuffs be moved, there was no sensation in my left arm and fingers now. The pain from the titanium staple was shooting up the back of my neck, the air in the closed-in back seat of the cruiser stale and stifling hot. The window was the roll-down kind, but the two cops up front ignored my request to stop and open it for me.

It didn't help that there were only about six inches of legroom down below, which forced me to sit in a contorted sideways position, my right foot squeezed in behind my left, neither of them with any space to move. And because of the way I was perched on the edge of the seat, every time the officer who was driving hit the brakes — and it seemed to me he did so with unnecessary suddenness and frequency — I was pitched forward repeatedly into the Plexiglass and steel-mesh security grille on the back of the front seat, my left shoulder slamming up against it so that the shooting pains in my shoulder, neck and head were so intense I imagined it was what you experienced if you were having a stroke.

I breathed a sigh of slight relief when the cruiser finally arrived at the station, a new building with landscaped gardens surrounding a pool and water fountain that had officially opened a year earlier, in spite of considerable opposition from various quarters. Crime rates in the area had been falling steadily for the past ten years, and the $10 million price tag for what the media dubbed a "public relations showpiece," with its cutting-edge environmental design and state-of-the-art energy-saving features, was felt to be excessive, particularly when other city departments were under severe budget constraints and when there was already a perfectly good police station only fifteen minutes away.

The patrol car headed to the back of the building and into one of the three receiving bays. After the bay door closed behind us, the officers took me out of the cruiser. I asked them if they could give me a few seconds to get some feeling back in my legs, a request that was ignored as they hurried me off through a door and into a glassed-in area where Carson and Nicky and their police escorts were waiting.

A female officer in her mid-forties was standing behind a chest-high white counter, a large six-by-six-foot dry-erase message-board on the grey wall behind her. She instructed us to position ourselves with our toes on the yellow line on the floor then look straight ahead at her. As ordered, we toed the line, which was set about four feet back from the counter. Starting with Carson, she asked us our names, then held up a hand and told us to hang on a minute. She took an eight-foot aluminum stepladder out of the corner, opened it below the message-board and climbed up with a black marker in one hand, a darkly smudged white cloth in the other, and asked us to say them again, slowly. Like Woz when he was recording our information, she too had difficulty spelling our last name, writing it as "Endrige," "Inglidge," "Hillidge," which I told her was close enough. She turned atop the ladder and asked our police escorts what we were being booked for. "P-for-P," one of them said.

The officer on the ladder wrote this down in the space to the right of our names.

"How much?" she asked.

"Under three," replied the officer holding Nicky.

The woman put a minus sign and the number three in the next square. As she climbed down from the ladder, folded it up, lugged it back to the corner then returned to the counter, I noticed there were no other names on the board. It looked as though we had the jail to ourselves that night.

"Do you understand what you're being charged with?" the woman asked.

Carson, Nicky and I looked at each other. "More or less," I answered for the three of us.

"Yes or no," she said, waiting till each of us had answered in the affirmative before signaling to our escorting officers that they could pass us off to six uniformed officers who'd just come in, fresh-faced young guys who appeared to be in their mid- to late twenties, not that much older than Carson; rookies, I gathered, from the fact they were wearing their dark-blue police caps inside the station.

Carson and Nicky disappeared with their escorts around a corner into the building proper; I followed a few minutes later with mine, the two cops taking me down a succession of corridors to a painted-grey cinderblock cubicle, a space slightly larger than your average shower stall. The officers removed my handcuffs, told me to stand facing them, take the laces out of my shoes and hand them over, then get undressed, underwear off, too.

Though the pain in my shoulder eased as soon as the handcuffs came off, my left arm hung limp and lifeless down at my side. As a result, I had to remove my clothes using only my right hand, which was shaking so badly that it took me close to five minutes just to get my T-shirt off, several more for my shorts and underwear. The officers were amused at my palsied fumbling to begin with, but the shorter of the two young guys lost patience, suggesting, in an irritated voice, that I "cut the crap" and get a move on because they didn't have "all friggin' night."

Naked at last, I was instructed to turn around, step up to the white line on the floor, bend over, spread my legs and touch my toes while they conducted a "cavity search." My head between my legs, I watched as one of the officers crouched down behind me, flicked on a small flashlight and, completing the indignities of the evening, peered at my anus.

Dressed again and out in the hall, the handcuffs still off, no sign of Carson or Nicky, I cradled my left arm in my right and shuffled in my laceless Top-Sider boat shoes down a long narrow hall, one of the officers walking in front of me, the other right behind. Our footsteps the only sound, we moved past doors with small, eye-level viewing windows, the sliding visors on most of them closed, until we reached one toward the end of the corridor where one of the officers took a key, opened up, ordered me inside then closed and locked the door behind me.

Alone in the high-ceilinged, fluorescent-lit room, I could feel myself coming out of shock (I guessed that's what it was), fear setting in at what might be happening to Carson and Nicky and whether Hannah had gone back to the house yet. My next thought was that I'd better keep moving, try not to think about things too much — things over which it was clear that I had absolutely no control — so I started pacing beside the grey walls, whistling as I shuffled along, finishing one tune then segueing quickly into the next. Pop songs, rock classics, show tunes — material from my repertoire in the days when I played cocktail piano at bistros, bars and lounges around Toronto.

After a few hours, I began mixing in some old favourites, marched in time to "Side by Side," "Oh! Susanna," "I've Been Working on the Railroad" and, the biggest time-waster of them all, "The Ants Go Marching." Amused at the picture I must have presented with my self-entertaining antics, I stopped in the middle of the room at one point and, to show whoever might be watching that the spirit hadn't been knocked out of me just yet, I hollered up at the security camera tucked in a corner of the ceiling, "I take requests, in case you're interested! Whatever you like — I whistle by ear!" Then waited quietly for five minutes or so to see if there'd be any takers. There weren't.

When I felt I'd had enough, and needed a break from the music and the monotonous pacing, I sat down for a few minutes at the room's only piece of furniture: a round metal barroom-style table, chest-high and bolted to the floor in the middle of the room, with a small disk-seat on a steel arm extending out from the base. As it was only the size of a dessert-plate however, sitting on it became uncomfortable after about ten minutes, at which time I took my partially functional right hand, picked my out-of-commission left one up off the table, crossed to the corner by the door and resumed the routine again, moving in the opposite direction to what I had been before in order to keep things interesting: "The ants go marching one by one, hurrah, hurrah . . ."

After about three hours of this, the pain in my left shoulder still very present, my cheek muscles sore from all the whistling, a blood-pressure headache pounding behind my eyes and my legs feeling as though they might give way beneath me at any time, I trudged over to the corner nearest the door, sat down out of sight directly below the security camera and made myself as comfortable as I could: legs stretched out in front of me; right arm cradling my left, my head leaning wearily back in the V where the cinder-block walls met.

Deep yawns seizing me as the nervous energy I'd had for several hours began to wear off, I forced myself to stay awake by whistling louder and faster, staring up at the ceiling until tears formed, then blinking rapidly several times to lubricate my contact lenses, a solution I'd come up with to prevent them from drying out and scratching the corneas, damage that my ophthalmologist had once warned me could be permanent.

I wondered to myself if Carson and Nicky were being subjected to the same kind of treatment, perhaps in one of the other rooms down the hall. Maybe Officer Val had been in to meet with them, now that I was out of the way. Maybe she'd laid some more of her cop-show scare-tactics on them, gotten them good and frightened and promised to let them off the hook if they'd just tell her the truth: that their father was the culprit, the main man and kingpin of the operation, a wily Fagin using children to do his dirty work for him . . . a notion that, like the others Officer Val's imagination had concocted in the course of the evening, couldn't have been further from the truth.

I did indeed buy Nicky a grow unit in March 2004, at a store on Lakeshore Boulevard in the west end, across the street from a Tim Hortons coffee shop. The innocuously named "Green Buddha Seeds" was a cute little place. A sleigh bell above the front door rang as I entered, three white-hooded plant-lights hung in the front window above a thriving indoor garden, a small water fountain, rocks and ferns, and a stream that trickled into a moss-rimmed pool where some good-sized goldfish were swimming around under real lily pads.

The owner was a broad-shouldered, barrel-chested but genial guy in his mid-thirties who, with a friendly smile, introduced himself as Richie. We shook hands. There was a floor-to-ceiling circular kiosk in the middle of the room with gardening supplies, plant fertilizers and horticultural brochures, information booklets and catalogues artfully displayed on it, narrow glass shelves running along the wall adjacent to the front window, each one lined with packets of plant, flower and vegetable seeds.

Directly across from this stood a chest-high Art Deco black counter, the latest issues of *Cannabis Culture* and *High Times* magazines arranged neatly beside the cash register, next to which was the debit-machine and a large glass snifter that was half-filled with colourful Licorice Allsorts, a milkshake spoon sitting inside to scoop them out with. A blackboard on the wall behind the counter had the words "Green Buddha Seeds" written ornamentally at the top in green, red, blue and yellow chalk, the names of different seed-strains, quantities available and their prices, also written in coloured chalk, listed below.

Richie listened patiently while I explained my situation. Told him I was a writer who worked at home, was a single parent to three teenagers, used pot recreationally and had done so since university. I said I felt I knew a certain amount about cannabis from my experiences (as well as from teaching high school for quite a few years) — a lot more than most parents out there, at least as far as I could see — but I'd never grown pot myself and it was something I was wondering about trying. Perhaps put a few plants in a cold cellar I had in my house. "Not a lot," as I said to Richie. "Just enough to learn what's involved, and maybe enjoy the results afterwards, if I'm successful. Or rather if *we're* successful," adding that I'd like to have my fifteen-year-old son do the growing along with me.

I explained that Nicky, like a lot of teenagers, was smoking pot pretty regularly, and like a lot of teenagers, he was curious about what the effects of harder and more exotic drugs might be: magic mushrooms, cocaine, LSD, and one called *ayahuasca* that had recently come onto the scene, a much more powerful hallucinogenic that is apparently used by tribes in the Amazon that puts the user in a mind-altering trance for up to twenty-four hours. The last time I'd been talking to Nicky about it, he let on that some of his friends were already starting to dabble with chemicals. "In fact," I told Richie, "they boasted about the results of their experimental efforts in such glowing terms that my son decided to drop acid at a party last Saturday night. A dealer nobody knew much about passed off some bad ecstasy as LSD. My son freaked out. Came home from the party a half hour after he'd taken it, confessed to what he'd done, and I spent till dawn the next day helping him weather the hallucinations, the shakes, the sweats, the vomiting. Took him for walks along the beach, talked him out of thinking he was going crazy, hugged him and reassured him that everything would be okay in a few hours' time; that this would just be a bad memory he'd look back on and laugh about, which I pretended to do, though I was scared shitless the whole time. Anyway," I continued, "I did quite a bit of thinking about it, about what might be the best approach to take with him in the future. Kids being kids, it's unrealistic for me to think he'll never touch anything stronger than marijuana again." This point prompted a sage smile and knowing nod from Richie.

I said I thought it might be good for Nicky to find out more about where marijuana comes from. Let him see how it's grown and, if nothing else, at least teach him how to tell good stuff from bad. "Who knows," I put it to Richie, "maybe he'll become more enamoured of growing it than smoking it," which I told him I could see happening. "He reads *High Times* and the various grow magazines all the time. Visits a bunch of sites on the internet, and a few months ago bought himself a book called *The Grow Bible* by Jorge Something-or-other that he's always reading me excerpts from."

Leaning against the counter with his arms crossed, Richie smiled, said he knew the book well, adding that he thought the plan was an excellent idea, a refreshing change from the way most parents dealt with their teenagers' drug issues. He said he couldn't see any reason why it wouldn't work out to everyone's benefit. And the timing was good, too. In the next couple of days, he was going to be receiving a new home-growing unit from General Hydroponics in California. There was a four-by-two-foot reservoir, a removable plastic cover on top of which you sit eight small buckets filled with Hydroton clay pellets, a bag of which he said he'd throw in with the unit. A pump, plastic hoses and drainage tubes were provided. He'd set us up with a 1,000-watt high-pressure sodium bulb, a ballast box and a circular hood, give us starter-bottles of the three nutrients the plants would need, along with something called pH Down, a water and phosphoric acid mixture used to balance the heavy alkalinity in city tap water — the whole package for $850 if I was okay with that. He said he couldn't really make it any cheaper or he'd be losing money.

Though I didn't have anything to base it on, it sounded like a pretty fair price to me, considering all that Richie was throwing in as part of the deal, so I had him write up a bill of sale. He processed my debit-card payment then explained that, to help us get going, instead of selling us ten seeds for $150, only five of which were guaranteed to be females when they sprouted (males have no THC properties and are thrown away) and which would take a couple of months anyway to grow big enough just to plant, he'd gladly throw in eight clones (cuttings) of Purple Kush, a new strain he was developing for one of the compassion societies downtown. It had 50% *indica* properties, and 50% *sativa* — indica pot produced stronger body effects and was good for alleviating physical aches and pains, while sativa effects were more cerebral, good for alleviating stress, anxiety and depression, promoting creativity and increased feelings of well-being. "All these years of smoking pot," I said, a little embarrassed, "and I had absolutely no idea there was any difference. I just thought pot was pot."

Richie laughed and said most people tended to think so. "The way I look at it," he said, "is why should you be drinking crappy boxed wine you bought from someone else, when you could be sipping Château Lafite of your own?"

As to legalities, he made a point of letting me know that everything in his store was legal for purchase, even the seeds. Which they weren't in the United States, he said, so a good amount of his business came from Americans, the store only two hours' drive from the Buffalo border. Green Buddha Seeds was a registered company, paid tax like any other business, and the only "dealing" he did was with manufacturers about their various products, with the publishers of the magazines in which he advertised, and with the webmaster who managed his site. The sticky point, he said, came when you planted the seeds. "The moment they start sprouting, they become illegal. At least according to Canadian law," he added in sardonic tones.

I gave him a look. "So it's okay to plant them, but they become illegal once they start growing?"

He chuckled, wryly, at my puzzlement. "That's about the size of it."

"The things hit the light, and then they go bad," I joked. "I'd like to know how that works."

He laughed. "The good news, though, is that cops aren't that interested in home-growers. They go after the commercial operators primarily; guys with three or four hundred lights and maybe 100,000 plants in warehouses out in the suburbs. The only thing you really have to worry about if you're growing in your house is nosy neighbours. Nine times out of ten, that's how people get pinched . . ."

A key clicking in the door to the interview room made me start. It swung open and hit my outstretched legs down near the ankles before I could move them out of the way. A short, scruffy-looking guy, maybe in his early thirties, hurried into the room. A small build, stringy long brown hair, three or four days' stubble on his face and the washed-out red T-shirt he was wearing soiled, stained and fraying around the neck, he had a ratty jean-jacket on over it, ripped badly in several places, makeshift patches in others, and one of the breast-pockets partially torn off and hanging down.

As I got to my feet, I caught a look at the beaten-up hiking-boots he was wearing, each from a different pair: one black, with light-grey markings, the other beige and moss-green, both boots done up with yellow skate laces. I remember thinking to myself as I went over and stood across from him at the round metal table that he looked more like a down-on-his-luck homeless guy than an undercover Toronto cop. Only the black Glock pistol on his hip under the jean-jacket gave him away; it was police-issue, identical to the ones the officers had been packing back at the house.

Restless, a little jumpy in the way he shifted his weight from one foot to the other every few seconds, he plucked a ballpoint pen and a small notepad from the one still-intact breast pocket of his jean-jacket, set the pad down and quickly opened it to a page covered in spidery handwriting. He licked his thumb, flipped forward to a fresh page and took down my personal information: name, date of birth, address, previous addresses, how many years I'd resided at each address; along with my occupation, previous occupations, marital status, number of children and their ages.

He finished up in short order, leafed back through the pages of the notebook, browsing momentarily here and there, frowning steadily while doing so, squinting at the words as if he was having real trouble deciphering them, like the notepad might actually have belonged to someone else. I wondered if maybe his superior officer had pressed it on him, with orders to come in and talk to me for a bit since I'd been there for close to four hours.

To my surprise, he abruptly closed the notepad, tapped his pen on it a few times then slipped it and the pad back in the pocket of his jean-jacket and, without having looked at me once the whole time he'd been in the room, turned for the door.

"So was that it for my statement?" I called over to him, confused because we hadn't even talked about the raid.

"No," he came back offhandedly, pulling the door open. "The arresting officer's not having you do that now. There's three of you involved, so she's booking you as organized crime. There's a different set of procedures."

"Because there's three of us?"

"That's right."

"Two is okay, but three makes us organized criminals?"

"That's the way it works, sir."

"What does organized crime have to do with anything?"

"Well," he said, shrugging, "that's what the arresting officer's calling it, sir."

"You mean like the Mafia, the Hells Angels? That kind of organized crime?"

"Not really my area, sir," he said, dodging the question, and was quickly out the door and gone, the interview apparently over.

No one in to see me in the course of the next hour, I continued with my pacing and whistling routines as before. I'd just finished the Beatles' "Ob-La-Di, Ob-La-Da" and was starting in on "Maxwell's Silver Hammer," when I realized I was going to have to use the bathroom soon. Just a pee, thank goodness, but with the way everyone had been avoiding me, I figured it wouldn't hurt to try to attract someone's attention before matters became more urgent.

I walked over and, as I had earlier, positioned myself in full view of the security camera, in a reasonably loud voice announcing that I had to go to the toilet.

I made my appeal three more times in the course of the next half hour, waving my right hand back and forth over my head at several points in hopes that it would catch someone's eye. But it didn't, so after another fifteen minutes of waiting for somebody to put in an appearance, I finally hollered, "I'll just go ahead and *piss* on the floor then!" meaning it as a bluff, of course, though crazily enough, the more I thought about it — about the treatment the police had been dishing out to the boys and me from the moment they pulled up in front of our house five hours ago — the more I came to feel there was nothing I'd rather do.

But it wasn't to be. After about ten minutes, the pressure mounting in my kidneys warning me that time was running out, a key rattled in the door. It opened, and an officer who looked to be in his early thirties stepped into the room. He was a clean-cut guy with close-cropped hair, about my height, in a blue, short-sleeved police shirt, the chest of a body-builder, imposing biceps and a metal band wristwatch on his left hand.

With his head down and his eyes averted for some reason, he nodded silently toward the door and had me leave the room ahead of him. He instructed me to turn left, once we were in the hall, and walked behind me down to the end, where he had me round the corner into another corridor, this one without any doors, that led toward an open area, a long, fluorescent-lit hall to my left intersecting with it, a dozen grey doors running down either side with steel-lever handles on them: the cell block, or so I assumed.

The officer pointed out a cubicle against the wall to my right, a waist-high cinder-block stall in which there was a low, stainless-steel toilet bowl, no seat, no paper. Whistling "Like a Hurricane" while I went to the bathroom, I turned my head and asked the officer — my voice loud enough for them to hear if they happened to be nearby — where my two boys were.

As I'd hoped, within a few seconds there was a response from partway down the cell row.

"Dad?"

"Carson?"

"Are you all right?"

"I'm okay," I said, using my foot rather than my hand to flush the toilet. "Where's Nicky?"

"In the cell beside me."

"I'm fine!" Nicky called out. "Are you in one of the cells, Dad?"

"No, I'm in a holding room of some kind on the other side of the building."

The young officer cleared his throat to let me know time was up, nodded for me to get moving back to the holding room. As he was letting me back in the room, I noticed on his wristwatch that it was a little before two. I thanked him for the bathroom break, which I told him came in the nick of time; mentioned, too, that I appreciated him giving me a chance to talk to my sons.

No response, his head down, eyes still averted, he closed the door, locked it and disappeared from the viewing window.

Alone for another hour, I calculated it was about three o'clock when the young officer appeared again. Still with his head down, eyes averted as before and saying nothing, he brought me out of the holding room and led me back down the grey corridor past the toilet stall and across the open area, directing me toward the cell row. Unlocking a door about halfway down on my left, he motioned with his head for me to step in. Sliding open the visor on the small viewing window after he closed my door, I noticed when I looked out that he did the same with the visors on two cell doors kitty-corner to mine across the hall: Carson's and Nicky's, as it turned out, the two of them popping into view when they heard me start whistling. Though we couldn't speak directly, we could see each other's faces in the viewing windows, our voices echoing off the cell walls if we spoke loudly enough, the combination allowing us to talk to one another at least.

The first thing we decided was that we had to stay strong; everything about the situation sucked, but we had to find a way to hang in. Stick to our story, and hope things somehow got sorted out. We agreed that it could've been a lot worse — though after thinking about it for a few seconds, we took that back. It couldn't have been. The cops had treated us like shit, wrecked our house and staged the bust so we were outed as criminals in full view of the whole neighbourhood. Yet there wasn't anything we could do about that now except grin and bear it, which Carson said wasn't going to be easy after dealing with someone like Officer Val, whom we had no trouble agreeing was one crazy nutjob.

Nobody having talked to them since they'd been put in their cells, they wondered if I had any idea of what was going to happen to us. I said I didn't, but that a guy had popped into the holding room earlier and explained that, because there were three of us, Val was booking us as a criminal organization.

"Come on," Carson said.

"Call me Tony Soprano."

"What is that woman's *problem?*" Nicky wanted to know.

"Maybe we better drop it for now, boys," I said. "The walls have ears, if you know what I mean."

"Right," Carson said, taking the hint.

"Anything you say, Tony!" Nicky quipped sarcastically.

"To the Bada Bing . . ." Carson chimed in, alluding to the club in the TV series where Tony Soprano and his mob crew hung out.

Their cells were larger than mine from what I could see through the viewing windows, their walls light yellow in colour, as opposed to the dark-orange in which my six-by-eight-foot space had been painted. Their lights seemed much brighter, too, whereas the low-wattage one encased in wire mesh on the high ceiling did little to alleviate the shadowy darkness in mine. There was an orange, molded-plastic slab running the length of the cell at knee-level, barely wide enough to accommodate my body if I decided to lie down; the slight bump at the end closest to the far wall intended to serve as a sort of pillow, I guessed. Beside the bed stood a low, stainless-steel toilet bowl, no seat, no toilet paper and no sign of a flushing mechanism that I could see, yet for some reason the cell floor was covered in about two inches of water.

With the air conditioning blowing steadily down from the vent in the ceiling like somebody had set it to "polar," I started wondering, through smarting eyes, how much longer my contact lenses would hold out in the arctic air. They were an old pair, and due for replacement. I'd had them on since seven that morning, eighteen hours or so; every time I blinked it felt like my lids were passing over ridges of coarse-grain sandpaper. My left shoulder was continuing to throb, my right hand getting sore from holding it. As there was no point in moving around because of the flooded floor, I sat down on the edge of the orange slab-bed. I rested my dead hand on my thigh, then let my right arm hang free at my side and began doing some slow breathing, hoping I could relax in spite of the fact I could feel my heart beating out of whack; fibrillating, as the doctors call it, due to the stress of the night's events. It didn't help that, along with everything else, Val had refused to let me take my evening blood-pressure pill before we left the house, telling me that I wouldn't need to, since Carson and I would be coming back home right after we'd made our statements.

Feeling restless, I got up from the bed after about twenty minutes, stepped back to the viewing window and talked with Carson and Nicky some more, keeping the conversation light by reviewing some of the night's more comedic moments. Nicky wondered, when we were on the topic of strip searches, how anybody could do something like that for a living — check out people's butt-holes with a flashlight. "What do they think they're gonna find up there anyway," he joked, "Oh Henry! bars?" Carson and I cracked up, and the three of us enjoyed the first good laugh we'd had all evening.

But the joke was on us, as it turned out. A few minutes after Nicky's Oh Henry! comment the door at the end of the hall opened and slammed shut a second later with such force that it rattled the cell doors up and down the corridor.

"Who's that?" Nicky asked Carson, whose cell was closest to the door.

"Beats me," Carson said, straining to see who it was.

Someone, a female, judging by the click of high-heel shoes on the concrete floor, started slowly down the corridor, the woman we'd later refer to as "Spike" coming into view several seconds later. In her early forties, about five-foot-five, even with the heels, she was dressed in a light-grey, double-breasted pantsuit, the shoulders of the jacket well-padded, a light-purple silk blouse underneath, lipstick to match, her designer horn-rimmed glasses, nail polish and pentacle-shaped earrings in light-purple as well. Her short black hair was gelled and slicked back against the sides of her head while standing in short, stiff spikes on top and dyed purple at the tips. It was quite the punk look in spite of the conservative grey pantsuit she was wearing.

Walking slowly toward us, her hands clasped together behind her back, her lips pursed and her face set in a deep frown like she was good and peeved about something, Spike stepped up to the door of Carson's cell, regarded his viewing window for a second, adjusted her glasses on her nose and then reached out quickly and flipped the visor closed. She moved next door to Nicky's cell and did the same thing, after which she wheeled around and came over to mine, gave me a sour look through the viewing-window, then put her index finger on the visor and casually flicked it shut. High heels clicking, she seemed to take her time going back down the corridor, opening the cell-block door and, after pausing for several moments, slamming it shut even harder than she had when she'd come in.

Since conversation wasn't possible with the visors shut, the boys and I stayed incommunicado for the next half hour or so . . . until the door to the cell-block opened again and we could hear someone entering, the door closing with its normal reverberations so we knew it couldn't be Spike. A man's footsteps, moving quickly. I saw, when the visor on my viewing window flipped open suddenly, that it was the young officer. Eyes averted as usual and not a hint of an expression on his face, he walked over to Carson's and Nicky's cells and slid open their visors, too.

Taking advantage of his presence, I put my face as close to the viewing window as possible and shouted as he passed by on his way out: "Is there any way you can get us some blankets, Officer — it's freezing in here!"

Not acknowledging whether he'd heard me or not, he kept walking, disappeared from view down the corridor and, a few seconds later, treated us to a bone-jarring slam of the cell-block door that, though it was no match for Spike's, was right up there on the Richter scale. "So much for the blanket request," I called across to the boys.

Oddly enough, however, he returned about ten minutes later, opened our doors in turn and tossed us each a pair of bright-orange, one-size-fits-all prison overalls. Because of the flood on the floor, I climbed onto the slab-bed to put mine on, not the easiest task with just the one arm, the vent directly above my head so the air-conditioning was blasting in my face. The legs about ten inches too long, made to fit someone seven-feet tall if necessary, I rolled the bottoms up several times to keep them from trailing on the flooded floor.

The overalls made a noticeable difference, but with no snaps or buttons on the front, they stood open down to my waist. My leather Top-Siders drenched, with no socks on, the cold water had chilled my feet to the bone. Standing almost ankle-deep in it again, I began shivering and couldn't seem to stop, holding the front of the overalls closed with my right hand against the air conditioning's frigid blasts.

The good-cop, bad-cop routine with our window visors continued for the next little while. Ten or fifteen minutes would go by, the three of us not talking because Spike had made her rounds — and then the young officer would show up, march quickly down the corridor and flick our visors open again, a routine that left Carson, Nicky and I baffled. Was this just night-shift hijinks, or a deliberately contrived tactic to mess with our minds? It was impossible to tell.

To our surprise, on one occasion the young officer actually brought food with him: Jamaican meat patties, mine landing with a splash in the toilet-bowl when he tossed it into my cell, sinking almost immediately. Something about the look of the dark-yellow blob of dough sitting on the bottom of the toilet bowl, the chemical-laced beef inside, I stepped up to the viewing window and told the boys that I knew they were probably hungry, but I thought it might be risky to have anything to do with the meat patties, especially if their toilets, like mine, were flooded and without toilet paper.

The boys made their "one phone call" first, Nicky telling us, while the young officer was putting him back in his cell after his, that he'd left a voicemail message for his mother explaining what had happened. As there didn't seem to be any point in Carson doing the same thing, he elected to speak with "duty-counsel," a defence lawyer affiliated with the court that takes jailhouse calls and dispenses legal advice.

There was a delay, for some reason, before I was allowed to make my call, the clock on the wall in the phone area showing 4:35 when the young cop brought me in and had me stand in a glass-walled booth, a black, rotary-dial phone extension bolted to a worn wooden shelf that was fastened to the wall. "No phone books," the young officer explained. "No directory assistance. Give me the number you want called and we'll connect you."

I'd like to have talked to Malcolm Hardy, an old friend of mine who practised criminal law and handled drug cases, but since we hadn't been in touch for a while, I couldn't remember his complete cellphone number. As a result, like Carson I asked to be put through to a duty-counsel lawyer. A man named McDaniel or Nathaniel, I couldn't make out which, came on the line.

A fast talker, McDaniel jumped right in and told me, like it was a matter of course, that the police listened in on these calls; warned me to be careful about everything I said, in case they tried to use it against me. "Forget lawyer-client confidentiality," he cracked with pointed sarcasm, then went on to say I shouldn't tell the police anything more than my name and address, adding that, above all, I shouldn't confess to *anything*, no matter what the cops threatened to do. He said the best thing to do was to keep my mouth shut.

I spoke up at that point and suggested it was a little late for him to be giving me such advice, as the arresting officer had extracted a story from us during the raid and, based on that, had booked us as an organized crime operation.

"Why's that?" McDaniel asked.

"Don't ask me. An undercover guy came into the holding room earlier on and told me that's what she'd decided. He said it was because there were three of us involved. What's P-for-P, by the way?"

"Possession for the purpose of trafficking."

"We weren't trafficking."

"Of course you weren't," McDaniel said, "but they'll try to say you were. How much stuff did they book you for?"

"They told us under three when they brought us in."

"That means anything up to three kilograms. They use range numbers."

"It couldn't have been kilograms."

"Cannabis?"

"Yes."

"Debt lists? IOUs? Bank records? Anything to indicate money was changing hands?"

"No money *was* changing hands."

"Okay. So how it works is, one of you will have to take the rap, you'll pay a fine and that'll be it," he said confidently. "I wouldn't worry. It's run-of-the-mill stuff. Just don't say anything more from here on in. They'll take you down to the Bail Court at Old City Hall in the morning, somebody will have to post a $5,000 surety for each of you, and then you'll be released. Why did you talk to the police, though?"

"The arresting officer didn't give us much choice."

"Drug squad. Right . . ." he said, like he knew exactly what I meant. He was silent for a few seconds. Thinking the call was finished, I thanked him for his help and was just about to take the phone away from my ear, when he launched into a passionate spiel about how much the police *hated* guys like him, the lawyers, the barristers and solicitors — big-time troublemakers for the cops, according to McDaniel. "A royal *pain* in the ass is what we are," he said, like he was proud of it, continuing for the next few minutes in an effort to have me understand the various factors behind this longstanding and bitter animosity. "Good luck," he finally said, reminding me once again not to give the police anything they could use against me before ending the call.

The clock on the wall outside the booth read 4:50 when the young officer led me back to my cell.

Too tired to stand now, I lay down on the bed and tried to get some sleep; tried to forget that the pain in my shoulder was worsening again with the steady flow of icy air from above, that the muscles in my lower back were knotting up and starting to spasm, that my feet were freezing in their drenched shoes, that my almost dried-out contact lenses were burning in my eyes as I stared up at the dim bulb in the wire-mesh cage on the ceiling in an effort to keep them open . . . until at what seemed like increasingly shorter intervals, usually at the same moment I started to drift off, I was jolted out of sleep-deprived delirium by Spike letting go with yet another of her seismic sound tsunamis. I sat up while still not fully awake, looking around the cell and waiting for the tremor in the walls to subside: cold, scared, dead-tired and desperate for just a couple of minutes of shut-eye. Like Winston Smith confessing all at the end of Orwell's *1984*, I began to feel that I had no choice but to do the same. Call out to Spike when she next came by, admit defeat at her tormenting hands and tell her that I couldn't take it anymore and was willing to do, or say, or sign whatever she and Officer Val wanted me to, if she'd *just . . . stop . . . slamming the fucking door!*

CHAPTER **THREE**
COURT SERVICES

At some point — not sure of the time, though I had a feeling it was morning — I heard a commotion in the corridor outside our cells. The door to the block had opened and Carson, Nicky and I, springing to our viewing windows, spotted six uniformed officers (caps on, in bulletproof vests) having a heated conversation as they came toward our cells. They stood outside for a good minute, griping about a work-related matter that sounded like it might have had something to do with us. The discussion continued while they opened our doors, cuffed our hands behind our backs then hurried us through the station corridors to the receiving area where we'd been brought in the night before. There was an oversize white police van marked "Court Services" waiting in the first bay; I'd picked up from the way our escorting officers had been talking that we were headed to a different station for fingerprints and mug shots.

"Plus," one officer reminded the others, "there's a pick-up over at 36 Division too."

"Yuh *see?*" another officer piped up. "*This* is what really pisses me off. There's *no* fuckin' way we can do that and make it to the courthouse by 9:30."

"Why the fuck is dispatch always pulling shit like this?" the first guy wanted to know.

The question hanging in the air unanswered, Carson was hustled into one of the van's rear compartments by himself, while Nicky and I were ordered into a unit two doors away, a space that was small even for one person: no window, galvanized-metal walls and floor, a single bench-seat that we had to share, the two of us hunching over since there was no headroom. "Good if you're a midget," Nicky said as we contorted ourselves, in vain as it turned out, to find a comfortable sitting position.

We soon heard the driver start the truck. He revved the engine while the electric bay door droned open above us, backed out of the garage, threw the van in gear and booted it down the station driveway. After making a rolling stop when we came out to the street, the driver made a hard left onto what I knew was Lawrence Avenue, hitting the gas the moment the van straightened out. There was a traffic light just ahead at Morningside that I knew the driver was trying to make. But at the last second he changed his mind, jammed on the brakes and brought the van to a squealing stop. Nicky and I were tossed forward into the galvanized-metal wall, turning our faces sideways just before impact, our ears taking the blow, our heads thrown back against the other wall in the whiplash.

Twenty minutes of continuous tossing-around, a dozen more body-battering stops that left us sore and disoriented

— my left shoulder taking repeated thumpings, one of Nicky's cheekbones and his forehead suffering cuts that had started bleeding — we found ourselves stepping on jittery legs out of the Court Services van in the fluorescent-lit receiving area of another police division. Nicky asked our driver if he could have a minute to clear his head, explaining that he was dizzy from all the bouncing around. Blood on his forehead, he was pale and perspiring, a bad attack of the motion sickness to which he'd been prone since he was a little boy.

But there was no time, according to the cops transporting us; we needed to be upstairs ten minutes ago. And with that, we were whisked up a long flight of stairs to the building's second floor and taken to the Photograph & Fingerprint Room. The three cops accompanying us removed our hand-cuffs, pointed out two chairs next to a small window and told Carson and Nicky to have a seat, while I was turned over to the officer who appeared to be manning the electronic equip-ment, a man the other officers referred to as "Stan."

Two of our escorts left the room while the other stayed behind to stand guard near the door. Arms crossed, he barked at the technician, "Make it snappy, Stan. We gotta be outta here in ten."

"If you're thinking minutes, you can forget it."

"That's ten, as in one-zero."

Stan rolled his eyes in exasperation and readied his equip-ment. He was in his early fifties, a thin, small-framed man with what some might call feminine facial features, small, delicate hands, a poorly fitted brown toupee on his head and, to my surprise, powdery traces of flesh-coloured cover makeup on the back of his neck, just above the collar of his short-sleeved, blue police shirt. A gentle manner and a simpering voice, with a tendency to pronounce his Rs like Ws, he chatted amicably as he took my mug shot and finger-prints, at one point remarking on what fine-looking boys my sons were. "The curly blond hair on *that* one," Stan raved, smiling up at me and nodding over at Carson. "I think we know where *that* comes from, don't we? And the blue eyes on *this* one," he cooed as he finished with me and, hands on his hips, asked Nicky to step up for his "photo-shoot."

Stan took Nicky by the biceps, walked him backwards and stood him in position in front of the camera for his mug shot, shifting him a little to the right and then back to the left before he was finally satisfied. "Mm-*mm*," Stan mur-mured under his breath after the flash had gone off. "Okay, handsome," he said, putting his hands on Nicky's upper arms again and guiding him, like a dance partner, over to the light-table for fingerprinting.

Concerned that Nicky might not be able to figure out his instructions, Stan made a point of standing directly behind him at the light-table, his crotch a little too close to Nicky's behind for my liking.

"Hey!" I protested to the cop standing by the door, motioning with my head at what was happening.

"Come on, Stan," the cop said casually, like it was no big deal.

Stan told the officer petulantly to take it easy; said he wasn't committing a federal crime here, for heaven's sake. "Like *some* people I know," he winked at Nicky, who just rolled his eyes, came back to his chair and sat down.

Buoyed by the successful *pas de deux* with Nicky, Stan waved Carson eagerly forward for processing. He asked him, in an overly flattering voice as he stepped into position, if he happened to be on the school swim team by any chance. "You've *certainly* got the physique for it!"

Carson, a good nine inches taller than Stan, replied, in surly tones, that he was just there for the mug shot and fingerprints, thanks very much. Stan made a face, clamped his hands on his hips and said in a teasing voice, "Ooooh, *somebody* sure got up on the wrong side of the bed today . . ."

Hands cuffed behind our backs again after the affectionate interlude with Stan, we were hurried back downstairs to the receiving area and loaded into the Court Services van for another high-speed drive, this one thankfully much shorter, though after a jarring, last-second stop that hurled Nicky and me yet again into the galvanized-metal wall and ended with our driver leaning on his horn for a good ten seconds, Nicky, closing his eyes and groaning as he resumed his seat, admitted he'd eaten the Jamaican meat patty after all last night and his stomach was starting to rumble.

No move made to let us out of the stifling hot compartment once we arrived at our next destination, I yelled to the driver when I heard him step out of the truck and begin talking to someone: "*My son's feeling sick in here and thinks he might throw up!*"

No immediate response to the news, maybe half a minute or so later the driver made a big deal of unlocking our door, gruffly telling Nicky that he could step out for a second. I took advantage of the situation and scrambled out behind him, asked the driver if he could have a drink of some kind because he was severely dehydrated. We were in the receiving area of another police station, uniformed cops coming and going, patrol cars arriving and departing, a couple dozen officers chatting, kibitzing and milling about not far from the Court Services van.

"No time," the driver said. "We're late as it is."

Nicky wavered on his feet, pale and perspiring, a few feet away from a black officer who was watching as two plain-clothes white cops brought a black prisoner — maybe in his late twenties, his hair in dreadlocks, his hands cuffed in front of him and leg-shackles around his ankles — toward the Court Services truck. The cops escorting him undid the shackles and had him climb into the compartment next to ours, then replaced the shackles before closing up and locking the compartment door.

"There any way you could get my son a glass of water?" I called over to the black cop. "It's been a bumpy ride and he's not feeling too good."

The cop glanced at Nicky and saw he wasn't in the greatest shape. "We might have some Tang."

"That would do," I said.

He cleared it with our driver's partner, with whom he'd been talking, and headed upstairs, taking the steps two at a time.

Not happy with the end-run, our driver barked up at him, "Make it snappy, Errol! I'm fucking *late* here!"

"Hold your horses," Errol said, standing back for a female officer coming through the door before disappearing inside.

The drive not so bad once we got on the Don Valley Expressway, the Tang settled Nicky's stomach somewhat, and we were downtown and poking our way through rush-hour traffic in twenty minutes or so, the driver laying on the horn liberally, though fortunately we were moving at such a slow speed that, when he stepped on the brakes, the impact with which we hit the galvanized wall was minimal.

We stepped out of the van in the enclosed courtyard behind Old City Hall maybe ten minutes later and were promptly hustled through the door to a small basement hall where the driver and his partner handed us off to several uniformed officers in caps and bulletproof vests, who seemed to have been waiting for us.

Two officers walking in front, two behind, they led Carson, me and Nicky and the four other prisoners from the van along a succession of barely lit passageways smelling of mildew that ran through the basement of the 150-year-old building. Things were a bit cleaner and brighter after we crossed an open area, but in the narrow corridor we turned down on the other side, the lights were out, so the lead cop flicked on a flashlight that allowed the rest of us to see where we were going. In a few minutes we emerged from the darkness and were marched along a passageway with stone walls, arriving shortly at a cell door that one of the officers opened. The others removed our handcuffs, stood back and ordered us inside.

I entered first, whistling a little nervously since I had no idea what to expect. I was surprised to see there was only one other person in the low-ceilinged, dingy cell besides us: a man in his late thirties with a hard-bitten look about him — scars in several places on his face, a number of his teeth broken, his head shaved bald, two dents in his skull, plus numerous Hell- and devil-themed tattoos on his thick neck and up and down his muscle-built arms. The tattoos were readily visible since he was wearing the same short-sleeved overalls we were, his pair yellow instead of orange as I recall, and the letter K, followed by six digits, was stenciled in black on the overalls where a pocket would normally have been. I guessed it was his penitentiary number, by the looks of him, probably maximum security.

Sitting in the middle of one of the wall-bracketed benches on the far side of the room, his hands in cuffs, his feet in leg-shackles, he made a loud hissing noise, like he wanted my attention. I turned and looked more directly at him.

"No whistling!" he hissed, his lips moving but his teeth locked together. "*Birds* whistle! But they're *free*! *We're* not! No *whistling*! *Got* it?"

"Got it," I said, suggesting to the wide-eyed boys that it would probably be best if we parked ourselves on a bench on *this* side of the room, at least for now.

In deference to "Hellboy," as we later dubbed him, we made a point of talking extra quietly for the next little while, careful even then about what we said so as to avoid his wrath; even more careful, in my case, not to emit so much as the hint of a whistle.

There were no further outbursts from our prison friend, however, and after about half an hour we were moved into a cell we later learned was referred to as "The Pit" — an even dingier room than we'd been in with Hellboy. A stainless-steel toilet stood beside a low cinder-block wall, ready to overflow, no toilet paper; graffiti had been scratched in every available space on the yellow paint on the walls, along with hundreds of names, doodles, scrawls and dates, a couple from several decades ago. There were about thirty people crowded into the twenty-by-twenty-foot cell, all male and all black except for two Asians.

Some of them huddling in the centre of the room, others sitting on the benches along two of the walls, some standing on them, stretching their arms over their heads with their hands pressed against the ceiling, everyone stopped talking and looked over with wary curiosity the moment the boys and I walked in. A boy in blue jeans, a black T-shirt and dreadlocks, maybe in his mid-twenties, asked us what we were being booked for.

"P-for-P," I told him.

"P-for-P?" he said. "*No way.*"

"Where'd they get you?" another kid put in, equally incredulous.

"In our house."

"No shit?" the first guy said.

"How much?"

"Under three."

The first guy nodded, shrugged at Carson and Nicky standing beside me, said everything should be okay. "The cops put their foot on the scale when they weigh the shit. Everybody knows."

"They count roots and soil, too, man," a boy beside him added.

"*Oh yeah*," another boy said, backing him up.

Other guys came forward in answer to questions I had about how things worked in Bail Court. Except for the two Asians — who appeared to be in their forties, looked like they might be brothers and kept quietly to themselves — all the black kids seemed to be between about eighteen and twenty-five years old. They explained that the main point was to get somebody to post your bail for you. Five grand the usual in a P-for-P, that's if you didn't have any priors. If nobody showed, you had to go to the Don (the city's nineteenth-century-era prison next to the Don River in the east end of Toronto). It was a complete hole, according to the black kids, some of whom had been there a number of times when they couldn't get anybody to post for them. "You don't want to go to the Don," one boy said ominously. Several of the others shook their heads to echo the sentiment.

After probably half an hour in The Pit, a police officer came to the cell door, called our names and we were taken through a series of corridors to a meeting in a more modern part of the basement, a long, narrow but brightly lit room with rows of walled carrels on each side, duty-counsel lawyers with armfuls of file folders sitting behind glass partitions in each one, with whom we were to consult for five minutes about our case. According to the woman who was coordinating the duty-counsel meetings, because of our "organized crime" designation, Carson, Nicky and I each had to be represented by a different lawyer, therefore when our turn came, we were escorted to separate cubicles, the coordinator reminding us we had five minutes in which to discuss particulars of the charges against us and make arrangements for someone to come to court and bail us out.

Between the police officers, court officials, the other accused and duty-counsel lawyers darting about, there were probably close to fifty people in the not overly large room. There was no air conditioning, and none of the three fans overhead was working. The atmosphere was tense and frenetic, the volume of noise considerable as people came and went constantly, lawyers calling out client names, those of us in the carrels shouting to make ourselves heard through the round, mouth-level holes in the glass partitions.

An armful of legal-size file folders under her arm, my duty-counsel lawyer, a woman named Laura, wasted no time explaining that in order to make bail I'd need somebody who could come right to court, post a $5,000 surety with proof of assets in that amount — car ownership, home mortgage, anything like that. Phonebooks unavailable and no directory assistance at her disposal, Laura said I'd have to give her numbers that I knew off by heart.

"Somebody who can get over here in how long?" I asked.

"About an hour," she said, "give or take."

I thought about it for a moment. My youngest brother Peter was not in any kind of position to help me (his photo-processing business was "hemorrhaging money" the last time I'd talked to him), my other brother John was in bankruptcy after some shady financial dealings a few years back and my sister Frances was living in Collingwood, a two-hour drive away, so I gave Laura my best guess at my pal Malcolm's cell-phone number, telling her he was an old friend of mine, that he'd been a criminal lawyer here at Old City Hall for many years, adding that there might be a chance he was somewhere in the building that very moment. Laura said she thought she'd heard of him, but that he wouldn't do me much good unless she could reach him by phone.

I provided her with the names of two other people whose numbers I was sure about, and who I thought could meet the court's requirements: Trionne Cooper, a friend I'd known since we were in junior kindergarten together, a well-established Toronto musician who owned a car and a good-sized home in the Beach where she worked most days, and who I was pretty sure wouldn't hesitate to get down to court and help me out; and Dean Tansey, a publisher-friend of mine whom I'd known since we were counsellors at a summer camp in Muskoka during the early 1970s. His office was on Peter Street, a fifteen-minute walk from the courthouse, if that.

On her side of the glass partition, Laura scribbled the names and phone numbers on a notepad, slid her pen and some forms under the partition and had me sign them. She let me know, as she was taking them back, that she'd do her best to reach at least one of my sureties before I was called up to Bail Court. She didn't know exactly when that would be, unfortunately; things were apparently busier than usual today. No mention of the charges against me, she gathered her stack of file folders together, stood up and scooted off.

The Pit still crowded when we returned from court, Nicky and Carson wondered if anyone would actually show up to post bail for us, whether people might be reluctant to, because drugs were involved. Nicky, who'd given the duty-counsel his mother's number, said he knew she'd go ballistic. Her sister Barb and her husband Roger would too, Carson pointed out; he'd given his duty-counsel their number to call, but said he wasn't expecting the most favourable of reactions. What concerned him more, he said, was who might be able to post bail for me. I admitted that I wasn't overly confident about my duty-counsel Laura, but let them know that the people whose numbers I'd given her were good friends who wouldn't think twice about helping me. If it turned out for some reason that nobody could today, I explained that I'd eventually be in touch with my friend Malcolm, who had been a successful defence lawyer for thirty years and dealt with cases a lot more serious than ours all the time. "I'll give him the story of the Officer Val horror-show. I can't believe it won't make *some* kind of difference in what happens to us," I told them.

Carson smirked, shaking his head. "She was something else, man."

"She was," I said and, the three of us managing to squeeze into a spot on the bench along the wall that a couple of the other guys had vacated, we waited in nervous anticipation for Bail Court to get underway.

CHAPTER **FOUR**
EMERGENCY HAM

As court adjourned for lunch at 11:30, the boys and I, along with about ten other prisoners whose cases hadn't been called yet, found ourselves being moved to a different cell, this one slightly smaller than The Pit, though there were still about thirty of us crammed into what was essentially an extra-long cell but with floor-to-ceiling bars instead of a door. It afforded a view of an open area across the way where half a dozen uniformed male officers in caps and bulletproof vests were sitting around a table. Three of them were leaning back in their chairs with their feet perched on it, eating foot-long submarine sandwiches and sipping Diet Cokes and bottled water. One guy, with his chair tilted precariously back on its rear legs, was engrossed in a story in the *Toronto Sun*. A few others besides me, I noticed, watched him to see if he'd fall.

Soon a female officer breezed up to an open slot in the bars of the cell carrying a cardboard flat piled with sandwiches.

She gave a short whistle and announced lunch. Everyone hungry, we crowded around, formed a makeshift line then took our turn placing a hand in the six-by-six-inch slot to receive our sandwiches: one per person, either a slice of processed cheddar cheese on plain white bread, or flaked red tuna, also on white, straight from the can, no mayonnaise.

One boy, who'd been with us since our arrival in The Pit, asked if he could trade his cheese for Carson's tuna, which Carson was only too happy to do. As I was at the end of the line, I had to make do with the tuna, the flakes of fish dark-red and oily, the sight alone enough to have me feeling queasy. I was famished, however, so I took two bites, chewed quickly as the taste of the oily flakes was revolting, so much so that when it came time to swallow I couldn't, my throat refused to take it down. I spit the mouthful as discreetly as I could into the cellophane the sandwich had been wrapped in. The boy who'd switched with Carson was ogling my still-uneaten lunch. He said he didn't mind that I'd taken a bite. Happy to get rid of it, I passed it to him and he polished it off in several sizeable chomps. The boy sitting beside him asked how he could eat that shit. "Not shit, man," the boy replied with a satisfied smile as he stood up and went hunting for more leftovers.

After an hour or so, word circulated through the cell that Bail Court had resumed. To our surprise, Carson, Nicky and I were first on the docket. We stepped from "The Cage" as it was apparently called, two fellows we'd gotten to know over the course of the morning calling "good luck" as the cops put our handcuffs on, in front for the first time. We were led upstairs in our orange prison overalls to Bail Court and into the prisoners' dock, a glassed-in area to the side and toward the rear of the small courtroom.

Police officers in caps and bulletproof vests stood guard over each of us, the three of us taking our time sitting down, searching the room for familiar faces, but there were none. The spectator benches were empty except for our duty-counsel lawyers, who were on their feet and making their way back to the prisoner's dock, presumably to tell us why.

Carson's reported that he'd had to leave a voicemail message for his mother.

Nicky's informed him that she'd had to do the same thing with his aunt and uncle. Laura, looking as flustered as she had earlier, said she hadn't been able to reach any of the people whose names I'd given her, even to leave a voicemail. She wondered if they were the right numbers. I admitted that my lawyer-friend Malcolm's had been a guess, but said that I knew the other two were accurate. She showed me the notepad on which she'd written them down, none of the numbers even close to the ones I'd given her, so I dictated them again, even included Dean Tansey's extension this time, which I'd remembered. I asked her, in what I hoped was a nice way, if she could be careful when she was dialing this time. She gave me a weak smile, said she would, however she broke off suddenly, turned and looked toward the bench.

In a hunter-green court gown and collar tabs, a red-and-green academic hood around his shoulders, the presiding judge, a man in his early sixties with a thin face, pinched features, reedy voice and glasses perched halfway down his nose, was talking something over with his court clerk and two attorneys for the Crown. The female Crown accepted some file folders from her male colleague, a man also in his mid-thirties whose thick neck, rugby player's physique and shaved-bald head seemed somehow familiar. He exchanged a few words with the judge then turned, a solemn frown on his face as he walked back to the Crown's table to retrieve his black briefcase and headed for the doors at the rear of the courtroom.

He slowed down as he passed the prisoner's dock, glancing our way with a sheepish smile and a brief, acknowledging wave: it was Tom Patchell, married to my brother John's eldest daughter, my niece Jennifer. Aware that Tom was a federal Crown Attorney in Toronto, I had no idea he was working here at Old City Hall.

"What are the odds of that?" Carson said under his breath, receiving a poke in the back from the cop behind him before I could answer.

"He's had to recuse himself," Laura explained, watching Tom go out. "There must be a conflict of interest with your case."

The duty-counsel trio assured us they were going to try to get through to our bail sponsors again, and they rushed over to the Crown attorney's table, gathering round and conferring with her for a minute as the judge looked on with an irritated frown.

The tête à tête finally breaking up, the Crown approached the bench and asked the judge if she could have more time to familiarize herself with the particulars of the file. "And as none of the people posting surety for the accused have been able to make it to court yet, Your Honour, perhaps the accused could be recalled in an hour's time."

Another irritated frown, after a muttered comment to the Crown, the judge granted the postponement as requested, though with a warning. He reminded the Crown that they needed to wrap things up that day by three o'clock. He hoped the delay wasn't going to pose any problems for him being able to do that.

The Crown turned to our three duty lawyers.

"It won't be a problem, Your Honour," Laura assured him on behalf of the three of them, and the court clerk called the next case.

Downstairs, in what I think was our fifth different cell, the only other person with us a short, thin and harmless-looking East Indian man in his late forties, Carson and Nicky were finding it hard to be optimistic about the chances of someone appearing to post bail for them. Knowing his mother's and her family's feelings about marijuana, Nicky in particular was worried they might use this as an opportunity to teach him a lesson.

Mindful of our run-in with the maximum-security Hellboy earlier in the day, the three of us agreed the prospect of being sent to the Don was not a pretty one. To shake off the anxiety a bit, I reminded them that no matter what their mother's or their aunt and uncle's personal opinions were about pot, there was no way they were going to let either of them stay in jail. The message would get through. Somebody would be there for them when we next went up to court. As to me and my dyslexic duty-counsel, I told them there was no reason for her to get the numbers wrong this time. "For all I know," I said lightly, "somebody's wending their way over here right now."

"I just hope they wend quickly," Carson said, chuckling.

As it turned out, when we returned to Bail Court again, 2:20 the time on the clock across the way, my ex-wife Julie, her sister Barb and her husband Roger were indeed present, seated a few rows back from the bar on the other side of the courtroom, arms crossed, glaring straight ahead, none of them looking over when we were led into the prisoner's dock. I hadn't seen or talked to any of them in a little over seven years, since the separation. Julie was forty-eight now, still blond and slim, eye-catching as ever. Barb, who was two years older, was still an attractive brunette, still keeping herself in shape by the looks of it, as was Roger, a former teaching colleague of mine at Upper Canada College, the one who had arranged the blind date that brought Julie and me together in January 1984.

Carson and Nicky, relieved that they'd now be able to make bail, grew frantic when they glanced around the courtroom and realized no one had appeared for me. They looked in appeal, as did I, at my duty-counsel Laura, who had hurried over to the prisoner's dock. In some distress, she apologized but said there was nobody with those names at the numbers I'd given her. A sick feeling in my stomach, I told her I didn't see how that could be, that she must have dialed them wrong — again.

The judge muttering in some disgruntlement at the front of the room, itching to get the proceedings underway by the looks of it, Laura terminated our discussion and started to walk away. I called to her, told her to try Dean Tansey again, the third number on her list. I shouted it out, included Dean's extension again, the judge throwing the two of us a peeved frown before he turned his eyes to the Crown attorney and asked her to present her case.

She read out a summary of our file, speaking quickly and too quietly for the three of us in the prisoner's dock to make out exactly what she was saying. About the only thing I heard distinctly was that the police had conducted an investigation in response to a neighbour's report of marijuana growing in our backyard . . . we were being charged with P-for-P, under three, and the Crown was requesting that bail for each of us be set at $5,000.

"*Marijuana growing in our backyard?*" I whispered to Nicky. "Where the hell did *that* come from?"

"No talking," the cop guarding me said, poking a stiff finger in my back to make his point.

Carson's Uncle Roger took the stand, agreeing to act as surety for him and, producing the ownership papers for one of his cars, posted the required $5,000 bond. Julie went up next on behalf of Nicky, offering the judge a copy of the mortgage on the house in which she lived, the mortgagor being her eldest sister, Carol. The Crown told the judge she was satisfied with the documentation and would let her stand as surety.

Among their bail conditions would be that they have no contact with their father in any form or by any means until the case was over; that they at no time discuss particulars of the case with me; that they reside with their sureties, attend school, attend at court as ordered or have their representatives do so, and otherwise keep the peace. They would have one visit to the house at 122 Friendship Avenue to retrieve any personal belongings, within two hours of bail being granted; they would agree not to possess or produce marijuana, or be on the premises of establishments where marijuana was present, and were not to be found in hydroponic establishments or marijuana growing-supply stores. The final condition, was that they were at no time to be on the premises of 122 Friendship Avenue once they'd removed their personal belongings. Breach of any one of the aforementioned conditions would result in their arrest and incarceration in a federal prison until the case went to trial.

The judge asked them in turn if they understood the conditions. When they said they did, he ruled that they be released after the necessary paperwork had been completed. Julie, Barb and Roger continued to sit with their arms crossed, glaring forward.

Noting that it was now approaching three o'clock, the judge had Laura present herself at the bar, asking if there was anyone present to post bail for the co-accused, Mr. Illidge. Laura explained that she'd left a voicemail message for a friend whose office was not far from Old City Hall. She asked for His Honour's patience; said it should just be a few minutes and they'd know one way or the other, her eyes going nervously to the clock as she walked back to the defence table.

The court was silent for a few minutes, most people with bored or indifferent expressions on their faces, while Carson, Nicky and I had our eyes trained anxiously on the minute-hand of the clock . . . until the judge, his patience wearing thin, piped up abruptly and told Laura he was going to adjourn the hearing. Standing beside her chair, she assured him that she was aware of the time constraints, pleading that if His Honour could bear with her for *just* a bit longer it was likely —

But her words were cut off at this point as the rear doors of the courtroom burst open and in rushed my friend Dean Tansey, perspiring heavily and badly out of breath as he made his way to the bar and announced that he was here to post bail for Paul Illidge.

After an exasperated glance at the clock — the hands showed 3:05 — the judge gave him a couple of seconds to recover before asking him to take the stand. He quickly verified Dean's documentation to act as surety (ownership of his two-year-old Dodge Magnum), then imposed the same bail conditions on me as he had on Carson and Nicky. As he had with them, he stipulated I could not be on the premises of 122 Friendship Avenue at any time, or for any reason, other than to attend immediately after the bail hearing to pick up my personal belongings, and as it was with the boys, I was required to live with my surety until the case had concluded.

"Excuse me, Your Honour," I called from the prisoner's dock. "I don't think that's right."

"What *you* think has no bearing here, Mr. Illidge," the judge said irascibly. "You and your sons have been identified as a criminal organization, and your house a crime scene subject to an ongoing investigation."

"It's a family home."

"Not for the time being, it isn't."

"This is ridiculous, Your Honour. It's not a crime scene, we're not a criminal organization."

"You were running a marijuana grow-operation, Mr. Illidge."

"An *alleged* grow-operation."

"Object as you may," he said, his irritation mounting, "those are the provisions in law regarding grow-operations, Mr. Illidge."

"That I'm not allowed to live in my own house?"

"You were running a marijuana grow-operation, as I said."

"An *alleged* marijuana grow-operation," I reminded him again.

"We'll let the court determine that."

"But you just told me it was."

"You're getting into contempt territory here, Mr. Illidge."

"That may be, Your Honour, but is the court prepared to pay my mortgage and my bills for me? And where am I supposed to work? I'm a writer. My office is in my house."

"That's not the court's problem," he shot back, his face reddening.

"My surety, Mr. Tansey," I continued, "lives in Clarkson, west of Toronto. About an hour's drive from my house."

"That's of no concern, Mr. Illidge, since you're not *living* at your house."

"I wasn't aware that posting bail required Mr. Illidge to live with me, Your Honour," Dean put in from the stand.

The judge turned and looked over at him. "Are you saying you'd rather *not* post bail?"

"No, Your Honour. Only that it could be months before the case comes to trial. I have a wife and two children, and I travel a fair bit because of my work."

"Again, that's not the court's problem. As his surety, you're expected to know of his whereabouts at all times."

"With due respect, Your Honour, I think it's asking a lot for Mr. Illidge, a man in his fifties and a father, to live with me and have to be treated like one of my kids —"

"Perhaps Mr. Illidge should find someone else as his surety then," the judge snipped at Dean.

"No, Your Honour, that won't be necessary. I'm sure we can work something out," he said, covering his frustration with a tight smile.

"Let's hope so," the judge said, returning just as tight a smile, then making motions like he was preparing to call it a day.

"Your Honour," I spoke up, all eyes turning to the

prisoners' dock except Julie's, Roger's and Barb's. "It seems to me by not letting me live in my house, you're impeding me from keeping up my employment, which I've been made aware is a condition of my bail."

"It is," he said.

"I'm a writer. I work at home. How am I to generate income and pay my bills if I can't be in my place of work?"

"Well," he said, "you'll just have to pull your computer out of there when you pick up your personal belongings, won't you?"

"It's professional belongings that I'm concerned about, Your Honour. It'll take me more than one visit to remove the things —"

"In that case," he cut in, "you'd better make sure you have a can of paint and a brush in your hand whenever you're doing so."

"A can of paint and a paint brush?"

"That's right," he said, gathering his papers together, darting his eyes up at the clock. "If you're found on the premises for reasons other than what we might call 'routine maintenance,' you'll be sent to jail until the time of trial." He peered over at me above his glasses. "Are we clear about that?"

"No, we're not," I said.

Floored by my insolence or my obstinacy, I couldn't decide which, the judge tilted his head forward, glowered sternly at me over his glasses and fixed me with a threatening look that clearly said: "Just try me, Buster." He kept up the testy glare for a moment longer, turned at last and consulted briefly with the Crown, the two of them, along with the court clerk and Laura, directing their gaze upwards and over to the side of the room where a large-size Grand & Toy office calendar for the month of August had been fastened to the wall beside the clock with strips of grey duct tape. The tape on one of the top corners having come loose, it was hanging at quite a pronounced angle.

Peering up at the lopsided calendar, the group decided, after a brief discussion on the matter, that I would "attend at court" again on August 8. No reason given for the hearing, the judge did let me know that if I failed to appear, a warrant would be issued for my arrest and I'd go to jail, again, until the time of my trial.

No further business, he adjourned the hearing, and everyone in the court sprang to their feet as His Honour, with a perturbed look on his face, stepped down from the bench and, the folds of his gown flowing out behind him, made a hasty exit through a door off to his right, my friend Dean still on the stand, waiting to be dismissed. It was 3:35.

Our police escorts returned us to the cell where we'd had lunch, The Cage considerably less crowded now than it had been earlier. We talked to several boys we'd met and got to know in The Pit. Four of them had managed to make bail and, like us, were waiting for their paperwork to come through; three were waiting for transport to the Don, and would be returning to court for the next few days until somebody showed up and posted for them.

One of these was a nineteen-year-old boy named Julian. A shy, soft-spoken guy, Julian had told us earlier in the day that he lived with his aunt (he pronounced it 'awnt'). She worked for a company that cleaned office buildings at night, and had no car, no extra cash and no credit cards. He said he was resigned to spending the next few nights in the Don, and his days here in The Pit, while she and his cousins worked on raising the five grand for his bail. The cops had caught him the night before with half an ounce of pot and $500 in his pocket. Most of the money was from his part-time job, where he'd just been paid that day. Though he hadn't told the cops this, he was hoping to sell the grass. Rent was due on his aunt's apartment and he knew she was going to be short. It was a bitch, Julian said, because he didn't even smoke pot. Soccer was his thing. He was playing in two leagues that summer, had an offer of a scholarship to an American college, but if he was convicted for the pot, with a criminal record he wouldn't be able to enter the U.S. He panicked when the cops grabbed him and started searching him. He broke away when they went to cuff him and outran them, took off into a ravine and went through the woods, thinking he'd made a getaway. But the cops were there waiting for him outside his aunt's apartment building when he got home: he'd forgotten they'd taken his wallet when they were searching him. They stood him against the side of the cruiser and told him that, along with possession and trafficking, they now had him for resisting arrest. Julian said that while one cop held his arms behind him, the other one took a can of mace, held his one eye open and sprayed the irritant. Then they did the same thing to his other eye. Like us, he'd spent the night in a police station cell and been brought to Old City Hall first thing that morning. He kept his head down most of the time when he spoke, not wanting us to see the whites of his eyes, which, the few times we did glimpse them, looked swollen, badly bloodshot and sore. He said, after we'd been chatting for a while, that he was "kind of surprised to see people like you here. You know . . . an older white man and his two sons."

"Well, Julian," I said, "we're kind of surprised ourselves."

He laughed. "P-for-P?"

"P-for-P," I said. He lifted his hand, made a fist and bumped mine when I held it up. "Cool," he said, smiled and bumped Nicky's and Carson's fists too.

It was a little before 5:30 when a uniformed officer opened the cell, held up a clipboard and read off five or six names. Ours among them, we bid Julian farewell, wished him good luck with his case and, as instructed, followed the cop into the open area across from the cell.

He had us remove our orange coveralls, turn them over to one of several cops eating takeout food at the break table, then directed us to follow him out of the cell area, through a door and along to a tiny office, where a female officer behind the counter in a cashier's wicket had us sign for our personal possessions: a large manila envelope for each of us containing our shoelaces, a police form to that effect in the envelope as well. The cop with the clipboard passed us off to a female officer who brought us out to the hall, around a corner and through another door into a high-ceilinged rotunda in the basement of the cavernous old building.

Julie, Barb and Roger were seated on a wooden bench to our right, arms folded and staring straight ahead in hostile silence as we walked over to them. They gave the boys cold looks and wouldn't make eye contact with me, so I went past them and over to greet my friend Dean, who was standing in the middle of the hall. We shook hands, had a quick embrace, during which I apologized for all the trouble and thanked him for coming through for me. I apologized, too, for the fact that I was going to have to live with him, his wife Lee-Anne and his kids Emma and Joey. Nobody told me about that part, I explained.

A publisher of law books, many of his authors prominent legislators, judges and lawyers — extremely knowledgeable about the justice system and the legal profession — Dean said he was appalled by the way the judge handled himself in the hearing; deplored, even more, the fact that I wasn't allowed to live in my house for the duration of the case, when these things sometimes took a year or more to resolve. He couldn't understand it; said he'd never heard of something like this happening at a hearing, and didn't see how the court could possibly justify it in law. I suggested it probably had something to do with the arresting officer, whom I explained was quite the bitch; and because there were three of us, had made a point of booking us as a criminal organization. "That's why we're not allowed back in the house. We're a crime family."

"Come on," Dean said.

"Goodfellas, as they say."

"Give me a break."

Julie called over from the bench along the way at this point to tell me, in scathing tones, that I had to call Hannah right away. She'd been hysterical all night, unable to sleep and frightened out of her mind. "You need to call her right now," she repeated. "She's *devastated* by what you've put her through."

Appreciating her anger and why it would be directed at me, I let the jab pass without comment, replying calmly that of course I was going to call Hannah.

As the police had emptied our pockets before we left the house, and Dean only had bills and plastic, I had no choice but to walk over to Julie and Barb and ask for a quarter. They carefully avoided looking at me, made no effort to check their purses for change. The same thing happened when I stepped in front of Roger. He kept his eyes elsewhere too, his hands firmly in his pants pockets and gave no sign that he was intending to take them out.

No other options, I continued standing there, turned to Julie after a few uncomfortably silent moments and asked what she wanted me to do. Between a rock and a hard place now, Roger finally took a hand out of his pocket and, careful to avert his gaze as he did so, held out a quarter.

Carson and Nicky having gone over to chat with Dean, I shuffled off in my laceless shoes until I found a payphone at the far end of the hall. My left arm out of commission, my right hand shaking whenever I lifted it, I cradled the phone against my shoulder, dropped the quarter three times trying to get it into the slot, was luckier on the fourth and the coin finally went down.

Hannah picked up after the first ring, shouted into the phone like she knew it was me, hysterical as she tried to explain how scared she'd been. She'd stayed awake all night and had no idea what had happened until her friend Christina called her at Holly's and said the police had raided our house and found drugs, thousands of dollars in cash and some guns. She was crying, apologizing through sobs for being so upset, but said she couldn't stop shaking, she'd been terrified and just wanted to hear our voices. She said she was just so relieved that we were all right, said so several more times as she tried to get her sobbing under control and calm down enough to talk.

Christina had called with news of the raid about nine, just after the police had taken us away. Hannah said she talked about it with Holly, and the two of them decided to go over to the house about eleven o'clock, when they figured the police would have gone. All the lights were off; there was a black SUV with a white trailer parked out front, its doors open but there didn't seem to be anything inside. She and Holly sneaked into the backyard, climbed through a window in the family room and walked around. The house looked like it had been robbed. She said they were too scared to go down the basement. "For some reason, though," Hannah laughed, "I made Holly come upstairs with me, went into the bathroom in your bedroom and picked up your contact lens case, the fluid and your glasses. Isn't that weird? It was just an instinctive reaction, I guess."

Holly started to get the creeps, thought maybe the cops were outside watching the place, hoping to arrest her too, so they decided to leave. The back doors of the trailer were open. They took a closer look, and there were a couple of empty cardboard boxes inside, some extension cords and two or three green garbage bags. She asked me what I thought might have been in them. I said I had no idea, but that it couldn't have been that important.

Hannah said that, for a minute, she and Holly thought about taking the bags, they didn't know why. But they spotted Mary-Ellen McCluskey standing at her front door looking over. "I don't think she saw us," Hannah said. "It was like she was keeping an eye on the trailer or something."

"I'm sure that's exactly what she was doing," I said, and gave her the story of Mary-Ellen's hollered declaration that she and Wes had played no part in the raid.

"It was *her* that ratted you out to the cops?"

"Apparently so. Anyway, I'm sorry I wasn't able to call you at Holly's last night and let you know what was happening. Things just weren't in my control, honey."

"I know," she said. "I'm just so happy! I'm so relieved you're all right."

I told her that we were tired and grungy, but otherwise fine; that I'd stop by her mom's house and see her right after I went to Friendship Avenue to pick up a few things.

"I'm just so glad you're all right, Dad!" she said once more.

"I'm just so glad *you're* all right," I said. "Having an arch-criminal for a father and all."

"I'll still love you, Dad. Don't *ever* worry about that."

"I knew I could count on you, sweetheart."

"Absolutely," she said.

"Why don't we break out the Celebration Ham when this is all over?" I kidded her.

"It'll have to be the Emergency Ham," she said, playing along. "We already polished off the Celebration Ham on Nicky's birthday."

"The Emergency Ham it'll be then."

'Breaking Out the Hams' was among our favourite comic bits from *The Simpsons*, ham being Homer's food of choice for important family occasions.

Hannah's light chuckle when she said goodbye let me know she was feeling better. Replacing the receiver, it was my turn to feel relieved.

CHAPTER FIVE
TO SERVE AND PROTECT

Borne along in the crowd of commuters streaming south toward Union Station to catch their trains, Dean and I made our way down Bay Street, along King and through the financial district toward his office. The temperature still a sweltering twenty-eight degrees, the light from the late-afternoon sun was so bright I had to keep my right hand over my eyes, my contact lenses in such a parched state that when I peeked between my fingers to see where I was going, everything appeared out of focus and blurry. I hobbled, stumbled and otherwise wended my way slowly behind Dean, who at one point told me to hang on and ducked into a convenience store.

He came out a minute later with two bottles of spring water, opened one for me, which I was on my way to draining when he spotted an opening in the passing crowd, seized me by my good arm and we joined the rush again. Leading the way a few feet in front of me, he called back as we moved along with the crowd. Told me what a fluke it had been that he'd even picked up the duty-counsel's phone message. Apparently he'd left the office mid-afternoon but had gone back for something he'd forgotten. He just happened to notice his message light flashing while he was rummaging around in his desk looking for whatever it was. He was thinking of ignoring it but saw "Federal Court" on the caller ID and thought it could be one of his authors, a federal judge from whom he was expecting a fairly important call. "The weirdest thing, though," he said, "is that I had my car with me so I could show the ownership to the judge. I almost always take the train into work. For some reason I decided to drive today. Serendipity, I guess," he said.

"Call it what you want," I said. "Without it I'd be spending the night in the Don Jail."

"Ugh," said Dean. "That's not something I'd wish on anybody. I've heard stories from some of my lawyer friends, and they're not very pretty. The place is supposed to be infested with vermin. And then there's the rats and cockroaches," he joked.

"No whistlers, though," I said, and described our brief encounter with the Hellboy earlier in the day.

"That's scary."

"We thought so."

Dean managed to find my lawyer-friend Malcolm's phone number in the Law Society Directory when we got back to his office. He thought it'd be a good idea for me to call and let him know what was going on. He'd phone Lee-Anne and give her the gist of the situation. He said not to worry, she wouldn't have any problem with me staying there; Joey was working at camp for the summer (Pinecrest, where the two of us had first met) and his daughter Emma was teaching swimming during the day at the local community centre, and out with her friends at night. He said he didn't think there'd be any issues and, when he saw the fingers of my right hand trembling over the telephone keypad, dialed Malcolm's number for me.

It was the first time I'd had to avail myself of his legal services since 1991, a night in late October when Julie called from a police station at two in the morning to say she'd been charged with drunk driving and wondered what she should do. Malcolm, as always, was guarded in his comments after I'd given him the lowdown on the raid. He was not as concerned about the over-the-top police tactics and rights violations as he was about my bail arrangements, in particular the conditions under which the Crown had released us. They were pretty stiff, according to him. He advised me not to stick around the house too long when I went over with Dean to pick up my personal belongings.

We arranged to meet at Friendship Avenue the next morning at eleven o'clock, so he could have a look at the "crime scene." Apparently I was allowed in the house as long as I was accompanied by my lawyer. He told me to hang in there, the worst was over; said I should make the best of a bad situation, he'd see if he could talk to the Crown about a bail change, adding that, though he didn't want to be alarmist and was just telling me for my own good, it was extremely important that I comply with my bail conditions "to a T." He said you could never tell with the cops; that for all we knew they had somebody watching the house right now. "They pick up most guys for breaching bail within twenty-four hours after their arrest, you know," he warned. "And don't think the nosy neighbour who squealed on you to begin with will have any compunction about doing so again. You can't be too careful here, Paul, remember that."

A combination of heavy rush-hour traffic and his unfamiliarity with the roads in east Toronto made the drive out to Scarborough a slow one, Dean and I pulling into the driveway at Friendship Avenue a little after seven. The trailer Hannah said the cops had left behind was gone. The front door was unlocked, a lucky break since I had no key. Stepping inside, the first thing I did was go over and check my leather billfold, which was still sitting on the hall table where the police left it when they emptied out my pockets. But the $80 in cash I'd had was gone, as were my driver's licence, birth certificate, health and social insurance cards, ATM and credit cards. Only my Toronto Public Library card was there, my sole piece of ID now. Not that it would do me much good, I picked it up anyway and, after checking the table drawers (a perfunctory gesture, as I was sure nothing would turn up), reported the missing cards and cash to Dean. He was outraged, of course; couldn't believe the police would do something like that. "It's just plain *mean*," he said.

"They were a mean bunch," I told him, and we started through the house: just as the bail judge had deemed it in court, it was indeed a crime scene. The living room and dining room had been turned upside down, the furniture tipped over, the rug partially rolled up, cushions from the armchairs and the sofa strewn about, lamps lying on their sides, all the artwork off the walls and spread around the floor, some of the frames damaged, the glass on my Robert Bateman "Church Doors" print now with jagged cracks in several places.

The flower vase, papers, file folders and books I had on

the dining-room table had been swept off and lay scattered on the carpet. The drawers in the sideboard had been pulled open and searched, cutlery, napkins and candles spilled out on the floor. The top of the piano was standing open, the panel down below by the foot-pedals had been pried off, the police using a crowbar or a large screwdriver to remove it, judging by the looks of the gouges in the wood. The bench was lying on its side several feet away, sheet music spilled around it. Dean and I stepped over it to get to the kitchen, but stopped before entering because of the scene that greeted us: flour, coffee, sugar and rice had been dumped from their canisters onto the countertops, the fridge and freezer doors were standing wide open, as were all the cupboards and drawers throughout the room, some of the contents still inside, but dozens of boxes, bags, cans, jars and bottles had been pitched to the floor, leaving shards of broken glass and different-coloured liquids pooling here and there on the white ceramic tiles. Lying in pieces, as well, were several china dinner plates, numerous wine-glasses, tumblers, coffee mugs, the ceramic jug that used to hold our bags of milk, a crystal salad bowl that had belonged to one of my grandmothers, along with the Limoges porcelain teapot, an antique from the early 1800s, that had belonged to *her* grandmother — its demise no doubt the source of at least one of the gleeful *"Oops!"* that the boys and I heard coming from the kitchen while the search was underway.

Not watching where he was going as we ventured through the mess to have a look in the family room across the way, Dean slipped while attempting to skirt a puddle of spilled olive oil, lost his balance and fell backwards — catching my outstretched arm as he was going down and just managing to stay upright, though not before his other foot shot out from under him and kicked the top half of a broken maple syrup bottle across the room so it burst into bits when it hit the wall beside the sliding-glass door.

The police had left it open so animals — skunks and raccoons probably — had come in from the backyard during the night, looted the open fridge of fruit, cheese and several containers of leftovers; dragged from the cupboards and broken into boxes of pancake mix and various breakfast cereals, leaving a trail of Honey Nut Cheerios, Frosted Flakes and Harvest Crunch granola leading across the floor out to the backyard. The spilled cereal mixed in with broken jars of soya, salsa and spaghetti sauce, artichoke hearts, olives and dill pickles, I worked my way over to the sliding-glass door and closed it while Dean removed his shoes, took them into the powder room just along the hall and washed off the olive oil.

Upstairs, in the bedrooms and the bathrooms, the doors to all the closets, cupboards and cabinets were standing open, as were all the drawers in our dressers, the contents, as had been the case downstairs, removed and thrown to the floor. All the books had been pulled off the shelves in my bedroom bookcases. Sheets and blankets had been stripped from the beds, the mattresses lifted off the box springs and leaned against the walls. The kids' school backpacks had been emptied, their clothes pitched on the floor, their trash cans emptied, and Carson's and Nicky's guitars had been taken out of their cases and were lying beside their beds, the middle strings on the two acoustics broken where somebody had stuck a hand in to search the hollow wooden bodies for drugs.

In our spare bedroom, the thirty or so Bankers boxes that I kept on shelves in the large floor-to-ceiling closet — boxes in which I stored all my old manuscripts, writing and

correspondence, business records, tax and financial information, as well as important family papers, old photographs and
childhood memorabilia — had been taken out of the closet
and dumped in the middle of the floor, leaving a mound of
paper about three feet high in the centre of the room, tapering
off closer to the walls where, in a few places, the carpet was
still visible, though just barely.

"Jeez . . ." said Dean with a pained look, taking in the
mess. "How the hell are you supposed to clean *this* up?"

"I think that's the point, Dean."

"This is disgusting."

"I'd say so."

Back along the hall, I checked Nicky's room to see about
Keke, his pet cockatiel, but clearly Carson and he had already
been by the house, as his cage and stand were gone. The door
to the wall safe that his grandfather had installed for him
was open, the lock-box in which he kept his lawn-cutting and
birthday money (the thousand dollars the police had seized
during the search) lying upside down and empty on the floor
just below.

With Malcolm's word of caution in mind — that I
shouldn't be in the house too long because you never knew
what the police could be up to — I headed back to the master
bedroom and, since I only had the use of my one hand, asked
Dean to help pack the suitcase; some clean clothes, underwear, toothbrush and paste, my shaving kit and three books
from the pile on the floor: Truman Capote's novel *The Grass
Harp*, a "definitive" biography of Beethoven I was partway
through, and *Zen Mind, Beginner's Mind* by Shunryu Suzuki,
a book that I just felt I needed to have with me.

Ready to go, I mentioned to Dean that my bottle of

aftershave lotion, *Bleu* by Givenchy, which Hannah had given me just a month ago for Father's Day, was missing from the bedside table where I always left it. The table drawer was open and the police had obviously gone through it, but there was no sign of the aftershave, or its blue box.

"Maybe they took it as evidence," Dean joked.

"That must be it," I said.

Dean closed up the suitcase, lifted it off the bed and carried it into the hall.

As we were heading downstairs, he said he wouldn't mind having a look in the basement, just to see what had prompted the police blitzkrieg, so we continued downstairs and I showed him into my writing office. All the books had been cleared off the shelves on the walls and tossed to the floor; the drawers of my two filing cabinets were standing open, the contents dumped out, file folders, bundles of old household bills, chequebooks, notebooks, office supplies, manufacturers' guarantees; the papers, writing pads and various manuscript pages that I'd had on my desk beside the computer had been swept off and lay mixed in with things the cops had cleared off the shelves in my closet: material for the writing, publishing and film production companies I'd operated over the years, most of it heaped in the middle of the floor: contracts, catalogues, business cards, book manuscripts, screenplays, storyboards, videotapes, 16mm film reels, a couple of the canisters open, the unspooling film creased in places where it had been trampled on.

Dean stood in the corner to the left of my desk and glanced down at the four-by-two-foot plastic reservoir where Nicky had been growing his plants. The eight small plastic bins filled with half-inch red clay pellets were still sitting in their openings on the white reservoir-cover, the small irrigating hoses coming from the pump still in place. But as the power cord to the unit had been cut, there was no water flowing through them. Three marijuana plants, maybe six inches high, which the police had for some reason left behind in the unit, had dried out, their stems curling over, their leaves still green but wilting and beginning to shrivel up, dead as far as I could see.

"This is it?" said Dean.

"This is it."

He leaned down and fingered the leaves of one of the dead plants.

"Why would they leave three plants behind?"

"No idea," I said, noticing that the pots in which Nicky's yellow beans, cherry tomatoes and green peppers had been growing were now lying on the floor, as were the pots with the pink, blue and orange miniature-cactuses he used to add colour to his "garden." Saddest of all, a small green, grey and brown clay Buddha that had been a gift from a student of mine at Upper Canada College in 1988, a present he'd brought back from a Zen monastery he'd visited in Japan during his summer vacation, lay in two pieces on the floor beside the grow unit, Buddha's head snapped off at the neck but still smiling against the red plastic milk crate beside which Dean was standing.

"So where's the light?" he asked, looking up at a metal hook in the ceiling.

"Taken as evidence I guess."

"What's illegal about a light?"

"Nothing, as far as I know."

"What's *that* all about?" Dean asked, pointing behind me. The police had written "69 PLANTS" in permanent black marker at eye-level on the white wall.

"A cop with a vivid imagination, I guess."

Back upstairs, I shut off the air conditioning and refilled the humidifier in the dining room beside the piano. The file folder containing my application for a Health Canada medicinal marijuana licence was lying open in the corner, the forms nowhere in sight. I wondered if Officer Val had taken them with her after all — so I couldn't use them as evidence at my trial maybe — but in case she hadn't, I told Dean I'd feel better if they were in my hands, rather than hers. After a few minutes of rummaging around we discovered them buried under the newspaper sports section and half a dozen of my Shakespeare novels. Twelve pages in all, still paperclipped together, some water damage to the top few from the spilled flower vase, but otherwise intact. "A doctor's signature and none of this would have happened," I said to Dean, handing him the application forms to put in my suitcase.

He did, then shook his head. "I know it's out of character," he said, "but I'm kind of at a loss for words, Paul."

"*Kind* of?" I said.

He chuckled, closed up my suitcase. "Let's just get outta here," he said. "The place is giving me the creeps."

The directions to Dean's place were a tad complicated (my unfamiliarity with west Toronto and beyond equaling Dean's here in the east), so the plan we worked out was that I'd follow him to his house in my car and, because my cellphone battery was dead and we'd have no way of getting in contact, the two of us would try not to get separated. When we went to leave, however, my car keys weren't on the hook behind the front door where I was pretty sure I'd left them. Not in the drawers of the table in the front hall, not in any of the rooms on the main floor, Dean did a quick check upstairs while I had a look around the basement, but there was no sign of the keys. My spare set, which I kept in the back of the cutlery drawer in the kitchen, was gone too. Maybe a good thing, as I said to Dean when we realized the keys were a lost cause, since I only had the use of my one arm, and my contact lenses were so dry that, as I told him, "I'm seeing everything through a miasmic blur."

"Not a miasmic blur!" he kidded, picking up my suitcase. "We'll go in my car. I'll be taking the train into work in the morning, so you can borrow it to drive back here and meet Malcolm. Maybe check at a Honda dealership about getting a new key. Won't be cheap though, if it's one with the computer chip in it. I think Lee-Anne paid $180 when she lost hers."

My hands still with their Parkinson's shake, an aftereffect of the handcuffing, Dean locked the front door with the spare key that I kept in a hole in the grouting under the living-room window, handed it to me and I followed him off the porch. I was heading down the front walk behind him when I noticed the garden shears lying on the grass off to one side of the weeping mulberry tree, right where the cop had made me drop them last night. I stepped over to the other side of the garden and picked them up. As I slipped them under the railing and set them on the porch, I heard a noise next door and, glancing over, saw somebody opening the McCluskey's front door: Mary-Ellen peering over at Dean's car in the driveway beside mine. My head down, I turned quickly to head over to it . . . but stopped when I saw on the grass, about twenty feet in front of me — like somebody had stood on the front steps and pitched them — the keys to my Honda.

Dean headed to the Tim Hortons near the highway for a coffee — the two of us were going to meet there in twenty minutes — while I drove to Julie's house, two blocks over. The drapes were open and Hannah was standing in the front window when I pulled up. She saw me, disappeared from the window and was outside running to meet me as I came up the driveway. We gave each other a tight hug, Hannah apologizing that she was starting to cry again . . . she was just so *glad* everybody was all right. Standing back and wiping her eyes with a tissue I'd handed her, she collected herself, smiled and said it would be weird living with Mom again. I told her that once my place was cleaned up, she could come over any time. "But no wild parties," I said.

"Not in much of a mood for parties right now."

"I'm sorry Holly had to get dragged into things." Holly lived next door with her parents and older sister. They treated Hannah as one of their family.

"She's fine," said Hannah. "She and her mom have been great, as usual."

"Thank goodness for the Raesides."

"I'll say. I'll go get your contact things and your glasses," Hannah said just as Carson and Nicky came outside.

"So get this, Dad," Nicky said, and took me over to his black 1995 Chevrolet Monte Carlo that was parked in Julie's driveway: a high-mileage, almost rust-free two-door coupe that he'd bought with his landscaping money the previous summer for $2,500. His pride and joy, Julie had been allowing him to keep the car in her driveway in return for lawn-cutting and snow-shoveling services. "I couldn't find my car keys at Friendship when we were picking up our personal belongings," he explained, leaning down and reaching under the Monty's front right bumper. "I figured the cops must have taken them," he said, and in a moment brought out the small magnetized-metal case in which he hid his spare key. "But check this out."

He hopped behind the wheel, started the engine and it roared to life, as it always did with its big engine, however this time it kept on roaring, revving in a high-pitched whine at what sounded like full speed, even though Nicky had stepped out of the car. Carson winced with the racket from the racing engine, a look of panic on his face — he said it sounded like it was going to blow up. Hannah was back with my contact lenses, standing in the driveway with her hands clamped over her ears, shouting at Nicky to "Turn the ruddy thing off before it explodes!"

He did, the four of us standing there in the sudden silence, miffed as to what could have happened. Carson wondered if the cops might have done a little tampering with the motor. Nicky pointed out that because the car was registered to him, they might have got his mother's address from his driver's licence, and decided to check it out.

I told him to pop the hood so we could have a look. Hannah took no chances and stayed back by the garage as the three of us peered in at the engine. Everything seemed fine . . . except I noticed the air hose that ran to the intake manifold had been detached. If the Monty had been put in gear, it would have shot out of the driveway at full speed, soared across the street, onto the front lawn and into the large bay window of the house across the street. Reconnecting the hose, I asked Nicky to start the car again. He turned the key.

The engine roared to life, and after a few seconds it kicked down to its normal idling speed. I signaled Nicky to shut it off and lowered the hood, a thought coming to mind as I spotted two small streams of what looked like oil that had trickled out from under the car. I crouched down, peered under the Monty's front-end and saw right away that both brake lines had been cut, a clean job about six inches back from the two front tires. "Huh," Carson snickered as I got to my feet. "And the cops are calling *us* organized criminals."

CHAPTER SIX
IN FLAGRANTE DELICTO

I arrived at Dean's house fairly rattled but in one piece a little before 8:30. I had a long shower, put on some clean clothes, and had a glass of wine with Lee-Anne and Dean in the kitchen while they made dinner.

With no sleep for thirty-six hours and several more glasses of wine at dinner, my lids were drooping and I was saying goodnight to the two of them by ten o'clock. I took my nightly blood-pressure pill, a couple of extra-strength Advil for the pain in my back and my left shoulder, then laid in bed reading until the pills kicked in.

Up early Friday morning, I had breakfast with Dean before he caught the 6:30 train into the city. He asked me how I'd slept.

"Fitfully," I told him.

He said he wasn't surprised, what with the host of things I probably had on my mind.

"It's a host all right," I said, and the two of us shared a laugh.

Knowing I had no money, Dean gave me the twenty dollars he had in his pocket, telling me Lee-Anne could let me have more if I needed it.

I told him that I didn't think there'd be a problem. As far as I knew, there was no charge to get a replacement driver's licence at the motor vehicle bureau (apparently there was one not far from where he lived). And I was confident that Maria, the manager at my bank, would let me take some money out when I reported my cards had been stolen.

Chuckling, Dean asked if I'd tell her by whom.

"You think she'd believe me?"

"I wouldn't," he teased, then took the last sip of his coffee and said he had to get a move on if he wanted to make his train.

Picking up a replacement driver's licence at the motor vehicle bureau with no trouble, I made good time on the drive across the city out to Scarborough to meet Malcolm. I stopped in at the bank on the way, explained to the manager, Maria, that my wallet had been stolen the night before and had her set me up with a temporary ATM card so I could take out some cash.

Malcolm was waiting for me when I arrived at Friendship Avenue a few minutes after eleven. He was leaning against his silver Mercedes, which he'd parked on the street rather than in the driveway. As he'd just come from a court hearing at Old City Hall, he was dressed in a light grey summer sportsjacket, white shirt, burgundy silk tie and tailored black pants. Though he claimed not to make a great deal of money as a criminal lawyer, it was a point of pride with Malcolm to look his best when he was in the courtroom — not like many in his profession, according to him, whose style he once described as "solicitor shabby." As I usually did, I commented approvingly on his natty wardrobe, expecting the regular story of where he'd purchased its various components and what a price break the salesman had given him, getting a good deal another point of pride with him. But he let the compliment pass that morning, and just glanced nervously up and down the street with an eye out for surveillance, or so I assumed from the wary look on his face as he headed me quickly across the lawn and up to the front door.

"What's the problem?" I asked him. "I thought you said this was legal?"

"You never know with the cops," he said anxiously, slipping inside and closing the door quickly behind him.

He checked my bail papers as we moved through the front hall. On our way downstairs I gave him a play-by-play of the raid as it had unfolded, the guns, the ransacking of the house, the forced confession, the sociopathic Officer Val.

"Nothing you can do about any of that," Malcolm said matter-of-factly as we entered my office. "It's just your word against theirs," he explained. "There's no remedy for breach of rights."

"This was a lot more than a breach," I said, and flicked the light on.

Malcolm took one look at the three dried-out plants the cops had left behind in the grow-unit, yelled "*Shit!*" and turned fast for the door. "We have to get out of here!" he shouted. "Come on!"

Taking the steps two at a time ahead of me, he stood in the hall at the top of the stairs catching his breath, looked down the hall to the front door, then the other way toward the kitchen. "Let's use the back," he said, and the two of us, with some fancy footwork crossing the messy kitchen floor, made it out the sliding-glass door into the backyard, tore around the side of the house and rushed out to the street.

We ran down the drive, over to his Mercedes and took a minute to catch our breath. "It's a set-up," Malcolm said, panting. "They catch you on the premises with pot growing, you go to jail. *In flagrante delicto.* No questions asked."

"It's not growing, Malcolm. It's dead."

"It's *pot*, Paul. A breach of bail." He handed me back my bail papers. "Remember I told you most bail-breakers are picked up within the first twenty-four hours? You can't be in the house. *Ever.* Get somebody to remove that stuff ASAP. Just don't do it yourself. You can't take any chances here. When's your next court date?"

I told him.

"I don't need to be there for that. Just let them know I'm representing you. Have you talked to Julie?"

"She let her feelings be known outside Bail Court."

"I'll bet," he said, taking out his car keys. We shook hands, he opened his door and threw me one of his lopsided grins just before stepping inside, the one he used to give me when we were twelve, line-mates on the same Pee Wee hockey team, and one of us had just scored a goal on a nice pass from the other.

"Just stay out of the house, okay?"

"Like I said, Malcolm, I'll do my best . . ."

As that night was the beginning of the Civic Holiday long weekend, Dean and Lee-Anne were heading north for the holiday. I'd been out on bail for less than twenty-four hours, and Dean, as my surety, was legally responsible for my "whereabouts and activities" at all times, so we agreed that it might be best if I came along to their cottage on Go Home Lake, two hours northwest of Toronto near Georgian Bay. The forecast was promising sun and high temperatures; it would just be the three of us, and Lee-Anne was hoping to do some baking. A good idea, as well, since there were some chores Dean had been putting off doing that he said he wouldn't mind a hand with. Since my left arm was immobile, still without much in the way of sensation, my fingers able to manage little more than a limp wiggle, I kidded him that that was about all he was going to get.

After a slow drive out of the city in the holiday exodus, by the time we'd transferred our luggage and food into Dean's boat at the marina then made the fifteen-minute ride out to the island cottage, it was after ten o'clock when we sat down to dinner. We talked a bit about the case while we were eating. Dean let me know that he'd been speaking to one of his authors earlier in the day, a judge in the Old City Hall courts who knew Malcolm. His Honour offered only good words about Malcolm, telling Dean to assure me that I was in extremely capable hands. In fact, only a couple of weeks before, Malcolm had conducted a successful defence in a complicated assault trial that hinged on a point of law even the judge wasn't familiar with. Malcolm's impressive jurisprudence was apparently the talk of the courthouse.

It was good news, to be sure — the first encouraging word about the case coming from a federal judge, and a ringing endorsement of my lawyer at that — yet as I confessed to Dean and Lee-Anne, I had some doubts. I found it a little hard to square Malcolm's courtroom aplomb with the petrified, paranoid guy whom I'd seen freak out so badly that morning because of the three dead plants in Nicky's grow-unit. "It wasn't exactly the kind of thing that inspires confidence."

Lee-Anne pointed out, quite rightly of course, that Malcolm, besides being a friend, *was* my lawyer, and probably just looking out for my best interests, then went on to say that she herself was open-minded about pot and, having raised two teenagers and worked in a high-school for twenty-five years, was sympathetic to the situation — even more so in this case after hearing some of the details of the raid. She said she didn't want to pry, and that it was really none of her business and she could understand if I didn't want to talk about it, but she was curious as to how I came to be growing marijuana in the first place; it wasn't something you really heard about people doing, certainly not at our age.

I agreed with her that you didn't, said I was happy to talk about it though, and gave Dean and her a condensed version of the story, starting with Nicky's bad LSD trip. I went on to explain that after our first crop was so successful, we decided to keep the unit operating and continued growing, eight plants every three months, nothing to speak of in terms of volume, however the quality, to quote Richie when he sampled our wares, was Château Lafite, just like he said.

I pointed out to them, as well, that Nicky had always been interested in gardening and horticulture, helping out his grandmother (Julie's mother) with her award-winning front and backyard gardens ever since he was a little boy. He was the only one of her five grandchildren who had any interest in what, for her, had been a lifelong passion, one that he seemed to really pick up on as he got older. As his Granny's arthritis worsened over the years, she had him doing more work around the garden for her, so the relationship became more of a mentoring one. It wasn't surprising to me in the least that he became so passionate about growing marijuana plants. He was gifted at it, dedicated to doing it, and after years of struggling academically at school, he was finding himself successful at something for a change. His whole view of himself, of his skills and his abilities, changed completely.

Because of the high-quality of the plants he grew, two, maybe three puffs was all you really needed for a comfortable and relaxing experience, and Nicky was able to cut his pot-smoking down to one joint a day, eliminating smoking altogether when he got into making his own canna-butter, a process where ground pot buds are simmered in water and unsalted butter for eight to ten hours to extract the THC crystals, the active ingredient of cannabis, which he'd then use to make baked goods of various kinds: peanut butter and chocolate chip cookies, muffins, brownies, carrot-cakes (with icing of course), treats that he'd share with his friends, as he did most of the marijuana he grew.

During a routine check-up in July 2005, our dentist discovered that fourteen of Nicky's baby teeth were blocking the adult ones from coming in and decided they'd have to be extracted. It was a complicated, three-hour operation involving our dentist, an orthopedic surgeon and a maxillo-facial specialist.

The pain, when the anesthetic wore off several hours later, was "torture," he wrote on the notepad we were using as a conversation-book, though with the gauze pads packed in his mouth, Nicky couldn't swallow any of the painkillers the surgeon had given him. Around midnight he managed to take a Percodan, but it was so strong he retched with the dry-heaves every five minutes for the next hour. He couldn't sleep because of the pain he was in; moaned, cried and wailed his way through the night somehow, then appeared in the kitchen a little after five the next morning and sat down at the table where, unable to sleep myself, I was having tea and cinnamon toast. His face was badly swollen, there was dried blood around his mouth, and his eyes were bloodshot from crying. He took the pen, turned to a fresh page in the conversation-book and wrote "G-13" in large letters. This was a strain he'd been cultivating for about a year, an indica plant originally from India, one that, in medicinal marijuana circles, was recommended for the treatment of physical pain. Nicky had some G-13 in the freezer, a dozen peanut-butter cookies left over from a batch he'd made a few weeks before, and maybe half an ounce of dried stuff. The cookies were a no-go because he couldn't eat solid food, so he rolled himself a G-13 joint, went out to the garage and had his usual three puffs — threw in a fourth for good luck, he said in the conversation-book when he returned to the kitchen, adding that he thought he'd get dressed and go for a "nice long bike ride by the lake."

When he returned, two hours later, he said the combination of the G-13 and the bike ride seemed to have reduced the pain so that it was just a dull throb in his jaw now, a bit uncomfortable, but that was about all. He went up to his room and started playing his guitar. Took his three "toodles," as he called them, every few hours during the day, managed to have some soup and lightly scrambled eggs at dinner, and slept for an uninterrupted twelve hours that night. Though his mouth was sore for about a week afterwards, it seemed that as long as he took his G-13 at regular intervals, pain was not a problem and he could get on with his life again.

Lee-Anne picked up her wine glass and sat back in her chair. "That's incredible," she said. "That he'd have to go through all that, and now the poor guy's being told something which was so good for him is bad, and he has to be punished for it."

"It's got to be confusing for him," said Dean. "I mean, from a certain point of view, you could say he was being charged for making his own medicine."

"You could," I agreed. "It's just not the point of view the police and the courts will take."

"Of course not," Dean said.

"It'll be interesting to make that contention if we ever do go to trial, though. See the looks on people's faces when Julie's mother takes the stand and tells the judge that Nicky dropped off a half-dozen of his G-13 peanut butter cookies at her house the day before the raid."

"Are you serious?" Lee-Anne said.

"Absolutely. She's been using them for the last six months to treat her arthritis. Nicky leaves them in a sealed, unmarked envelope in her mailbox once a week. According to him she finds them 'surprisingly effective for the pain, and delicious too.'"

"And how's Julie's family taking to the new regimen?" Lee-Anne asked.

Dean smirked. "By the looks on their faces in court yesterday, I'd say not very well."

"They're not exactly a pro-pot bunch," I said.

As it was after twelve when we finished dinner, we decided to leave the dishes until morning. I was given Dean and Lee-Anne's son Joey's bedroom, small but cozy, a comfortable single bed beside the room's double-window. I read for a little while by the light of a *Star Wars* lamp on his bedside table: parts of *Fear and Loathing in Las Vegas* by Hunter S. Thompson, a paperback copy of which I'd spotted on Joey's bookshelf alongside some Stephen King and John Irving novels, mysteries by Ian Rankin, Michael Connelly, Ngaio Marsh and Agatha Christie.

Through yawns and drooping lids, I was as amused as ever rereading Thompson's account of the speech given by America's foremost expert on marijuana, Dr. E.R. Bloomquist, to the National District Attorneys Convention at The Dunes hotel in Las Vegas in 1972, which Thompson was covering for *Rolling Stone* magazine: "There are four states of being in cannabis society: Cool, Groovy, Hip and Square. The square is seldom if ever cool. He is 'not with it.' He doesn't know 'what's happening.' But if he manages to figure it out, he moves up a notch to 'hip.' And if he can bring himself to approve of what's happening, he then becomes 'groovy.' And after that, with much luck and perseverance, he can rise to the rank of 'cool . . .'"

Saturday dawned sunny and hot, the temperature a balmy twenty-eight degrees by 9:30 when we were having breakfast in the screened-in porch. While Dean tended to some of the lighter maintenance tasks (mending screens, putting a new belt on the water pump, patching a hole in the sunroom wall where mice appeared to be getting in), I kept Lee-Anne company down by the lake. We sat on the dock in the sun, read the weekend *Globe and Mail*, discussed books, movies, our children, the current (deplorable as far as we were concerned) state of the education system, sipped lemonade, snacked, napped and dove in the water every twenty minutes or so to cool off.

As planned, Lee-Anne did some baking after lunch, while

I helped Dean build a new set of stairs for his equipment shed and repair several wooden shutters on the windows at the back of the cottage that had rotted at the hinges and fallen off, then I got into my bathing-suit and went down to the lake to give him a hand with the "heavy lifting": a long-overdue shoring up of the wooden crib under the front part of his dock, which was tilting at enough of an angle that Dean was worried people would slip on the wet planks and hurt themselves.

Though my left arm was still too weak to be very effective, thanks to the laws of physics whereby objects under water weigh substantially less than they do on land, in the course of the next hour I managed to dive down, retrieve twenty- and thirty-pound boulders off the bottom, heft them to the surface then slide them in place atop the rocks already in the crib, while Dean straight-armed the eight-foot section of cedar dock over his head. When we'd completed the job and Dean's level showed the deck was close enough to perfect for his liking, we were both relieved. "Time for some drinks," he said.

"Here, here," I agreed but, as I was still in the water at that point, decided that I'd squeeze in a final swim. I planted my feet against the newly leveled crib, put my arms out and pushed off, rolling over as I glided away from the dock, watching Dean make his way slowly up the stone stairs to the cottage (massaging his arms, rolling his stiff neck around) then closing my eyes, floating along on my back for several minutes, the water lapping lightly against my chin, the late-afternoon sun warm on my face: as relaxed and peaceful an organized criminal as you're ever likely to find.

Not anticipating the conversation would be an easy one (I'd sent Julie a message, through Hannah, that I'd phone

Saturday night to discuss the case), I waited until Lee-Anne, Dean and I had finished dinner before putting in the call to Fernwood, the family cottage on Jack Lake, north of Peterborough in the Kawarthas, where I knew Julie and the kids, her parents, her sisters and their husbands were having a powwow about the unfolding crisis.

Hannah answered. We had a brief conversation in which I let her know I was having a great weekend with my friend Dean and his wife. She said, when I asked how the mood was over there, that things were a little on the tense side. "Like they usually are when mom's clan gets together, Dad," she said, chuckling lightly, telling me to hang on and that she'd go get Mom.

I heard the screen door to the front deck bang shut in the background, Julie saying something to Hannah and then her footsteps as she crossed the living room, had a seat on the couch beside the phone and picked up. "I just want you to know," she started in, "that my family's been devastated by this. You have no idea how hard they're taking the whole thing. It's a complete disaster, and everyone is just sick about it, especially my parents." Her mother and father, she pointedly reminded me, weren't in the best of health and it was anybody's guess what the impact on them would be. Their only consolation, if you could call it that, was that I'd be taking the rap for all the charges, something she and her family felt I absolutely had to, since there was no way they were going to let Nicky go to jail for something I was responsible for.

As far as the house was concerned, her lawyer had told her it would have to be put up for sale immediately; that I'd have to retain a divorce attorney and give her a final separation agreement as soon as possible in order for her to get her money from the house sale before the government seized the property. She had a real-estate person already lined up, she said; a guy named Lenny who'd taken a course on how to handle the sale of houses that had been used as grow-ops. In his opinion it would go fast if we had it on the market by the end of August, and offered a quick closing as people would want to purchase so they could move in before their kids went back to school.

Resistance was pointless when Julie had been drinking, and from her rapid-fire, stammer-free delivery — the stutter she'd had since childhood disappeared when she'd had a few drinks — as well as the imperious, accusing tone in her voice, I could tell that she had been, and so rather than countering or questioning anything she'd said, I suggested that we talk again after I'd had a few days to mull the situation over. Putting the house up for sale might be the thing to do, I conceded, yet I told her not to forget that I was out on bail and not allowed on the premises. "Who's going to be the one to clean the place up and get it ready to put on the market that soon?" I asked her, my feeling that this was something we'd have to work out before any decisions could be made about the house. My own first priority, I explained, was making sure we got capable lawyers for the boys — at which point Julie cut in and, in even sharper tones, let me know that her family was taking care of all that. It was going to be very expensive, according to her, but she said that whatever her family had to pay would be deducted from my share of the proceeds of the sale of the house.

As good a time as any to draw the line, I told her that that wasn't something I was prepared to go along with, not when my friend Malcolm, whom she knew of course, could get two of his partners to represent Carson and Nicky pro bono. "What's the point of wasting money when we don't have to?"

"It's out of the question!" she shouted into the phone. "*My* family is taking care of getting them lawyers, and that's all there is to it!"

As diplomatically as I could, I said that I wanted Carson and Nicky to at least meet these friends of Malcolm's so they could make their own decision about who they wanted to handle their case. "There's a good chance we can get the charges dropped if we take the case through to trial."

"You were caught in the *act*, Paul! You're not going to get off!"

"As I say," I came back patiently, "if we have good lawyers, and they take the case to court, show abuse of process and violation of rights, there's a good possibility we will."

"No!" she shrieked into the phone. "Absolutely not!" and without pausing, screamed, "How could you *do* this to me!"

"Nobody's *done* anything to you, Julie," I said.

"You em*barrass* and hum*iliate* me!" she shrieked again. "You've been doing this to me for *years*! You have *no* idea how destructive it's been. You're pathological, getting your kicks by bringing shame down on everyone else. Why can't you just leave me and my family alone? And what kind of example are you setting for the children — drug trafficking out of a *house* in which I have half-ownership? If *anything* happens and we lose that house, we'll sue you. The bank will sue you . . ."

Dean and Lee-Anne shooting me concerned looks as I held the receiver away from my ear, I waited till her threat- and accusation-filled harangue began to lose steam and I could interrupt her to say that I'd be happy to meet her, and her real-estate friend Lenny, at the house on Tuesday morning, maybe about eleven o'clock, adding that I'd look into getting a divorce lawyer and tossing around some settlement amounts once we knew how much we could expect to receive on the sale of the house.

Calming down at the mention of money, she acquiesced, said she'd give Lenny a call, and that she thought eleven o'clock Tuesday would probably work out.

Assuming the conversation was at an end, I asked if I could have a word with the boys, just to see how they were doing.

"You've got *some* nerve," she snapped. "You *know* they're not allowed to have any communication with you — I can't believe you'd even ask," and with that, ended the call.

Eyebrows arched, letting out a breath and shaking his head, Dean came over with my wine glass and the bottle of Cabernet we'd been having with dinner. "That didn't sound like a whole lot of fun," he said, handing me my glass and topping it up.

"The word 'grueling' comes to mind," I said, had a healthy sip of wine, then the two of us headed back to the table where Lee-Anne was slicing one of the pies she'd baked that afternoon.

CHAPTER **SEVEN**
THE DOCTOR

After a relaxed and restorative weekend with Dean and Lee-Anne, I headed over to Friendship Avenue first thing the next day, wracking my brain as I bided my time in the city-bound, stop-and-go traffic, trying to think of someone I could live with whose house was closer than Dean's, at least until I had a better idea of how things were going to play out in the court case. And with the house going on the market (I was kidding myself if I thought I could keep Julie at bay on that front when Lenny would be touting the possibilities of a "quick sale"), I knew that I'd be the one who would end up doing all the post-raid clean-up, the painting, decorating, repairs and everything else required to have the place ready, at least from the way Julie had been talking, in the next few weeks. The amount of work in store for someone with only one good arm was daunting enough; that I'd be breaking bail every time I stepped onto the premises made the prospect seem downright perilous. Moving along Lakeshore Boulevard at a crawl, it seemed to me that a slog in traffic like this every day was the last thing I needed with my nerves still frayed from the bust.

As I was passing St. Joseph's Hospital, just before the National Exhibition grounds, my friend Callum "The Doctor" McConachie came to mind. He'd been in the process of separating from his wife Allison for the last nine months. He was living in a basement apartment not far from his house, waiting for Allison to figure out what she wanted to do. I remembered him telling me, when I'd talked to him in June, that it looked like she might be out of the house by the end of July, in which case he could have moved back in by now with their son Angus, who was Nicky's age and, according to Callum, keen to live with his father for a while. I knew he went to Nova Scotia during the last two weeks of July every year to visit his East Coast friends and relatives, and attend a few of the folk and bluegrass festivals held around the province during the summer. On the chance he might be back in town, I gave his cellphone a call.

Picking up on the second ring, the Doctor answered in his polite-but-firm business voice (it was his work number I was calling) but he broke into an enthusiastic, "Great to hear from you, Sledge!" when he realized it was me.

"Sledge," a nickname that evolved during my elementary school years, was a variation of 'Slidge' which had been printed, instead of 'Illidge,' on my hockey equipment bag when I was twelve, the year Malcolm's and my Pee Wee team competed in the "Tournoi International d'Hockey" in Quebec City. After the tournament, word about the new nickname spread from my teammates to my other friends, who changed the *I* to an *E* in my last year of high school, when

Burt Lancaster starred in the movie *A Man Called Sledge*. The nickname had stuck with me ever since.

Callum was dubbed "the Doctor" because of the white labcoat he took to wearing at parties as a gag when we were in high school (slipping into conversations with people and holding forth eloquently and authoritatively on topics about which he knew absolutely nothing), then afterwards as a bathrobe in the little house on Hazel Avenue in the Beach where he, Malcolm and a few of our other friends lived for several years following university.

Traffic moving faster now, Callum regaled me with the highlights of his East Coast jaunt, on which he'd taken Angus this year to help with the driving, but as well so they could have a look at several universities in Nova Scotia that he was thinking of applying to in January.

On the road and just leaving Montreal, Callum said he was planning to be back in Toronto later that afternoon. More good news, he added quickly, was that he'd just talked to his "erstwhile wife" Allison. The gentle reminder he'd asked his lawyer to send her had apparently done the trick. She'd promised to be gone by the weekend, which meant that he'd probably be moving out of the basement bunker he'd been living in by next Monday at the latest. "But enough about me," he said. "What's up with you, Sledge? I haven't talked to you in a while. How've you been?"

Sparing him the more harrowing details, I gave him the précis version of our brush with the drug-squad the previous Wednesday. I told him about the charges against us, the bail condition that we weren't allowed to set foot in the house till the case was over, and explained that Nicky and Hannah were living at Julie's, Carson at his Aunt Barb and Uncle Roger's, and that my friend Dean Tansey (whom Callum knew) was acting as my surety, the judge having ordered me to live with him, his wife and kids in Clarkson.

"That's no good," Callum said. "Clarkson. Jeez. That's about an hour and a bit from your place, isn't it?"

"If there's no traffic."

"Why can't you live in the house?"

"It's considered a crime scene."

"Come on."

"I'm serious."

"Did you call Malcolm?"

"He came over to the house yesterday and had a look around."

"What's he think?"

"He doesn't want me going near the place."

"Hang on," he said, and went off the line for a few seconds.

"Why not move in with Angus and me?" he said when he came back on.

"Is that a possibility?"

"*No*, it's what's going to happen. You can help me bring my stuff over from Stewart's and move your things into Angus's room. He's going down to the basement, where he spends every waking hour anyway. It'll be a great set-up."

"I'm happy to pay you rent, Doctor."

"Don't be silly," he came back. "I wouldn't think of taking any money from you."

"I'm going to insist."

"*No you're not.* Just take the room, Sledge. It's yours."

"You're sure it's okay?"

"It's a done deal," he said. "Only one problem though."

"What's that?"

"My lovely ex-wife is leaving her three cats for the time being. I know you're not exactly a lover of the feline species."

"I guess I'll learn to be, Doctor."

"*That's* the spirit, Sledge!" he said with a boisterous laugh. And as he was wont to do at the end of phone conversations, laid on a joke, one that he'd just picked up down East in fact. "So," he began, "a leprechaun walks into a bar with a pig under his arm . . ."

Julie and a man who I assumed was her real-estate friend Lenny were standing beside their cars, talking in the driveway, when I pulled up in front of the house. A few years older than me from the looks of it, Lenny was wearing a beige summer suit, pale-yellow sports shirt and brown loafers. He was on the short side, stout, and bald on top but still with a fringe of brown hair around the sides — a feature that, along with his moon-face, apple cheeks and beaming smile, had me thinking I was about to meet Friar Tuck.

I checked the street for signs of the police as I walked up the drive and joined them. I shook hands and exchanged nice-to-meet-you's with Lenny when he introduced himself, accepted his business card when he offered it, but hung back as he and Julie started for the front door. I told them it would be a lot safer for me if we had our meeting at a Tim Hortons rather than here at the house, just in case the police happened to come snooping.

Lenny, having heard about my bail conditions, felt that made good sense, as it did to Julie, but she said she wanted to have a look inside so she could see where the pot had been. Something about her lawyer needing to make sure everything was as I'd said . . . whatever that meant. I doubted her lawyer had given her any such instruction, but looked to Lenny for a deciding vote. He changed his tune about going inside somewhat, said that as the agent of record it probably wouldn't hurt for him to have a look too. I said okay, but that we'd have to make it quick; checked the street again as we headed up the steps and, the coast clear, unlocked the front door, led them inside and took them straight downstairs to my office.

"This is it?" Julie said when she saw the grow-unit.

"This is it."

Lenny glanced down at the three plants that had been left behind. "So what are these doing here?" he asked.

"According to my lawyer, it's a trick the police like to use. A little 'planted' evidence in case I get any funny ideas about coming into the house."

"But they're dead," Julie said.

"Wow, these guys sure don't fool around!" said Lenny.

"No, they don't," I said, "which is why we really should be getting out of here."

And with the two of them looking on in surprise, I found a plastic grocery bag filled with books, dumped them out on the pile the cops had left in the middle of the floor. I plucked the dead plants out of the grow-unit, stuffed them in the grocery bag, tied it up then headed Julie and Lenny back upstairs.

I ditched the dead plants in a garbage can at the neighbourhood shopping-plaza on my way over to the Tim Hortons at Morningside and Kingston Road. Lenny and Julie passed on coffee and took a seat, while I went over to the counter, about to ask for a regular coffee when I changed my mind and ordered decaf instead. I had a feeling I wouldn't need the caffeine.

Lenny and Julie took turns explaining that they'd already

talked it over and had decided the house should be advertised, at least online, as of the second last week of August, the lawn sign to go up the following Friday, the 31st, in time for the Labour Day weekend. Though Julie was adamant that our asking price should be $499,000, Lenny diffidently suggested that, while the house might have been worth that much, the figure was a little steep, about $50,000 more than what houses in our area were currently selling for. This seemed to be information that he hadn't yet shared with Julie. She gave him a sharp look, threw me one as well, then folded her arms in front of her and, shaking her head, declared that her price was $499,000 and she wasn't budging a cent.

After ten minutes or so of what came across to me as obsequious pleading, Lenny turned the tide when he pointed out to Julie that if she went with a lower price she could easily have her money by Christmas. She relented, telling him (I was but a bystander during negotiations) that she might be able to live with $479,000 but that was her absolute bottom line. She wouldn't accept any offer lower than that.

I spoke up at this point, said I hated to rain on the parade, but three weeks wasn't nearly long enough to clean up after the raid, *and* do all that was involved in making the house look like it was worth $480,000. It would have been out of the question even if I hadn't been out on bail; three weeks just wasn't a doable proposition.

As to asking price, I reminded Julie that when I had the house up for sale three years ago, the highest the real-estate agents would go then was $439,000, and even at that price, they had their reservations. The furnace was still old, as were all the windows, and the kitchen cupboards were the original ones, which we'd just painted over when we moved in ten years ago. "These are things people are going to take into account, aren't they, Lenny?"

He agreed they were certainly important factors, however to placate Julie, suggested we run with the $479,000 price and see if it attracted any interest. We could reconsider things if it didn't.

Arms folded still, her legs crossed, Julie had been giving me acid looks ever since I mentioned our previous attempt to sell the house. Or rather *my* previous attempt. "The problem three years ago," she said stiffly, "was our not having a final separation agreement in place. *You* were the one who took the house off the market, remember?"

Another piece of news she hadn't shared with Lenny, judging by his puzzled expression, I clarified the comment for him, explaining that Julie had agreed fully with me when I put the house up for sale in 2004; said she had no problem accepting the terms I'd made in a written offer I gave her: our assets split 50-50, and joint custody of the children. However she waited till I'd spent six weeks and a ten-thousand dollar demand-loan from the bank getting the place ready to sell, then announced that her lawyer wouldn't let her sign any offers until we knew exactly how the money was going to be divided between us: her attorney's position that Julie receive 100% of the proceeds from the sale of the house; $500 a month in child support, even though the kids were living with me; and $200,000 from my teacher's pension, which I'd cashed out in 2001, at which time she was only entitled to $100,000 according to the actuaries. The deal about as bad as it could get for me, nowhere near what she'd initially agreed to and legally untenable as a lawyer-friend counseled me, I took the house off the market immediately. "If Julie's going to pull a stunt like that again," I suggested to Lenny, "this whole exercise is just another waste of everybody's time."

My candour rewarded with a withering go-to-hell glare from Julie, she sat back in her chair, crossed her arms and turned to Lenny. "I'll accept $479,000 on condition that the house is ready to go up for sale by the end of August, no later."

"That's not going to happen, Julie," I said. "Unless you'll be coming over to help me out, of course."

"And why would I do that?" she said. "*You're* the one who got busted, and *you're* the one living in the house."

"Not anymore," I said.

Lenny intervened, suggesting that we might be getting a little off-track here. He said we had to remain realistic; keep the big picture in mind and not lose sight of our objective. He recommended that I do as much of the work as I could by the end of August, but asked Julie to understand that if it took longer, then it took longer. "Why doesn't Paul keep in touch with me," he proposed. "In the meantime, we'll look at going online with the listing toward the middle of September, just to be on the safe side. We'll hold off on the lawn sign till the week after, when we have the agents' open house."

Hostile silence from Julie, she turned away and gazed indifferently out the window.

Lenny seized the opportunity to take us through the various sections and key clauses of the listing agreement, asking the two of us, when he was done, to sign in the places that he'd highlighted in yellow.

Julie went first, pitched the pen to me when she was finished then got up from the table and, without a word, left the coffee shop, Lenny and I watching through the window as she hopped in her car, backed out and roared off across the parking lot.

Lenny shook his head, smiling diplomatically. "I guess it'll be my job to keep the two of you on speaking terms."

"I guess it will, Lenny," I said and, after returning his smile with an encouraging one of my own, bent down, picked the pen up off the floor and started signing the papers. A nice guy, who I could tell had the best of intentions, with his jolly, monk-like manner and easy optimism, I wondered if he had any idea of what he'd just gotten himself into.

I helped the Doctor move back into his house the following Saturday morning, record high temperatures and tropical humidity not helping things any between Callum and his now ex-wife Allison. There were some prickly disagreements over who had the right to certain antiques and mementoes that had been bequeathed to them over the years by both their families. There was some heated discussion, too, about Allison leaving a few larger and more unwieldy pieces of furniture in the house until she had somewhere to put them (she was staying at a friend's apartment until she found a place of her own).

As forewarned, there were the three cats to contend with as well. Two of them, spooked by the commotion, had fled the house by the time I arrived and disappeared nobody knew where; the third, a kitten named Shadow, had scatted to the top of the forty-foot blue-spruce tree on Callum's front lawn. Inured to little Shadow's plaintive mews after twenty minutes or so, the Doctor and I carried on bringing in his stuff, but the kitten's continuing cries of distress proved too much for Allison. Putting her moving on hold, she stationed herself at the base of the spruce tree and, assuring Shadow that everything was all right, pleaded with her to come down; cajoled her, offered toys, pet treats and opened cans of her favourite cat food, though none of these was enough to induce the distraught Shadow to descend. When Callum asked Allison, after maybe an hour or so of this, when he could expect her to be all moved out, she got angry with him and roundly declared that, until the three cats were safely back in the house, she had no intention of going anywhere.

Tension mounting between the two of them over letting the cat come down on its own (Callum) or putting a call in to the fire department (Allison), their son Angus arrived home from his part-time job mid-afternoon and saved the day with some subtle pet-whispering, something that it turned out he was so good at that he succeeded, in fairly short order, in getting all three cats into the house, cozy in their regular snoozing spots, their food, water dishes and kitty toys nearby, and let Allison see for herself that her animals were going to be just fine. After some parting reminders to Angus, to Callum and even to me about some of the cats' peccadilloes, she and her loaded station wagon finally pulled away from the curb. Callum had the house rearranged the way he wanted it within the next hour, at which point he slipped a roast in the oven, a prime-rib dinner with all the trimmings. He found some classical music on satellite radio, opened a bottle of his favourite wine, a red Burgundy he'd been saving for just such an occasion.

Angus raised his glass to make a toast as we sat down to eat. "Here's to my dad's return to the fold, and to Sledge moving in. To the Three Musketeers!" he added ceremoniously, clinked his glass against mine and moved to do the same with his father's.

"*No-oo . . .*" the Doctor corrected him in a reprimanding tone, his wine glass still sitting on the table. "To the Three *Stooges,* Angus. Curly," he said, pointing his finger at me. "Larry," he pointed at Angus. "And Moe," he said, pointing to himself.

"Wait a minute," Angus complained. "Wasn't Moe the one who bossed the other two around all the time?"

"Ex*act*ly!" the Doctor said in mock seriousness, raised his wine glass and, just as Moe would have, ordered us two knuckleheads to make it snappy, hoist our glasses and toast the Stooges — *or else!*

It was going to be an interesting stay.

CHAPTER **EIGHT**
PLAYING WITH FIRE

On Monday morning, awake since 4 a.m. because of a night-mare in which Officers Val and Spike were working me over in a jail cell, I left Callum's house before he and Angus woke up and drove to The Amazing Ted's, a 1950s-era diner about fifteen minutes from Friendship Avenue in Highland Creek, a place where the kids and I, like a lot of other local families, sometimes went for breakfast on weekends.

I browsed the *Toronto Star* while I ate my western omelette, lingered over the paper for several refills of caffeinated coffee and chatted with Denise, the diner's resident waitress. The *Regis & Kelly* morning show was just starting on the television mounted to the wall behind the counter when I went up to the cash register to pay my bill. Denise and I watched a beaming Regis Philbin and Kelly Ripa slip through an opening in the curtains and, hand-in-hand, make their entrance onto the brightly lit set, smiling and waving to the cheering and wildly applauding studio audience as they sat in their chairs and looked out over the crowd until the ovation died down.

"I liked him better in *Who Wants To Be a Millionaire*," Denise said.

"Same here," I said, and told her I'd see her tomorrow.

"I'll be here," she said. "Have a good day now."

"I'll try to," I said, chuckling to myself a little grimly as I made my way over to the door.

No ovations came my way, but it was show time nonetheless. In no particular hurry, I drove over to Friendship Avenue, parked my car on the street — half in front of Wes and Mary-Ellen's house, half in front of my own — then, with a glance around to ensure that I wasn't being watched, made it snappy crossing the front lawn, opened the door, slipped inside and quickly headed downstairs to the basement, the storage-room next to my office, where I rustled up painting supplies: a nearly full can of white latex semi-gloss, a brush, a roller, a rag and plastic paint tray, as well as a screwdriver, a hammer and a wooden stir-stick that I discovered tucked away in my tool box.

I brought the equipment upstairs to the front hall and set it down on some pages of newspaper I'd spread on the floor in front of the coat closet. I ran up to my bedroom and picked out a red T-shirt that had seen better days, an old pair of navy-blue Dockers and a pair of black low-cut running shoes I hadn't worn in years then raced back down to the living room and changed into them.

I went out to the front hall, picked up the paint can, gave it a brief shake and, after prying it open and stirring a bit, stood on a section of newspaper, dipped the brush in the white paint and splattered it liberally on my clothes and shoes.

Done, I cleaned off the brush in the laundry room, replaced the lid loosely on the paint can and laid the brush beside the roller in the paint tray. As I was tucking a white cleaning-rag in my back pocket, I remembered something that I thought would add a convincing touch. I rummaged among the gloves, hats and winter scarves on the upper shelf in the hall-closet, and came up with a white "Benjamin Moore" painter's cap that had been there since we moved in. In the event the cops ever did stop by, my plan was to race from wherever I was in the house at the time to the "routine maintenance" station I'd set up in the front hall. I'd take the paint can and brush in hand, tip the bill of my Benjamin Moore cap and greet them brightly as I opened the door, "Just doing a little routine maintenance, Officers. What appears to be the problem?"

During an exchange of phone calls late Sunday afternoon, Malcolm gave the okay to Callum becoming my "proxy surety," so it was now his responsibility to see that I complied with my various bail conditions, didn't possess or produce marijuana and otherwise kept the peace. It seemed like an unnecessary exercise to me, but Malcolm, knowing one of the reasons I'd made the switch was to be closer to the house, used the opportunity to remind me of the seriousness of the situation and to warn me again about the ramifications of the police catching me on the property. He said it would be no skin off their noses to just take me into custody and talk about it later. Maybe they'd find the Bail Court judge's note permitting me to be there for "routine maintenance," maybe they wouldn't. Either way, according to Malcolm, I was playing with fire to even think of setting foot in the place. Dean would lose his $5,000, and until the time of my trial I'd be living in a federal jail; a year if I was lucky, longer if I wasn't. His firm feeling was that Julie and her sisters were putting the house sale in jeopardy by not accepting some responsibility for fixing it up, especially when they were the ones who wanted to unload it so badly. "Ask them," he said to me before he let me go, "how they're proposing to conduct a real-estate transaction with one of the parties in a prison cell."

Even if he was going overboard a bit with the paranoia, I knew the risks were considerable. But I was between a rock and a hard place, as I saw it, damned if I did, and damned if I didn't. As a result, I never let on to anyone, not even Callum, when I was going to be working over at the house, and from the time I showed up till the moment I was out the door, I followed a strict, meticulously planned routine: I first did a quick drive-by to scout the street for surveillance, then parked the car, scooted across the lawn and, once inside, changed into my painter's get-up and got down to business.

I never went out to the backyard, never turned on the radio or TV, and wherever I happened to be working, I stayed alert for the sound of the front doorbell. I checked out front for police vehicles about every fifteen minutes or so, just in case, made no calls from my cellphone or the two landlines; if they rang, I didn't answer, and though sometimes I was tempted to do so to let off a little nervous energy, I resisted the urge to sit down at the piano and play something.

I kept track of the time using a stopwatch I wore on a cord around my neck. At the forty-five-minute mark I'd change back into my street clothes, hop in the car and drive over to Mr. Beans, a coffee-shop in the neighbourhood plaza. Mr. Beans himself was usually behind the counter. He was a friendly guy named André who was maybe in his late forties; he'd left his job as a floor-trader at the Toronto Stock

Exchange in 2001 to start his own coffee and sandwich shop. Still the only place of its kind in the immediate area, "Mr. Beans" had been a roaring success since the day it opened.

The drill on these make-myself-scarce missions never varied. I'd head straight to Mr. Beans, have a decaf coffee and a muffin, a sandwich and some soup during the early afternoon, chat with André a little bit about life in general, local politics or the Blue Jays, of whom he was a huge fan, then head back in the direction of the house. However, instead of turning left where Lawrence Avenue comes to an end and taking Rouge Hills Drive over to Friendship, I'd veer right and go down the hill and along the gravel road past the marsh, to the beach at the mouth of the Rouge River, where it empties into the lake, the park a provincial wildlife sanctuary that stretches thirty miles upriver, almost to the town of Markham. When the kids were younger we'd come down here on many of our walks. The "Loud-Train Park" they called it because in order to get to the beach from the parking lot, you have to pass under a CN railway trestle, a 1930s-era bridge that looms high above the river — rusted iron spans, curving arches and thick steel girders rising sixty feet from weathered concrete foundations on either side of the river. The din made by the wheels when trains were on the trestle was so loud you couldn't hear a thing — always an exhilarating experience for Carson, Nicky and Hannah, and, to be honest about it, me too. They used to race up from the beach whenever they heard one approaching so they could stand under the bridge, laughing and shouting at the tops of their voices with their hands clamped over their ears against the noise, unplugging them once the train had gone by, standing astounded in the sudden silence until somebody spoke up and said, "*Wow*, was that ever *loud*!"

The beach quiet and deserted most days I was there, I looked upon these breaks as cheer-myself-up time, whistling (something I couldn't do when I was working at the house) tunes from my cocktail piano repertoire, according either to the weather, or to the progress I was making that day. I whistled, sang or hummed my way down the beach for about a hundred yards or so, then climbed the large rock cairn that extended out from the side of the railroad embankment marking the end of the beach: a twenty-foot high mound of enormous cubes of grey cut rock, known around the community as "The Boulders." I'd find myself a place to sit, usually somewhere toward the top, give the music a rest, have my coffee and muffin and, more than anything else, just try to keep my mind off the turmoil into which my life seemed to have fallen: my head back, my eyes closed, my face up to the sun or into the wind for maybe twenty minutes or so. When I judged it was time to be getting back to work, I strolled quietly along the beach toward the river and headed back to my car.

In the event a train crossed the bridge while I was there — which they did, more often than not — I'd run to make it underneath the trestle in time, stand with my hands clamped over my ears and yell at the top of my voice as it thundered overhead, reveling in the sudden silence for a few moments after it had gone by, saying to myself sometimes, as the kids used to, "*Wow*, was that ever *loud!*"

Driving back to the house after the break, I'd do some reconnaissance up and down the street before parking the car, darting inside, throwing on my painting duds, re-setting the stopwatch alarm for forty-five minutes then continuing with items on my to-do list, which, despite my best efforts, never seemed to get any smaller. As a rule, I'd call it a day between about 5:00 and 5:30. Most nights I'd stop in for dinner at Kelsey's Bar & Grill, a restaurant about fifteen minutes from Friendship, just off the 401 about halfway back to Callum's house. The Doctor didn't begrudge me eating his food, and never would have, however, as he was good enough not to be charging me rent, I didn't want to impose on him any more than I had to. Plus there were differences of opinion between him and Angus over a new set of house rules and I thought it was just easier if I wasn't around during the dinner hour, when "hostilities" tended to break out.

Still early for the dinner-time crowd, when I arrived at Kelsey's I was often the only one there besides the bartenders and the wait-staff, a hard-working, happy crew, many of whom I got to know that August at my table in the corner. Sometimes jotting things down on a notepad while I was eating, sometimes browsing a book that I'd brought along, sometimes the daily newspaper, a copy of which someone always managed to rustle up for me, it was a couple of hours of down time with a welcome amount of easy-going social interchange, something I increasingly felt the need for after seven or eight hours in the house by myself.

With the exception of the shrimp pasta and alfredo sauce on which I occasionally splurged, my regular order consisted of a banquet burger with French fries, a small Caesar salad and one glass of Australian red wine, with tax and tip just under twenty dollars . . . and worth every penny, as I sometimes joked with the assistant manager, Monroe, an animated black gentleman in his early forties who, on learning about my situation after I'd been eating there for several weeks, let his staff know that I was to be given the twenty-five percent "loyalty" discount.

If he was working, Monroe would make a point of stopping by to shake hands and say hello, ask me how things were going. "Things are looking good, Monroe," was my usual response. Sometimes, "Couldn't be better, Monroe."

"*That's* what I like to hear!" he always replied enthusiastically, giving me a jovial smile and laying on another hardy handshake — sometimes calling back, as he was walking away from my table, to tell me he was sending my server over with a glass of wine, a dessert or a liqueur, on the house of course. Waving away my protests every time, he'd flash a smile, point an emphatic index finger at me and say, "You de*serve* it, my man. You de*serve* it."

Most nights I'd be back at Callum's place by about 9 or 9:30, exhausted, my knees sore, my head aching, my left arm limp and numb, the muscles in my back so stiff that I might as well have been working on the Sistine Chapel. I was often afraid to bend over and take my shoes off when I came in the door in case I wasn't able to straighten up again. I might chat with Callum or Angus if they happened to be around, but most of the time I just washed my face, brushed my teeth, closed the door to my room then fell into bed, dead to the world until the alarm went off at six o'clock the next morning and, while having a shower with the water hot enough to assuage my aches and pains from the day before, I'd plot my strategy for the day ahead.

Though I came and went freely from Friendship Avenue every day without incident, had no run-ins with the police and was able to make slow but steady progress on the numerous renovation and repair projects Lenny and Julie had deemed necessary for the proper "staging" of the house, my promise to Malcolm and my legal obligations to Dean and

Callum kept me from being complacent about the actual state of affairs. I stuck closely to my stringent security measures, continued taking an assortment of carefully worked out precautions (avoiding Mary-Ellen and Wes at the top of my list). If, in my more weary and frustrated moments, I did find myself slacking off on my routines, wondering whether fear had maybe got the best of me and this prospect of the police busting down my door and hauling me off to the slammer was all in my mind — like Hamlet, a case of "thinking too precisely on the event" — I only had to picture the gloating smile Officer Val would have on her face when they brought me in to the station, Spike hurrying off to oil the hinges on the cell-block door for maximum reverberation, and I became more vigilant than ever in my fugitive ways.

There was hardly a time when I was on the premises that I didn't feel like an outlaw, a wanted man, at large and on the lam . . . whatever you want to call it. Unarmed and no threat to anybody one way or another and yet, in the eyes of the court and the police, apparently still dangerous enough to keep me out of my house until the case was resolved.

Holed up in my hideout, I'd ponder how that might go. A plea-bargain was something that I'd resolved never to accept, and I didn't want Nicky accepting one either. Even if it was just our word against whatever the police would say had happened during the raid, there was a little something called due process, the statutory procedures police are expected to follow in enforcing the law. Arrest me, tell me what I'm being charged with and then take me off to the station and book me. It's not designed to be a complicated process, and intentionally so, to preserve the "innocent until proven guilty" assumption on which justice is supposedly based. If a judge was going to convict me and send me to jail for growing some marijuana for myself, tell me that the guns, threats and abuse of my legal and human rights had no bearing on the verdict — that following due process was no longer a requirement for conviction in Canadian law — then I wanted to hear someone say that as a matter of public record. I wanted to make sure the media got their hands on it, too, and spread the word, just so people would know where things actually stood with our justice system.

At the same time, I had a right to a trial. I didn't have to accept a plea deal if I didn't want to. In a trial, the police would have to take the stand, present an explanation of their activities in our house that evening and justify what they were up to for two hours before they shipped us off to jail, His or Her Honour perhaps finding a grain or two of truth in what we had to say, perhaps enough to see that due process hadn't been observed after all.

I went back and forth in my thinking almost daily. If I held out for a trial, where would I live for the next twelve to eighteen months, in my car? Where would I work, and what at? Writing wasn't the sort of job where I could make the kind of money I'd need to pay the mortgage, bills and taxes every month, let alone on a house that I wasn't even living in. What could possibly be the point of that, some of my friends wanted to know. As far as anyone I talked to about it was concerned, a plea bargain was a no-brainer. Malcolm, as my lawyer, said he was obliged to support me in whatever decision I made. As a friend, however, he put things more incisively: "Do you really want your children to see their father living that way?"

I had no trouble conceding his point, but as I tried to

explain in what I thought was an appropriate analogy, if I'd been cited by the police for speeding, like most people would, I'd have taken the ticket to court and fought the charge, or at least tried to have the fine reduced, or points kept off my driving record. Though I'd broken a law and been picked up in a police radar trap doing so, there hadn't been any accident as a result of the infraction, no one had been hurt or put in harm's way. In the grand scheme of things, the offence was not a big deal. But again, like most people, I'd feel it was worth something to at least tell my side of the story and let a judge, rather than the police, find me guilty as charged.

The parallel, as I saw it, was that I'd been cited for drug trafficking. The police had delivered their notice of infraction at gunpoint, the only danger to anyone posed by the aggression with which they'd conducted themselves. They'd harmed us in ways that had, and would continue to have, a significant and perhaps lasting impact on our lives. If I was willing to fight a simple speeding ticket, how could I not fight the much more serious one that I'd been given for drug trafficking, something that I was not, nor ever had been doing? Was it such a bad thing that I wanted the case tried in open court, not sitting in handcuffs in my own living room?

I wondered, and had no fear of taking the stand in my own defence to ask the judge if, in view of the venomous attitude Val and her crew seemed to have toward cannabis and those who used it, the real purpose of the whole police exercise might have been to scare the boys and me into never touching marijuana again. Scare the crowd of spectators who'd gathered from around the neighbourhood too; show them what they could expect to happen to them if the police ever found out they were growing marijuana inside their homes. Go ahead and put me in jail, I was ready to say. Fine me, publicly humiliate me if you feel you have to, yet after what my children and I had been through, who'd be surprised if it didn't make us — and maybe others who heard about our experience — want to possess and produce marijuana all the more? Newton's law of equal and opposite reaction, let's say. And in the event that the justice system's determent strategies *did* work, the boys and I turning into born-again, anti-drug crusaders who'd sworn off the vile weed forever, weren't there still thousands out there growing it? Millions possessing it? And more people climbing on the bandwagon all the time? It didn't seem right to me that Carson, Nicky and I should have been subject to any more penalties for having been caught with marijuana than we'd already paid, simply because we'd had the misfortune of living next door to a nosy neighbour. Most important of all, with a trial I'd have an opportunity to meet Officer Val in person, face-to-face, no handcuffs. I'd have Malcolm put her on the stand and show her Defence Exhibit "A": the roll of date-and-time-marked colour snapshots that I'd managed to take of the ransacked house with my old Samsung film camera before I started to clean the place up. I was dying to hear what she'd have to say.

It was about six o'clock on a Thursday evening toward the end of my second week on bail. I was upstairs cleaning the carpet in Nicky's bedroom when I heard the front door-bell ring. My heart racing instantly, a sinking feeling in my stomach, I managed to keep my composure and, having prac-tised for just such an occasion in my mind so many times, went quickly into action. I dropped the wire brush I was using, ran quickly down the hall into the spare bedroom, had a look through the curtains. Sure enough, a police car was down below in the driveway, headlights on, the engine running, the passenger seat empty and no one behind the wheel.

The bell ringing again as I reached the bottom of the stairs, I hustled over to the painting station by the hall closet, grabbed the can and brush and, putting on a calm front as I stepped toward the door, took a last nervous breath, readied a pleasant smile and opened up.

A female officer, in uniform, bulletproof vest and cap, with glasses, maybe in her early thirties, looked up from a file folder she was holding and asked me, in an official voice, if I was Mr. Robert Allan Hughes.

Trying not to let my relief appear too obvious, I paused like I was letting the name register, but told her no, Bob Hughes lived up the street at 221 Friendship; this was 122, an error that I explained even our postman sometimes made. She pushed her glasses up on her nose, squinted and regarded me suspiciously for a moment. Checked the address against the one on her documents, shrugged casually and said sorry, her mistake. She noticed the paint can in my hand, the brush, my paint-spattered clothes and the Benjamin Moore cap sitting at a jaunty angle on my head, but made no comment. "Have a nice evening, sir," she said, and turned to go. I said I would, closed the door gently behind her and, when I was sure that she was gone, set the painting gear down, shot both my fists into the air and let go with a silent but no less euphoric: *"Yes!!"*

CHAPTER NINE
ARE WE HAVING FUN YET?

Our first court appearance was scheduled for the Thursday before the Labour Day long weekend. I arrived at the Old City Hall courthouse shortly before 8:30, cleared the police security checkpoint just inside the front doors then set off across the grand, Victorian-era lobby. I turned right at a "To Courtrooms" sign and started along a wide hall, checking numbers on the tall, brown-oak doors until I located the room I was looking for: #110.

Several dozen people were milling about in the hall, a few checking the list of names posted on a small bulletin board beside the double doors, still closed at this point since the morning session didn't start until 9. Lawyerly type men and women holding briefcases and cellphones were huddling here and there with clients, frantic duty-counsel attorneys were scrambling about, talking on their cellphones, checking their case files, calling out the names of individuals they'd been assigned to represent.

I took in the commotion: the frenetic discussions, flurried conversations, the steady stream of distressed-looking people hurrying toward courtrooms further down the hall, the sense of fear and desperation in the air almost palpable — becoming even more so when, at 8:59, the court clerk was sighted moving down the hall. A woman, perhaps in her early thirties, wearing black horn-rimmed glasses, a black court gown, white collar and tabs, she made her way through the growing crowd outside Room 110 pushing a two-tiered trolley loaded with plastic bins containing what I guessed were the morning's case files.

Her appearance signalled that court would soon be getting underway, as a result people thronged around her as she moved, jostling for position behind her as she took out a set of keys, found the right one and unlocked the door to 110. A police officer, who had suddenly materialized, held the door for her while she wheeled her trolley inside, then stood in the doorway, his arms crossed in front of him bouncer-style, and instructed people to proceed in an orderly manner, though he was no match for the surging crowd, who more or less ignored him and shouldered their way forward into the room on the heels of the court clerk.

With just two church-style wooden pews at the back of the room, which looked like they might have accommodated twenty-five or thirty people between them, the charge into the room quickly turned into a game of musical chairs, as maybe fifty or sixty of us rushed to find somewhere to sit down.

All the lawyers having raced to the far side of the room and up to the lectern to speak with the Crown Attorney, nine o'clock came and went but the judge still hadn't shown up. The lawyers and duty-counselors chatted casually with each other in a line back from the Crown's lectern; two police officers sat behind the bar on either side of the file-trolley; the court clerk shuffled papers at her table; and the court stenographer was in place in front of her machine, earphones on, hands folded in her lap.

The late arrivals hurrying into court grimaced when they realized there were no seats. After one last, hopeful look around, they turned and walked out past the bouncer cop, who was standing to one side of the door with his chin in the air, his arms crossed, looking surly and unapproachable. Some who'd been lucky enough to find a seat stared uneasily at the front of the room, some scared, some distraught. Some had indifferent smirks on their faces, like this wasn't the first time they've been here.

Thanks to a feisty larger woman who'd propelled me from behind in the crush to enter the room, I'd managed to obtain one of the last available spots in the front pew, about halfway along. I was fully prepared to give it to the first person who seemed to need it more than me — more than the guy in his early thirties who grappled me for it when we first came in but lost, complaining, as he backed off and watched me sit down, that he needed it because his knees were bad. Telling him they seemed fine when he'd been body-checking me a moment earlier, I said I was staying put. Hovering in the doorway now with a scowl on his face, he monitored the pews, ready to pounce.

Not knowing what to expect in this, my debut performance in Drug Court (maybe not the only organized criminal in the room but, from the looks of it, certainly the oldest), like everyone else I waited a little restlessly for the judge to arrive, whistling quietly and thinking nothing of it — a number of people around me were talking freely — until a police officer standing duty on the far side of the room beside the windows, marched over, leaned down and, with a stern frown on his face, gave me a hard, two-finger poke in the left shoulder and ordered me to stop.

"What's the problem, Officer?" I asked lightly. "The judge isn't even here yet."

"Doesn't matter," he shot back. "You keep it up, and I'm gonna ask you to leave." As he stood there making sure the message had sunk in, I caught a look at the name-tag on his chest: *Endicott.*

I canned the whistling as instructed. Officer Endicott returned to his post near the windows, crossed his arms and, with a pointed stare, made sure I knew that he was keeping his eye on me.

An elderly, fairly overweight woman stepped into the courtroom, glancing frantically along the spectator pews looking for a seat. I caught her eye, stood up and waved her over, guarding the spot from several other people who'd noticed my gesture (including the chump with the supposedly bad knees) until she came slowly across the room and, with a grateful smile, took the seat. I then retreated to an open area at the back of the courtroom, where there seemed to be all kinds of space if you were prepared to stand.

But Officer Endicott was on the move. Leaving his post, he hustled over, stood with his face about a foot from mine and informed me that nobody was permitted to stand in the presence of the judge; if I couldn't find a seat, I'd have to wait in the hall.

"But the judge isn't here yet," I reminded him.

"Out!" he said, and pointed to the door.

My ejection apparently the cue for His Honour to arrive, I delayed my exit long enough to get a look at him. Suntanned, grey-haired and well-groomed, he was a man in his late fifties, wearing a tailored grey business suit, a white shirt and emerald-green tie beneath his black court gown, which he finished throwing on as he hurriedly mounted the bench, sat down and, a little out of breath, announced that court was now in session. It seemed to me he might have apologized for having kept us all waiting (it was 9:13 on the courtroom clock); or that someone might have at least announced his name, though as I thought about it, maybe that only happened in movies and on television crime shows.

People in the hall continued to come and go from Room 110. I looked over at one point and recognized the lawyer I'd been told Julie's family had retained to defend Nicky: Larry Heffernan, a man in his late forties, a full head of dark-brown wavy hair, blue blazer, white shirt, wine-coloured tie, grey dress pants and black oxfords. Like many in the city, I knew Larry as the host of a local cable TV show called *Legal Matters*, a phone-in program in which he dispensed free legal advice and, for people's convenience, had his web address and phone number displayed at the bottom of the screen, in case callers wanted to take up their "legal matters" with him off-air. Nicky had told me a few nights earlier, when we were out for a walk at the Loud Train Park, that Larry had asked Roger and Barb, who were going to be footing his legal bill, for a $15,000 retainer. "Nice work if you can get it," was Malcolm's only comment when I told him the figure.

Pacing back and forth with his cellphone pressed to his

ear, Larry seemed to be stewing about whatever the person on the other end was saying, staring intently at the floor one moment, scuffing his foot in frustration the next, wincing, frowning, grimacing and shaking his head in stern disagreement about something, yet never, at least while I was watching him, saying anything by way of reply. All he seemed to be doing was listening, something he was probably good at as host of a call-in TV show, I guess. However when I noticed, in the course of watching him, that his cellphone screen wasn't lit up, I began to wonder if he was actually talking to anyone, or merely putting on an act to make it look like he was.

I was in the process of manoeuvring to get a closer look — to confirm my suspicions that he was faking the calls — when a young woman came up to him, introduced herself and, once Larry was off the phone, shook his hand. My assumption that this was the lawyer acting for Carson (to whom Roger and Barb had apparently given a $5,000 retainer), I sidled over, said hello and explained who I was.

Clearly annoyed at my presumption, Larry shot me a haughty frown, made a dismissive *"Puh!"* sound when he heard my name and then promptly looked away, leaving me to talk with the young woman, whose name turned out to be Leslie. In her late twenties, unsmiling and obviously a little nervous (Malcolm told me later she was a junior at her law firm), she let me know that she'd be standing in for Carson's lawyer during our court appearances.

Still off his phone, back to pacing and not giving me the time of day (I wondered if he knew I'd cottoned on to his cellphone charade), Larry glanced at his watch after several moments, huffed impatiently, turned abruptly to Leslie and snapped, "We'll be called any time now. We better get in there . . ."

I caught up with him on our way over to the courtroom door and asked him what the procedure would be when our case was called, mentioning that Malcolm, whom he apparently knew, was doing a trial in Mississauga and so I was there on my own.

No reply to my question, he held the courtroom door open for Leslie, stepped in quickly behind her and, without turning around, muttered indignantly that he "wasn't at liberty" to give me that information.

Inside, he and Leslie scooted over to the other side of the room toward the Crown's lectern, while I lingered beside the bench that was closest to the door and tried to look inconspicuous, scanning the pews for the next available seat. When the judge put off a black youth's case until mid-September, a woman in the second pew, possibly his mother, got to her feet and started for the door.

With Endicott giving me the eye, now that I was back in court, I made a beeline for the second pew, excused myself with people along the row when they stood up to let me by, shuffling as quickly as I could toward the open seat — only to hear, just as I was about to sit down, the court clerk announcing our case at the front of the room.

Leslie and Larry duly presented themselves to the judge on behalf of Carson and Nicky. The judge noted this down, paused for a moment, peered over his reading glasses and, seeing only two lawyers, inquired in some consternation as to the whereabouts of their co-accused. He glanced down at the file in front of him. "A Mr. Illidge," he said, looking up again, "whom I'm assuming is the father?"

"That would be me, Your Honour," I blurted as I walked up the aisle to the bar, squeezed in between Leslie and Larry and presented myself — a move that prompted the police officer on the other side of the bar, one of two guarding the trolley with the case files on it, to jump to his feet, reach over and, with a hand to my chest and a firm shove that sent me stumbling backwards, tell me that only *lawyers* were permitted to stand at the bar.

With what happened in the space of the next two minutes, however, it didn't appear to make much difference where I was standing. The court clerk, His Honour, the Crown Attorney, Larry and Leslie, all raised their eyes in unison and gazed at the large calendar for the month of September which, like the one in Bail Court, had been duct-taped at a noticeably crooked angle on the wall to the left of the clock.

The subject of their conversation was the date and time of our next court appearance. They quickly reached agreement, and the clerk scribbled details down on a piece of neon-orange paper that she walked over and thrust across the bar for me to take: a "Notice" that I was to appear on September 26, again in Room 110, again at 9 a.m. The Crown Attorney called the next case. My "appearance" having lasted all of three minutes, I turned, made a point of catching Endicott's eye and, whistling loudly, headed out to the hall. No wonder Malcolm hadn't felt it important to attend.

With the real estate listing slated to go online as of September 14, I had to call Lenny the day before and tell him that, due to circumstances beyond my control, there was no way I could have the house ready. I apologized, but explained that there was just too much to do, and too little time. Disappointed, the news definitely a letdown, Lenny said maybe he'd be able to push things back another week, though it would really piss Julie off, a reaction he'd like to avoid if he could. Feeling a bit mercenary yet not sure what else I could do, I took the bull by the horns and asked him if, to be realistic about it, there were any chance he could push back two weeks. He groaned at the suggestion and said that was sure to upset Julie even more. I told him I knew that, and sympathized with the position I was putting him in, and for that reason would commit to the end of September, the 28th at the very latest. I said he could count on it this time and go ahead and order the lawn sign for then, too. I kidded him that maybe it would bring us good luck with the sale, since the 28th would have been Julie's and my twenty-third wedding anniversary if we'd still been married. "I wouldn't be too sure about that," he said with a dubious chuckle, but conceded that there really weren't any other options available at that point; he'd just have to send it up the flagpole and see what happened. He added, before letting me go, that he needed me to guarantee there would be no more holdups of any kind; otherwise we'd "lose our window" and might have to wait till the New Year. Whether this was the case or not, I couldn't have said; however I promised him as firmly as I could that there would be no more delays, thanking him for his peace-keeping efforts with Julie, who I knew was riding him pretty hard. I assured him the wait would prove worthwhile, that the house, when I was finished with it, would more than meet his and Julie's expectations. "It'll look absolutely spectacular, Lenny," I told him.

"It better," he said, "for both our sakes."

What I didn't tell him, figuring that it would only have complicated things more than they already were, was that aside from major fatigue, pain in most parts of my fifty-five-year-old body and growing trepidation that my luck with the police was going to run out at any time, one of the reasons for the holdup on the real-estate listing was that I'd been driving to Oakville, forty miles west of Toronto, since the last week of August. I was spending my days in the studio at Simply Audiobooks, a company that was having me record four of my Shakespeare novels for them.

All things considered, it might not have been the best time to have committed to such a venture, but Simply Audiobooks had made me an offer that I felt I "simply" couldn't refuse. They were going to include me in their CD downloading service, which had 350,000 subscribers in the northeast United States, Florida and California. They contracted to pay me $2,800 to record the four novels, cash that I knew would come in more than a little handy in the next few months. On top of which, Cindy, the woman who was heading up the project for Simply Audiobooks, said I could expect to make a minimum of fifteen- to twenty-thousand dollars in royalties in the first year alone — double that once I'd recorded the three remaining plays in the series. It'd be the biggest-ever payday of my career; the revenue stream, as Cindy explained it, would be ongoing and, according to her, Simply Audiobooks was signing up new members at a rate of five thousand a week: if even a small percentage of those people bought or rented my Shakespeare CDs, royalty payments could easily top six figures within a few years.

Cindy worked under the supervision of the Chief Financial Officer of the company, a genial, laid-back gentleman in his early fifties named Dell Parsons. A chartered accountant by profession, Dell didn't look like my idea of a "financial officer," let alone the chief one. With his longish, sandy-brown hair, the blue jeans, Tommy Bahama shirts and cowboy boots, he looked more like a roadie for a rock-and-roll band. In fact, according to Cindy, Dell played electric guitar in a bar band with some friends of his from high school, and indeed he had worked in the music business for a while: he'd been manager of the Tragically Hip's road crew for a number of years before he went into accounting. He might have been a late starter, Cindy told me, but he was a whiz with numbers, brilliant at marketing, and apparently it was Dell who'd single-handedly orchestrated the company's recent rapid expansion.

Dell not only backed up the royalty estimates Cindy had given me, he let me know in no uncertain terms that he was "super enthusiastic" about the Shakespeare project and behind me all the way. Behind it so much, as things turned out, that once the recording sessions got underway, he made a point of popping into the studio every few days to see how Colin, the recording engineer, and I were making out.

Usually in the sound booth when he stopped by, I'd watch him walk over to the table where Colin manned the recording equipment. Dell listened to my voice on the studio speakers as I read my versions of *Hamlet*, *King Lear*, *Twelfth Night* and *Midsummer Night's Dream*, the plays Cindy had selected for the first series of CDs. He'd stand with his arms folded, chuckling here, nodding appreciatively there, frowning reflectively during more serious moments, dissolving in laughter if I was delivering a bit of comic nonsense, until I'd wrapped up whatever scene we were doing. He'd flash me a beaming smile and an energetic two thumbs up through the booth window once Colin signaled that the take had been a good one.

He'd call over to me the moment I stepped out of the booth: things like "Hey, hey, *hey*, don't you just *love* Shakespeare?";

"Out-*out* damn spot!"; "My horse, my horse, my *king*dom for a horse!" But his most frequent greeting was "Are we having *fun* yet?" Whether he asked this in ironic sympathy for the high-energy work I was doing behind the microphone, or out of a genuine enthusiasm for the works of the Bard, I couldn't say. But Dell was firmly in my corner and had no problem letting me know it. He was one of the most down-to-earth people I'd ever worked with — open, easy-going and fun to be around.

When it was time for us both to get back to work, Dell's habit was to hitch up his jeans, tell me that things were "sounding terrific" or he was "really pleased with how it was going," or he'd plant a friendly mock-punch on my shoulder and say: "Hang in there, Romeo." After which he'd hold a hand in the air, we'd exchange high-fives, and as he turned and sauntered happily toward the studio door, he'd start whistling, which of course endeared him to me all the more.

As I was spending five days a week in Oakville, any work at the house had to be done at night, the principal task the regrouting of the ceramic tiles in the kitchen and the main-floor hall, which, even though I was sure we could get by with them as they were — the grouting between some of the tiles was splitting and chipping off, and a few of them, in the heavier-traffic areas, were starting to crack, but the damage was noticeable only from certain angles and, as I saw it, not particularly unsightly — I'd agreed in a moment of weakness to undertake the regrouting, a favour to Lenny for pushing back the listing date. "It's just not a good idea for a cracked floor to be the first thing people see when they walk into your house, Paul," he had advised. I couldn't disagree with the point in itself, but it ticked me off that Julie would be so implacable about the floor needing re-grouting when, except for the brief visit on her lawyer's alleged instructions to inspect the grow-op with Lenny, she hadn't been inside the house for almost seven years. How did *she* know what condition the ceramic tiles were in?

I warned Lenny that it would be a do-it-yourself job; confessed that I'd never regrouted ceramic tiles before and the outcome might not be of the Michelangelo quality that I knew he and Julie were expecting. "How hard can it be?" he asked, rather blithely I thought. I told him I'd have to get back to him on that, and soon made the first of what turned out to be numerous visits to Home Depot for various grouting supplies, as well as some free in-store video instruction on the finer points of ceramic tile repair.

Back from Oakville by 6:30 most nights, I'd stop in at Kelsey's, chat for a bit with Monroe or one of his servers while I waited for a bacon cheeseburger and fries, or a pasta dish to go. Arriving at the house around seven or so, I'd change quickly into my routine-maintenance garb and have my dinner at the kitchen table by the light of a pillar candle, rehearsing, while I ate, the scenes I was going to be recording the next day.

I usually got down to work by about eight, except when I was preparing for a longer or more complex scene the next day. Dell, Colin and I had agreed that since it was basically a live performance I was giving, its dramatic effect would be maximized if I was able to record a scene in one take: no do-overs, no matching up voice levels, no overdubs to correct mistakes. This necessitated some rehearsal and the making of sometimes extensive notes, directions and reminders on how best to deliver my lines.

Since having the lights on might bring the police sniffing around, I left them off. I closed the California shutters on the living-room, dining-room and family-room windows; covered the sliding-glass door and the windows in the kitchen with dark-green sheets and a couple of old drapes that once belonged to Julie's mother, which I'd come across in a box in the basement. I shut the doors to the laundry room and the computer room, did a final walkabout of the main floor in darkness, using duct tape to seal up any cracks where street light was seeping through, then got to work mixing up a batch of grouting compound in a plastic pail in the laundry-room sink.

All this was carried out by the beam of a small Mag flashlight. I set my big twelve-volt, pivoting head light on the floor in the hall, the bulb jerry-rigged with a flimsy but serviceable cardboard-and-duct-tape shade to illuminate the two-by-two-foot space that I was grouting. Using a chisel, a metal scraper or sometimes a straight-head screwdriver, I chipped the old grout plaster from between the tiles, swept it up with a whisk and dustpan I kept on hand and emptied it into a white plastic grocery bag that I had tied to one of my belt loops.

Painstaking and tedious was the best way to describe the process: three or four hours crouched over on my hands and knees, spreading plaster slurry, similar in colour and consistency to melted French vanilla ice cream, over the two hundred or so twelve-inch tiles; wiping the excess off with a damp sponge, rinsing it in a bucket of warm water that needed to be changed every fifteen minutes to be effective; rubbing the dried residue off the tiles, buffing them until they gleamed then carefully sliding the operation several feet back and setting myself up in front of the next patch of tiles.

Whistling, humming and voice-strengthening exercises helping keep my mind off the onerous work for the most part, in my weaker moments, when my knees, arms and back were aching and beginning to cramp up, my eyes straining in the minimal light to see exactly where I'd grouted and where I hadn't, there were moments when, if I wasn't saying them to myself, you would have heard me in full Shakespearean mode calling "vile imprecations" down on Mary-Ellen McCluskey's "foul head" for putting me through all this, simply because she was incapable of minding her own business. If her nosiness hadn't caused enough damage already, on one of her recent nightly strolls around the neighbourhood, she'd apparently cornered Nicky, who was out walking Julie's dog, and made a point of mentioning, a little too snoopily it seemed to him, that she'd heard we were out on bail and not living at the house — however she'd seen me coming and going at odd hours lately, and wondered if everything was "all right," a dead giveaway, or so Nicky felt, that she was up to her old tricks again. Hence the Battle of Britain blackout conditions; you just never knew where Mary-Ellen's next bomb was going to land.

Once that evening's grouting was done (when my arms, back and knees were unable to take the punishment any longer) I'd clean up in darkness, remove all the window-coverings and open the shutters, just so anybody looking at the house during the day wouldn't suspect anything untoward was going on inside.

Back in my regular clothes, I'd leave through the sliding-glass doors in the kitchen, climb my back fence, run along half a dozen backyards to the house on the corner and jump to the sidewalk, my car parked halfway down the street, another precaution I'd decided to take after the latest "Mary-Ellen Alert." These fence-top getaways required careful and, for the first while, pretty fancy footwork to avoid the over-hanging branches of fruit trees, vine-covered latticing and birdfeeders, no easy task even if you *weren't* attempting to do it in the dark, as I was. However, as with the other routines I'd adopted as part of my take-no-chances strategy, after a few precarious moments early on, I managed to get this one down to a fine art too.

Or so I thought. One night midway through the third week, scooting along with maybe ten feet to go before I reached the corner fence, a dog started barking in the backyard to my left. It rushed the fence and leapt up, snapping viciously at my heels. I panicked, lost my balance and then my footing. The dog was barking louder than ever. With no time to think, I leapt the remaining six feet to the corner fence in an attempt to dive over it. Not a pretty sight, I'd underestimated the distance, my body bouncing on the edge of the fence, flipping over and falling to the sidewalk on the street-side.

The dog still barking, I lay there on my back for a second, wincing with the pain I was experiencing in my chest and all four limbs — even more when I sat up, looked across the median and saw a police cruiser parked by the curb, the cab light on, two officers inside, the one behind the wheel with his window down, looking over at me. He turned to his partner, said something, the partner leaning forward with his head down, peering over as well. A short discussion, they put the paperwork they were doing aside, opened their doors and stepped out of the cruiser.

Hurt badly in a few places, still disoriented from the fall, I tried to appear calm and at ease as I watched them approach, like it was not out of the ordinary, in a quiet, residential neighbourhood like ours, for a fifty-five-year-old man to come flying over a backyard fence at eleven o'clock at night and land in a heap on the sidewalk.

The officers moving across the median, they reached the sidewalk and stationed themselves in front of me, several feet apart, one a few feet back from the other.

"So what's going on?" the first cop said, his voice raised over the sound of the dog's still-rabid barking.

"You all right?" the other cop called.

"I think so," I said, "though all the damage reports aren't in yet."

The first cop chuckled. "So what were you doing up there on the fence?"

"Oh," I said, after the barking stopped, the owners having taken the mad dog inside. I pointed behind me. "I live about five houses down on Friendship. I locked myself out. Thought I might have left the back door open, but apparently I hadn't. Rather than walk all the way around, I thought I'd just take the shortcut down here to my dog-walker's house. Get him to give me his key."

The two of them looked me over.

"What kind of dog do you have?" the second cop asked.

"Irish setter," I said.

Their faces expressionless, they continued looking me over.

"So that's it?" the first cop finally said.

"That's it," I answered.

"What's your number on Friendship?" the second cop piped up.

"122," I blurted after a momentary pause, hoping they hadn't noticed. I'd been thinking of telling them 127, across the street and several houses down from my place, but for all I knew they were going to park out front, just to make sure I got in all right.

The two of them studied me some more, glancing up at the lattice-topped, eight-foot fence I'd fallen from.

"Better be more careful next time," the first cop said, bringing his eyes back to me.

"I think you can count on that, Officer," I said.

"Hope the rest of your evening goes a little better."

"Thanks," I said. "Is it okay if I get on my way?"

He nodded, his partner stepping forward to stand beside him, thumbs hooked on his belt, the two of them with their eyes on me as I set off down the sidewalk.

Whistling lightly, limping slightly from a wrenched right knee and a burning pain at the base of my spine, I carried on past my car, the only one parked on either side of the street at the time. No idea whether they were still watching me or not, I wasn't about to look back and check. I walked slowly to the end of the block, rounded the corner but immediately doubled back, hid behind a thick juniper bush on somebody's lawn and peered down the street.

When they pulled away from the curb, in about five minutes or so, I buried myself in the branches of the juniper, watched and waited as they cruised slowly up to the corner, the cruiser maybe twenty feet away from me when they rounded it, then drove slowly off down Blueking Crescent, like maybe they were heading over to Friendship Avenue to confirm what I'd have been the first to agree was a pretty far-fetched story.

Once the cruiser was out of sight, I slipped from behind the juniper, cut across the lawn and hobbled as fast as I could up the street to my car. I did a quick three-point turn, made my way up Greybeaver Trail, in the opposite direction the police had gone. I stayed off the main streets until I reached the highway, then with a considerable amount of difficulty headed back to Callum's, the cruise-control on whenever possible, since the muscles in my right leg had gone into spasm and I couldn't keep my foot on the gas pedal for more than a few seconds at a time.

Callum and Angus were in bed when I got home, shortly before midnight. I took two of the prescription anti-inflammatory pills I knew Callum kept in the cupboard above the stove, had a shower with the water as hot as I could stand it, brushed my teeth then slid into bed. It was 12:45 on the clock-radio when I set the alarm. Switching off the bedside light and getting under the covers, it dawned on me, while I was adjusting the pillow under my head, that today was my birthday. I was turning fifty-six. Feeling my age, as they say, yet I could sense the heavy-duty pain pills and the jets of hot water doing their work. A little light-headed, less sore and in a more relaxed mood, I chuckled to myself as I thought about my Humpty Dumpty performance in front of the police. Thought of them in their cruiser parked in front of the house, waiting for me to show up with my key. Mary-Ellen would be having a bird.

THINGS GO BETTER WITH COKE

My progress on the tile grouting was such that I was able to call Lenny on September 24 and let him know that, as it turned out, there had been some method to my madness after all: the house was now going to be "ready for viewing" on the 26th, two days earlier than the September 28 date that I'd promised. With Julie threatening to replace him and hire another agent if he didn't "make something happen soon," I knew it would boost Lenny's spirits to hear the news. He'd confided to me earlier that he was actually quite worried about losing the listing. Things had been slow for him lately, he said. He could really use this sale to get out of the slump he was in. He admitted, as well, that Julie's calls were finally starting to take their toll: he was almost at his wit's end trying to explain to her that he "wasn't a miracle-worker, for Christ's sake." He'd pleaded with me to keep my part of the bargain and have the house ready by the agreed-upon date. "I *really* need you to come through for me on this, big fella," was how he put it. I told him in the message that he could let Julie know we were good to go; that the two of them could meet me at the house for the grand tour on the 26th if they wanted, adding, on a lighter note, that maybe it wasn't a miracle . . . but it was the closest this "big fella" was ever going to get.

My recording session was canceled on the 26th so that I could make my second appearance at court. Things proceeded at Old City Hall more or less as they had the first time: the crowd limbering up outside Room 110 for the imminent shoving match; a different cop on duty at the door this time, though sporting the same belligerent look; Larry pacing about, wincing, fussing and fuming over several lengthy, but what I was now sure were fake, phone calls; his sneering response, when I dared to approach him with another procedural question, a louder and even snootier "I'm not at liberty to give you that information" than he'd laid on me before.

"No Whistling" Endicott didn't seem to be present in the courtroom — a bit of good news, as I saw it. As was the announcement by the court clerk that our case was first on her docket. The Crown Attorney informed the judge, a blond, pleasantly smiling woman in her late forties (who managed to take the bench only seven minutes late) that police disclosure (their case against us) wasn't ready yet. Thus Her Honour, the Crown Attorney, the clerk, Larry and Leslie, turned in unison and, as they had previously, cast their eyes up to the lopsided calendar high on the wall so they could settle on a date for my next appearance. Their decision that the last week of October would work best for everyone, the clerk nodded, filled out and then handed me a notice to that effect (a neon-green slip of paper this time), a cue for me to leave I guessed, the whole process, as before, having taken maybe three minutes, if that.

And who but Officer Endicott was standing just inside the door when Larry, Leslie and I were on our way out. He recognized me immediately, leveled a cold glare and watched as I passed in front of him. I threw him a sarcastic wink just as I was leaving, whistled at full volume the opening strains of "The Hills Are Alive" from *The Sound of Music*, not bothering to look back when I entered the hall but quickening my pace just the same. As Malcolm was always reminding me, you just never knew with the cops.

As I hadn't eaten breakfast, I stopped in at Mr. Beans on my way back to the house and ordered a cinnamon-raisin bagel with peanut butter along with my decaf. I had some time to kill, so I ate in the coffee shop. I browsed the complimentary copy of the *Toronto Sun* and chatted to André about the recent woes of the Blue Jays who, once again, weren't going to make the World Series.

All in all, I was feeling pleased with myself, happy at how things had worked out, proud of what I'd accomplished in spite of less than favourable circumstances; confident that when Lenny brought Julie over to see the place at eleven o'clock — only their second visit to the crime scene since the raid — they'd be impressed with how bright, spacious, clean, cozy and comfortable I had the place looking, worth every penny of the $479,000 we were asking for it, even if it *had* been headquarters to an organized-crime operation.

I came out of Mr. Beans, popped into the flower shop on the other side of the plaza and picked out three colourful bouquets of fresh flowers, one to put in the crystal vase on the dining-room table, another for the coffee table in the living room, a third for the island in the middle of the kitchen — the floral finishing touch one that I knew Julie would appreciate.

Because Lenny and Julie would be there with me, I parked in front of the house, rather than around the corner on Greybeaver Trail. I grabbed the flowers, ran across the lawn, ducked under the overhanging branches of the still untrimmed weeping mulberry tree, and hurried up the steps onto the porch . . . and stopped dead in my tracks upon glimpsing a notice that had been posted on the front door, on red 8½-by-11-inch paper, the printing in large, bold-font black letters:

TOXIC WARNING!!
PREMISES UNDER QUARANTINE!!

Too stunned, at first, for the information to register, it hit me like a body blow after a couple of seconds. I stood there staring, the muscles in my neck knotting up, my stomach churning with a sick feeling. "This can't be," I said out loud. "It just can't *be*." Had Mary-Ellen decided to report me to the health department now? Was it something the cops had dreamed up? I stepped closer to the door and read the notice: that by order of the City of Toronto Public Health Department, the building had been quarantined due to the presence of bio-hazardous materials. No one was allowed on the premises, for any reason, until further notice. Fines and imprisonment could result from violation of the order, the property was being monitored regularly by Health Department officials, and it was a criminal offence to tamper in any way with, or take down, the order as posted. The

TOXIC WARNING was repeated again at the bottom; there was a phone number in the lower right-hand corner that I could call for further information.

"Toxic warning? Bio-hazardous materials?" What the hell could they mean by that? The house was probably in the best shape it had ever been in. I'd washed, scrubbed, vacuumed, polished, dusted, disinfected and deodorized for three days straight, after all the work had been done — Mr. Clean wouldn't think twice about moving into the place with the condition it was in now.

Curious, I moved closer and had a look at the tape they'd used to put up the notice, thinking maybe I could take it down; call the information number and complain that somehow a mistake had been made, that it had been posted on the wrong house. But whoever had put it up had taken no chances. All four edges of the sign were expertly tacked down with two-inch-wide strips of clear scotch tape, a second series of strips overlapping the edges of the first, in case anyone got a notion to try peeling it off.

Realizing these people meant business, the words "premises monitored regularly" leaping out at me, I memorized the information number, turned casually, stepping off the porch and, as if nothing was amiss — like I'd merely stopped by to bring someone flowers but they weren't home — walked calmly across the lawn back to my car, scouting the street for a vehicle in which Health Department officials might be sitting, staking the place out. It was only 10:30; the sign couldn't have gone up too long ago. For all I knew their strategy might be to hang around for a while after a notice had been posted, just to make sure people took it to heart.

The coast still clear on the street, from what I could see,

I opened my car door, set the fresh flower bouquets in the passenger seat, calmly hopped in, started up and drove off, heading around the block and parking in my usual spot, part way down Greybeaver Trail. No one about, I sneaked into the backyard of the house that was kitty-corner to mine and, not worrying whether anyone saw me or not, climbed onto the wooden fence, made my usual way along the top for about thirty feet or so, and then jumped down into my own yard. I ran to the sliding-glass doors and slipped inside.

I made it snappy across the kitchen, cut through the dining room and stood next to one of the living-room windows, peeking through the shutters to see if there was anything going on out front. For a few seconds there wasn't — but then a small white sedan came into view, driving at normal speed . . . but it was only a woman with a baby-seat in the back. When she'd gone past, I flipped open my cellphone and dialed the Health Department number.

Steadying myself while it rang, resolved to stay level-headed and keep things matter-of-fact, I let the woman who answered know the situation, said I wondered if there was someone from whom I could get more information. She asked for my name and address, which I gave her; went off the line for a moment then came back on and told me she was putting me through to the inspector handling the case.

A man picked up after several rings, identifying himself in a robust East Indian accent, "Dar Arulanadam."

Dar listened while I explained the reason for my call, gave me a suspicious, accusing and, I realized immediately, crafty response to what I'd told him: he wondered why I was calling him from inside my house, in defiance of the posted order. I told him I wasn't defying anything, I was on my cellphone.

I'd seen the sign on the front door when I arrived at the house, but left without going inside. The grilling continuing, he asked where I was calling from. "A coffee-shop nearby," I came back quickly. "Mr. Beans it's called."

"Mister what?"

"Beans."

Still not convinced apparently, he warned me the premises were monitored regularly to make sure the Health Department order was being upheld; informed me in stern tones that I could be arrested if I was calling from the house, which he went so far as to say he thought I was. "Most people have a tendency to do so when orders are posted," he let me know.

I conceded that, although it might be the case with most people, I liked to think I was smarter than that: the kind of person who did his utmost to cooperate with the authorities in circumstances like this.

My cloying obsequiousness enough to mollify him, at least for the time being, he got down to the business of explaining the quarantine order. It had evidently been posted in connection with a house search by the Metropolitan Toronto Police in late July that had turned up a marijuana grow-operation at 122 Friendship Avenue, the report by the officer in charge of the search indicating that black mould, a toxic contaminant, had been found on the premises.

My first impulse was to ask him why it had taken two months for the Health Department to determine the house was contaminated enough to be quarantined, but I kept my sarcasm in check and assured him that there was no mould of any kind in my house, and never had been. I asked him exactly where the purported mould had been found.

"One second," said Mr. Arulanadam, went off the line,

shuffled through some papers then came back on, clearing his throat before he spoke. "According to the police," he said, "and here I'm referring to their report, which I have in front of me, officers at the scene detected patches of mould about . . ." he paused while he read more, ". . . halfway down the main-floor corridor . . ." I scooted from the living room and walked halfway down the hall, ". . . on the baseboard," Mr. Arulanadam continued, "directly across from the basement door."

It took me a moment, but sure enough, when I crouched down and peered at the white baseboard, there were indeed two spots about half an inch off the floor, dark brown, one the size of a nickel, the other about the size of a dime. I must have overlooked them in the low-light conditions when I was grouting the tiles.

"On closer inspection," he carried on, "and I'm reading from the report again, 'officers were able to determine that the patches were of the black mould variety, the type commonly present in buildings where marijuana is grown.'"

While he'd been talking, I'd taken my thumb and rubbed the two spots with the toe of my shoe — splashes of Coca-Cola that probably spilt from a glass when one of the kids was heading to the basement to watch TV — and they came off with no trouble. I didn't tell Mr. Arulanadam, but I'd cleaned up many such spots before.

"Anywhere else?" I asked him, the relief in my voice evidently reigniting his suspicions as to my whereabouts.

"Are *you* in the house, Mr. Id-leridge?" he demanded.

"I told you, Mr. Aru-lana-dam," I said patiently, enunciating the syllables clearly so as to emphasize the correct pronunciation of his name, "I'm in a coffee-shop. Do you want me to pass the phone to the owner and have him vouch for me? And by the way, my last name is pronounced Illidge, one D, no R's. *Illidge*."

Chastened, perhaps, by my setting him straight on my last name, he paused for a moment. "I don't think that will be necessary," he said.

"So what am I supposed to do at this point, Mr. Arulanadam? My house is set to go up for sale later today. How can I do that with a red toxic-warning sign posted on my front door?"

"Well, you can't," he said sharply. "*No one* is allowed on the premises until you've taken corrective measures and had the house tested."

"But like I told you, Mr. Arulanadam, there's no mould. No corrective measures are necessary."

"Well, according to the police they are."

"Be that as it may," I said, "how soon can you come and do the testing?"

"Oh, *we* don't do it," he explained. "You have to call an approved environmental testing company, preferably one of those that our department works with, which are listed on our website. They forward us the results of their tests and, if they meet our criteria, then we schedule an onsite inspection, another officer and myself, and if we determine at that point that the quarantine has been observed in all respects — namely that no one has been on the premises in violation of a posted order — then we lift it, and you're free to proceed with the sale of your house."

"How long does the process take?"

"Well," he said, "that of course depends on the length

of time required to clean up your house, repair any water or structural damage and eliminate the mould."

"There *is* no water or structural damage," I pointed out for a second time. "And as I told you, there *is* no mould."

"No water or structural damage?" He sounded confused.

"*None.* It's a family residence, Mr. Arulanadam. One of my sons had some plants growing in a room in the basement, that's all."

"Let me be clear, Mr. Id-leridge," he bridled out of the blue. "*No one*, and I can't stress this enough, is to be in that house, under any circumstances, until we have verified that all hazardous substances have been eliminated."

"I quite understand, Mr. Arulanadam. As far as my being on the premises is concerned, and maybe I should have pointed this out to you off the bat, I'm presently out on bail, one of my conditions that I'm not permitted to be in the house at any time."

"And you're not calling from there now?"

"No, I'm not," I said, trying not to sound impatient with him. "But tell me one thing, Mr. Arulanadam, out of curiosity more than anything else."

"Yes?"

"Since no one is allowed on the premises, for any reason, if I happened to be in a position where the house needed repairs or cleaning up in order to pass inspection, how exactly could that be done?"

"Well," he chuckled, "the house can't very well clean itself up now, can it?" This was a little Health Department humour, I supposed, Mr. Arulanadam appearing to have entirely missed the point of my question.

"No," I agreed, "it certainly can't."

"Best just to call one of the environmental companies and go from there," was his advice. "But I remind you again, we monitor these situations closely."

"You've made that very clear, sir."

"I hope so," he said. "At any rate, speak to one of the environmental testing companies. They'll be in touch with us when they have their results."

"Just out of interest," I said before hanging up. "What do these companies generally charge for testing?"

"That's a matter for you to discuss with them," he said. "I do know that it varies. One thing I could suggest," he added, "would be that you open some of the windows in your house; two months is a long time for them to have been closed. Let some ventilation in; it could affect the results significantly."

Whether this was a worthwhile suggestion or not, I couldn't say, but I had reason to suspect it was yet another ploy by Mr. Arulanadam to catch me up in my ruse, so rather than comment, I merely thanked him for his help and said, "Goodbye, Mr. Arulanadam."

"Goodbye, Mr. Id-leridge," he said, and ended the call.

Clearly not a good idea to hang around — if he didn't have a vehicle watching the house now, my hunch was that he'd dispatched one the moment he got off the phone with me — I left the house through the sliding-glass doors in the kitchen, scrambled over the back fence, went out to the street and headed down Greybeaver Trail to my car. I put in a call to Lenny as I was driving away, "So much for miracles" being the opening words in my message, after which I gave him the lowdown on what had just transpired and told him to meet me as soon as possible at Mr. Beans so we could decide which one of us would break the news to Julie.

On Wednesday of the following week, a technician from TH Harrison Environmental showed up at the house at ten o'clock sharp. Introducing himself as Dennis, he was a friendly guy who ventured around the house for about half an hour using various different digital devices he had with him, not saying much while he did his testing, most of which consisted of holding his monitors in the air for a few seconds at a time, or attaching probes and sensors to the walls. When he was done, and we were standing at the foot of the basement stairs, I asked him if he could give me some idea of the results. He said the data had to be processed in their lab, and the health department never publicized what its acceptable levels were. As far as he could see, though, everything seemed to be normal, the readings maybe slightly high in the basement, because some of the windows were open.

Miffed by him mentioning it, I told him the health inspector handling my case had suggested a little fresh air might improve the test readings.

Dennis made a face and shook his head. "It's just the opposite," he said. "The contaminants come in from outside, especially at this time of year. Mouldy leaves, pollen, dead plant-matter, that sort of thing. I don't understand why he'd tell you something like that."

"I just assumed he knew what he was talking about."

He shrugged. "I wouldn't worry about it too much," he said. "I don't see it being an issue."

When we came upstairs, I pointed out the place on the baseboard where the police claimed they'd found black mould. "Turned out to be a few drops of spilled Coca-Cola," I said lightly, careful not to sound too ironic, as I didn't know where Dennis's proclivities lay when it came to the police.

He gave a wry smirk and shook his head again. "Cops," he said, not with any particular affection.

We went outside to the front porch and I handed him his cheque for $1,500, Callum having loaned me the money. I told him, when he finished writing me out a receipt, that Dan, with whom I'd booked the appointment, had said he'd try to forward the results to the health department by Friday if at all possible.

"Should be able to," Dennis said, putting his pen away. "Normally it's three or four business days, depending on the complexity of the job, but this was pretty straight-forward. Plus I know he's put 'Rush' on it. Dan's usually pretty good about that."

"Sooner the better," I said.

"It's kind of a bummer, I know."

"Kind of?" I kidded with him.

He shook his head and offered another sympathetic smile. "Cops," he repeated. He thanked me for the payment, said he hoped things worked out for the best and we shook hands. I watched him drive off down the street — past a small, silver-grey two-door sedan which happened to be parked across the road now. About four houses down, no one behind the wheel, there was a bald man who looked to be in his fifties sitting in the passenger seat, pen in hand, writing something on a clipboard.

Not waiting around to see whether it was in connection with me or not, I pulled the door closed and locked up, hustled down the walk and across the driveway, ducked around the side of the garage and played Hopalong Cassidy over the backyard fences until I reached my car. Before starting up, I called Lenny, telling him, when he answered, that the testing was done and all we could do for the moment was hope the readings passed muster with Mr. Arulanadam. Lenny asked if I'd given any thought to what we'd do if for some reason they didn't.

"No," I told him, "I haven't. But burning the place down might not be a bad place to start."

"What?" he said, sounding shocked.

"We'll cross that bridge when we come to it, Lenny. For now, just keep your fingers crossed. And your toes too," I kidded him. "We'll need all the help we can get."

"Right," he said, chuckling lightly, and asked me to give him a call the moment I heard anything.

I made a U-turn, headed down Greybeaver, turned right onto Friendship and drove slowly up the street toward the house, just to see how noticeable the red *TOXIC WARNING* sign was from the street. The bald man was still sitting in the passenger seat of the silver sedan writing on his clipboard. A white panel-van had pulled up in front of the house, two guys on the front lawn hammering a *FOR SALE* sign into the ground with Lenny's picture, name and phone number on it. And, not surprisingly, Mary-Ellen McCluskey was standing on her front porch now, cellphone in hand, adjusting her glasses as she peered over at the real-estate sign. Always the first to know what people in the area were asking when their places went up for sale, she punched in what I knew would be Lenny's number. Wouldn't she be surprised, I thought to myself as I carried on up the street, when she snooped over to the front door and had a look at the *TOXIC WARNING* sign — but then again, in her community-minded way, Mary-Ellen would probably just take it as further evidence that she and Wes had done exactly the right thing by turning us in to the police.

CHAPTER ELEVEN
MAKING MY BONES

According to Lenny, Julie and her lawyer had "gone Chernobyl" when they heard the house sale was on hold because of a Health Department quarantine order, coming right out and accusing me of creating these delays over the past two months on purpose; as if I actually *wanted* the government to seize the house so she and her family would lose their share of the money. Nothing Lenny could say would disabuse them. They assumed that this was why I was stalling on the Final Agreement and were demanding that I retain a divorce lawyer immediately. There was no reason, according to them, we couldn't negotiate a "global settlement" by the time the quarantine was lifted and the sign came down. Lenny said he hated to mention it, but they wanted a picture of it, so they could verify that I wasn't just making the whole thing up.

I assured him that he had nothing to worry about on that

score; sabotage wasn't one of my preferred lines of work. As to retaining a lawyer, though, I told him not to get his hopes up. I wouldn't have the money to hire one until my recording sessions were done in a month or so; and as far as reaching an agreement with Julie was concerned, let alone one within the next two weeks, I suggested that as he could understand Julie's negotiating style, now that he'd been dealing with her for the past two months, he'd have a good idea of how successful any negotiations were likely to be. Lenny didn't say anything, but the slight smile on his face and the way he nodded gave me the impression that the point hit home.

I discussed the situation with Callum, who agreed to advance me money for legal fees against my upcoming Simply Audiobooks payment; I then talked with Malcolm, who said he didn't practise family law himself, but was happy to recommend a friend and former partner of his, someone named Stephen Arkoff. He was not a family lawyer either, but Malcolm said he knew what was required, was a good guy and, better yet, had reasonable rates.

Stephen told me, when we talked on the phone to set up a meeting, that he'd be happy to "handle the paper" for a final separation agreement between my wife and me, though he made a point of letting me know that he didn't do court work any longer. "You'll have to find somebody else if it gets to the point where you and your wife start duking it out," he joked. I said that was fine with me; I was already dealing with the drug case (which Malcolm had apparently spoken to him about) and had no intention, not to mention the financial resources, to get embroiled in another one. "*Ha-ha!*" I remember he burst out laughing when he heard that. "Famous last words!"

It was late morning when I arrived at the address Malcolm

had given me, a ten-storey yellow-brick office building on Eglinton Avenue just west of Yonge Street, two large "For Lease" signs of a commercial real-estate company prominently displayed in the ground-floor front window. With no tenant listings on the glass-encased directory board in the lobby, no furniture in the foyer across from the elevators (though from the discolouration of the carpet it looked like recently there had been), nobody around except me and the building looking for all intents and purposes like it was vacant, I had to wonder if Malcolm had given me someone else's address by mistake. He was usually on the ball about things like that, though, never enjoying it when he had to be corrected (a defence lawyer trait, he once told me) so I went ahead and pushed the button for the elevator.

When I stepped off at the fifth floor, there was a tenant directory behind glass on the wall straight ahead, white letters on a black background with the names and suite-numbers of several individuals, the odd letter and number missing. Stephen's was listed as #5_2, a small white arrow pointing to my right along the hall.

It was not 512, which I came to first (the door was locked). I turned along a different hall and opened the door to "502."

No one was in the waiting room when I entered the office. There were a couple of chairs with a low, round, chrome-and-glass table with nothing on it between them, a framed Georges Seurat gallery poster on one wall, and on the adjacent wall the light-faded outline of where another picture had been. The doors to the four offices across from me and to my right were all closed. I noticed an open one off to my left and heard somebody in the room. As I was stepping over to make my presence known, a wheeled office-chair rolled into view in the doorway and a slim, very attractive young woman beamed me a glossy red-lipstick smile. "Hey there!" she said cordially.

"Paul Illidge," I said, introducing myself. "I have an appointment with Stephen."

"Sure," she said, leaned forward in her chair, stuck her head out the door and shouted across the waiting-room: "*Ste*-phen!" The doors to the offices across the way remaining closed, she hollered again, louder this time, adding: "*Somebody's here to see you!*" Still no response, she muttered something under her breath, swiveled the chair around and stood up. "Sorry about this," she said, hurrying over to one of the doors. She gave it a firm rap, opened up and poked her head in.

Stephen not there apparently, she muttered something about "the boardroom" and walked me to the office at the end of the row, just raising her hand to knock when the door was opened from inside and a man who I took to be Stephen Arkoff was standing there. About my height, high cheek-bones, gold-rimmed glasses, a slightly beaked nose and frizzy, blondish hair brushed back on his head, he could easily have passed for Jerry Springer.

He stepped forward smiling, threw his arms in the air, palms open like he might be about to bow down in homage, and greeted me with an extra-effusive "Paul Illidge! The famous writer!" He shook my hand, hanging onto it while he turned to the young woman and made introductions. "Tess, this is Paul. Paul, Tess," he said.

Tess threw me a dry smile. "The famous legal secretary," she quipped.

"Not much longer, though," said Stephen. "She's cracking the books as we speak. Gonna be a paralegal, then before you know it a legal-legal, a legal-beagle, a —"

"Okay, okay," Tess said, playing down the flattery. "He gets it, Stephen."

"So, you able to rustle up a couple of coffees for us?" Stephen asked quickly. "Not Starbucks. What's that other place?"

The apparently unexpected request drawing a pointedly cool look, Tess said she'd "see what she could do" — more for my benefit, I think, than because she had any intention of snapping to it and "rustling up" the coffees. "Nice to meet you, Paul," she said, her pleasant smile returning, then left the two of us and headed back to her office. Stephen brought me into the boardroom.

A couple of dozen legal books, several stacks of file folders and three or four bankers boxes were crammed with papers on the shelves around the not overly large room. The walls were bare, though there were hooks and rectangles of brighter paint where pictures had obviously been. There was a window overlooking the street at one end of a teak conference table that seemed too big for the space, a couple of matching teak chairs on each side and two at the end in which Stephen and I took seats: me with a notebook in which I'd jotted down some questions I wanted to ask, Stephen with a razor-thin burgundy-coloured cellphone on the table in front of him, his legs crossed, dressed today in a double-breasted Hugo Boss suit, Gucci leather loafers and a colourful silk tie that he stroked appreciatively from time to time as we talked.

Or rather, as Stephen talked. After a few friendly cracks about Malcolm and his amusing eccentricities, his first order of business was to thank me for saving his seventeen-year-old son's ass with my novel version of Shakespeare's *Othello*, which they'd found by accident — the last copy — in the Chapters bookstore over at the Yonge-Eglinton Centre, just a couple of days before his son's final exam last June. "And because of *you*," Stephen said, "the kid ends up getting 86 in English — not bad for a guy who didn't start reading till he was ten!"

"That's good news," I said deferentially. "I didn't know the stores were still selling them."

"It was amazing, man. I even read it myself. That Iago character, what a prick!"

"I'm glad you liked it," I told him, a little overwhelmed by the extravagant praise.

There was something else he wanted to mention, too, before he forgot, which was that a client-friend of his named Angelo had an incredible story about some things that had happened to him that nobody was going to believe, though every word of it was apparently true. It was incredible, according to Stephen, what Angelo had been put through. The CBC profiled him in a documentary they made about the Mafia in Toronto. The RCMP raided his house, confiscated "everything he fuckin' owned" and started to investigate him. "Complete guilt by association," Stephen said, getting more wound up as he talked. "They fingered Angie for being in the mob because of his connection to Paulie V., his first cousin, who many claimed was a boss in the Magaddino crime family out of Buffalo — the ones who *supposedly* ordered the hit on Paulie in the Pearson airport parking lot back in '83. You remember that?" I told him that I was in fact familiar with Paulie V.'s story and the CBC documentary. "Ange and Paulie were close," Stephen continued, "but not *that* close, if you know what I mean. Ange was never a made man, at least as far as I know." He said *of course* Angie and Paulie saw each other a lot, why wouldn't they? They were cousins. They'd grown up together. So what if they went in on some business deals together. They'd been doing it since they were kids surviving on the mean streets in downtown Toronto.

"Because of the organized-crime allegations in the CBC program, Ange got pinched by the RICO Commission not long after he started working in Atlantic City during the late '70s. But he was never actually *charged* with anything, let alone convicted, as the CBC documentary basically came right out and said he had been. They hit him with *racketeering*. Ange and Paulie had been racketeering all their lives, for Christ's sake. Paulie's old man walked out on his wife, Angelo's father's sister and their eight children, who moved across the road to live at Angelo's house, with him and his eight brothers and sisters. As kids, Ange and Paulie helped out together at the shoeshine stand Angelo's father ran on Lombard Street. You imagine what it must have been like raising seventeen kids, running a shoeshine stand in the 1930s? Shit," Stephen said, "I can't pay *my* bills, and I only have one kid to look after. Anyway," he surged on, "CBC does this investigation on Paulie for this program about organized crime in Canada, and who happens to end up in the footage they shoot — at the Hampton Court Hotel on Jarvis Street no less, right across from the fucking CBC building, and two down from RCMP headquarters, how fucking convenient was that? — but Angelo, who'd stopped by the hotel that day to have coffee with his cousin Paulie out by the swimming pool — while the CBC-types had their hidden cameras rolling of course, and next thing you know, Angelo's a major underworld crime figure."

I told Stephen I remembered the documentary, *Connections* it was called.

"That's the one!" he said, and resumed the story. "Angelo lost a hundred million dollars worth of real-estate over that, his wife divorced him, his kids wouldn't have anything to do with him — still won't. But he's in his seventies now, still alive to tell the tale, and that's what he wants to do. Put out a book to set the record straight, tell his side of the story and, maybe along the way, throw mud in the eyes of a few people who ruined his life for him, thanks very much. You'd be the perfect guy to write it," Stephen said enthusiastically. "The two of you could make a fortune on it. You should give him a call, Paul. Here," he said, took a slim gold pen from the breast pocket of his suit-jacket, a business card from the inside pocket, wrote down Angelo's name and phone number on it then passed it across the table. "You *gotta* give him a call, Paul. I'm serious. He's looking around for a writer. Hang on," he broke off, picked up his cellphone and dialed. "I'm gonna give him a call — I think I know where he might be."

"It's all right, Stephen," I said, pocketing the business card.

"*No*, I'm gonna call him and put you on the phone."

No one answered, so he left a message: "Ange, it's Stephen. I've got some good news for you. Call me." He closed up the phone, looked at his watch. "You wanna grab some lunch?"

"I thought we might talk about the settlement agreement with my ex-wife," I said, to jog his memory.

"Right . . ." he came back, getting to his feet. "Why don't you give me $750 now, and that should cover it. When you sell the house, come on back in and we'll get things rolling. But like I said to you on the phone, I don't do court stuff any-more. The paperwork kills you. It's *all* paperwork. You're just charging people for paperwork, which I gotta hire people to do. It's endless, and it's all bullshit. He-said, she-said, who-did-what-with-which-and-to-whom shit. *Every*body gets fucked, and nobody enjoys it. That's family law."

Figuring I'd discuss my questions with him another time, I closed my notebook, pocketed my pen and stood up. I took the $800 I'd brought with me and, I don't really know why, handed over the eight hundred-dollar bills and told him, as a joke, to keep the change.

"Why don't I buy lunch then?" he volunteered, breaking into an animated grin. Pocketing the money without counting it, he threw a friendly arm around my shoulder and said, "Come on!"

We rode the elevator down, Stephen telling me the building was a virtual ghost town. The owners were having mortgage problems. He'd be out after Christmas, moving into an office in his house, he said, which was just two blocks up the street.

"Speaking of which," he said when we came outside, "maybe I better whip home and see if my son brought the car back. It's a Lexus. It's leased, though who knows for how much longer. Nah," he said, changing his mind. "Fuck it. Let's check the California Sandwich Shop. Ange likes to hang out there sometimes."

Two guys in open-necked white shirts and white aprons were making deli sandwiches behind the counter in the Yonge Street shop. Maybe a dozen customers were sitting at tables, but none of them Angelo, according to Stephen, and so we headed back up the street, crossed at the lights and entered the Yonge-Eglinton Shopping Centre through the revolving doors.

We rode the escalator down to the underground mall and made our way over to the food court, busy because it was lunch hour. Stephen surveyed the options available around the court then asked if I was feeling heroic.

"Heroic?"

"Yeah. You want the best hero sandwich in the world?"

I'd never had a hero before, at least that I knew of, but I took his word for it. "Why not?" I said.

There was no line-up at the place selling heroes, so he hurried over to the counter and ordered the sandwiches, two coffees and two bottles of spring water. He brought the food on a tray over to the high round table that I'd nabbed. Perched on tall stools, we sat across from each other and started in on our sandwiches.

I was partway through the first half of mine, Stephen laughing as he talked again about some of Malcolm's peccadilloes, things that he didn't let on to too many people, but that Stephen liked to tease him about, when he suddenly broke off and shouted, "Johnny C., get over here, you fat bastard!"

Johnny C. recognized Stephen, put on a good-natured smile and sauntered over to our table. He was a heavy-set man in his mid-fifties, a tailored olive-green suit, a brown peaked cap on his head, huge shoulders under a fawn-brown, expensive-looking camel-hair overcoat, his round, slightly tanned face dark with five-o'clock shadow, even though it was just coming up to noon.

"Hey, you skinny prick," Johnny said as he shook Stephen's hand.

"Get yourself a hero sandwich and join us," Stephen said. "Paul, this is Johnny C. Johnny, this is Paul, a soon-to-be client. Friend of Malcolm's."

Johnny C. and I shook hands, Johnny's completely encompassing mine, his grip strong but genuinely friendly. "Lemme take a look," he said, and strolled over to the counter of the sandwich outlet.

He returned in a few minutes, set his tray down and sat next to me. Unwrapping his sandwich, he snapped open a can of iced tea and inserted a straw, listening, as he ate, as Stephen gave him the latest on what some of their mutual acquaintances were up to. Johnny C. followed with news of his own. He was a straight-talker, well-spoken, a dry sense of humour. He and Stephen started bantering back and forth, poking fun at each other's respective backgrounds, Stephen ribbing Johnny C. about his Italian origins, Johnny with quick rejoinders about Stephen's "Hebraic ancestry" — taking back a further genealogical zinger a few moments later, kidding Stephen, deferentially, that maybe they should cut it out, what with a distinguished WASP gentleman like me sitting at their table.

"You want distinguished?" Stephen said, nodding across the table at me. "*This* guy translates Shakespeare into modern English for high school kids."

"No kidding?" said Johnny C., impressed, wiping the corners of his mouth with a serviette.

"No kidding," I said.

"That hard doing something like that?"

"It has its moments," I said.

Johnny nodded again, took a long sip of his iced tea. "I always liked Shakespeare," he said and paused. "Though I didn't know him personally of course," he said with a straight face. Stephen and I broke into laughter at the quip, Johnny C. cracking a dry smile as he threw me a wink and had another sip of his iced tea.

The wisecracks and friendly gibes continuing as we finished our heroes, Stephen made a point of lauding my writing talents several more times before we were done. (You'd have thought I deserved a Nobel Prize in literature to hear him tell it.) He raved, too, about me being just the right guy to do a book on "The Pooch," their mutual friend Angelo. He was still talking about The Pooch even after we'd said goodbye to Johnny C. at the subway entrance. We took the escalator up to the main floor and went outside to the square, Stephen pulling out his phone and dialing Angelo's number, saying he was going to try putting me on the phone with him again.

"I can't, Stephen," I said, "I've got to be on my way."

"Don't you want to talk to the Pooch?" he asked, sounding hurt.

"I do, just not right now."

But after a minute of waiting, it became clear Angelo was still unavailable. Stephen ended the call, closed up his phone and gave me the first serious look since I'd walked into his office. "What about this as a title for the book," he said. "Making My Bones." He gestured with his hands as though picturing it on a theatre marquee. "Making My Bones," he repeated. "Don't you think that'd be good?"

"I thought you said Angelo wasn't in the Mafia?"

"He *wasn't*. But that's the point. Because of the cops and the media, everybody thought he was. That's what got him into so much trouble. With the book, he can tell the true story and clear his name."

"It's not bad," I said, liking his explanation.

"See?" he said with a kind of preening grin. "You got your $750 worth after all."

"I guess I did," I said, laughing at his smooth segue onto the topic of his retainer.

"So," he said, "what I'll need you to give me is a copy of the Interim Agreement you have with your wife, plus all the case documents, files, legal correspondence, that sort of shit."

"I wish I could, Stephen," I said, "but everything was thrown out in the clean-up after the raid." I kidded him that, on the positive side, it would cut down on the paperwork he'd have to do.

"What about writing something up for me then? Not Shakespeare or anything. Just something that'll bring me up to speed on where we stand."

"Who did what, with which and to whom?" I said, quoting one of the phrases he'd used during his harangue about family law.

"That's it," he said, cracking a smile.

"I thought you might want me to," I said, took the brown envelope that I'd brought along with me and handed it to him. "It's a chapter from a novel I was working on in 2003," I explained, watching as he opened the envelope, removed the paperclipped manuscript and gave the title page a curious glance.

"'*Closing Time?*'" he asked, looking up.

"It's a version of what happened between my wife and me when we separated in January 2000, with a few additions to bring it up to date, but I wrote the book as a factum" (a brief used by lawyers to convince judges that if they find in favour of their clients they will be legally correct, will have done the fair thing, and that the factum and its author are credible).

"Ah," Stephen said wryly. "The bull without the shit."

"Exactly," I said, explaining that I was seeing an old girlfriend from university at the time I was writing the book, a Crown Attorney in the Ontario Court of Appeal who was always reading thousand-page factums for the cases she was prosecuting. "She let me browse through them once in a while, showed me the ins and outs, gave me some pointers on writing them. I realized, once I got the hang of it, that the fairest way to write about the break-up of my marriage was to do it as a factum."

"That must have been fun," Stephen said with a sardonic chuckle.

"It was no walk in the park, I can say that. It's tough writing something when your word-choice options can't include more than a handful of transitive verbs, no adverbs, adjectives, subordinate clauses or compound-complex sentences. But it'll give you the gist."

"Jeez," he said, throwing me a mock-guilty look. "Maybe I should give you back a coupla hundred dollars from the retainer . . ."

"Why don't we talk about that after you've read the factum," I said, tongue-in-cheek, since, from what I knew of Stephen so far, I couldn't see a refund of any kind coming my way anytime soon.

We shook hands; I thanked him for the lunch, told him I'd keep him posted on the matrimonial front, then turned and started across the square. "Think about that title!" he hollered after me. "*Making My Bones!* And don't forget to phone Angelo when you get a chance!!"

"I won't!" I called over my shoulder, and thought, with some amusement as I headed off along the sidewalk back to my car, that if he was anything like his friends Stephen and Johnny C., "The Pooch" might just turn out to be quite the character, too.

CHAPTER TWELVE
INSPECTOR HONG

Letting Julie know, through Lenny, that as requested I'd found a lawyer to work on the separation agreement for me, the other legal matter requiring my attention was the power-of-sale proceeding that the Royal Bank of Canada was threatening to bring against me for delinquency on my mortgage account. Joanne, the woman in the bank's collections department who was overseeing the file, had been leaving me increasingly irate messages since the middle of September about the urgency of the situation. We were into October now; I'd told her in late August that the house had gone up for sale, yet it was going on three months now and she still hadn't seen a real-estate listing. Joanne was wondering why that would be: was there something I wasn't telling her? She'd waived two months of payments already, now she'd had to let a third go by. It was time she had some answers, she said, otherwise things would be out of her hands; as much as she didn't want to, she'd be forced to notify legal and have them start the foreclosure-ball rolling.

After a menacing-sounding message one morning, in which she informed me in the stiffest tones yet that if I didn't return her call by the end of business that day, she was sending the papers up to legal and that would be that, I decided I couldn't put her off any longer and phoned her back.

I began by apologizing profusely, telling her that I'd been working outside Toronto on a writing project that was proving more complicated than I thought it would be. Sending her the listing had just slipped my mind. I promised to have our agent fax a copy of it to her ASAP.

"Well, just be sure he does," said Joanne, but then hesitated. "I don't know why, Paul, but I get the feeling you're not telling me the whole story here."

"It's the whole story," I lied, reminding her that I was also in the process of working on a final separation agreement with my ex-wife. I explained that that was slowing things down; that as there often were in these cases, my ex-wife and I had some fundamental disagreements about how the proceeds of the house sale should be divided up. But I assured her, in my most earnest-sounding voice, that everything was on the up-and-up, hunky-dory as they say, and we were expecting offers to start coming in at any time.

"Okay . . ." Joanne said, like she might be buying it. "But why wouldn't you have just called and told me that?"

"I know I should have, Joanne," I said penitently, "and I feel badly. As I was saying, though, I've been so caught up in —"

"Just get the listing to me, Paul," she cut in curtly, and ended the call.

By myself in the Simply Audiobooks lunchroom, where I'd gone to call Joanne while Colin made some adjustments to his equipment before we recorded our next scene, I stayed sitting at the table, put the phone down and worked on bringing my thoughts back to "Shakespeare mode" before heading into the studio, something I was finding increasingly hard to do. The court case and the business with the health department were never far from my mind, my voice was wearing down from the stress of our all-in-one-take recording strategy, the two of us working even faster now that Colin had told me he was probably going to lose his job because of the cash flow problems the company was having. Cindy, the woman who'd been supervising our project, had already been mysteriously let go two weeks earlier, as had about seventy percent of the other full-time employees, with a month's salary overdue and no severance pay. And since late September, Dell Parsons, the CFO, had been making himself so scarce around the office that none of the few remaining staff knew whether he was still with the company or not.

Rumours afoot in the office as to why the business was in trouble went from the problem of slumping subscription sales (the audiobook niche was apparently shrinking in the face of new media like YouTube and MySpace), to financial mis-management at the corporate level: the CEO was said to have been drawing large amounts from company bank accounts in recent months, though there were questions, too, about whether the company's stock price had been manipulated to misrepresent its true value over the last few years, the actual value of the business being a great deal less than what share-holders had been led to believe.

It was a mess any way you looked at it, but since no one

had told us not to, Colin and I simply carried on with our recording sessions, the precarious state of the company's finances progressively more nerve-wracking, since we never knew if or when someone would pop into the studio while we were in the middle of one of our one-take scenes and announce that the show was now over for us too.

With all that was going on "backstage" in my life at the time — a Shakespeare drama in its own right, Colin commented after I'd filled him in on what was happening — the last thing I needed to hear was that he might lose his job, and that with cash-flow problems myself, there was a good chance I wouldn't be paid for my nearly three months of hard work either.

There were days when I told Colin I'd had it; I was outta there, the suspense of not knowing how things stood in yet another area of my life making it impossible for me to focus on my performance at the mike. He said he felt exactly the same way, huffed and puffed about it himself for a minute, and then we'd carry on. There were days when I stepped into the tiny sound booth and had absolutely no idea where I was going to find the inspiration, let alone the energy, to put on King Lear's madness, Goneril's conniving, Edmund's lechery, the Fool's increasingly ominous jests that if Lear didn't wake up soon and see himself for who he really was, there was going to be hell to pay. On those occasions when I could muster up enough to give my creative all to a scene — raging, kibitzing, cursing, cajoling, rhapsodizing, agonizing, philosophizing and soliloquizing as the characters in the play do — there were times when my voice, already in rough shape from the two months of eight-hour days I'd been putting in, would suddenly crack from the strain and sink to a hoarse, laryngitis-like whisper.

Colin and I ran through every throat-reviving remedy we could think of — hot water and lemon, various fruit juices, salt-water gargling, ginger ale, ice cream, cough drops, even Trident Tropical Fruit chewing gum at one point — as we worked to bring my voice back so we could carry on; both of us frantic and particularly anxious to finish things up while there was still some money in the Simply Audiobook coffers to pay us.

After a succession of nervous phone calls to Mr. Arulanadam in which I ended up leaving what I know were desperate-sounding voicemail messages, I was finally able to reach him on October 12, Dar informing me, in a slow, matter-of-fact voice that, after having reviewed the results of the TH Harrison tests, he found the readings too high for his liking, especially those in the basement and so would be unable to lift the quarantine order on my house.

"You suggested I open the basement windows to let in some fresh air," I pointedly reminded him.

"You went into the house and opened them?"

"No," I came back, ready for his question, "I had one of my sons open them from the outside. More to the point," I went on, "what am I supposed to do now?"

"There isn't much point in doing anything," he said. "You've had the house cleaned up, repaired the water and structural damage, and yet you still have higher-than-normal readings."

"Nobody's been in the house, Mr. Arulanadam. It's perfectly clean. And as I told you before, there wasn't any water or structural damage. Except for the open windows, the house is exactly the way it was on the night the police raided it."

He pondered the situation. "Well, I suppose you *could* have it tested again," he said, not sounding optimistic.

"Then that's what I'm going to do," I said. I asked him to keep an eye out for a new set of test results, and hung up.

I talked to Dan at TH Harrison and explained what had happened, which he said he was disappointed to hear. I asked him, as part of the $1,500 I'd already paid, if he could see his way to giving me a second test at no charge.

Dan said he was sorry, but that wasn't how it worked. He'd need to bill me $1,500 to send his technician out again, reminding me that he'd given me a break on the regular fee of $2,000 as it was.

I gave him the lowdown on what was happening, said I'd borrowed the money to have the first testing done, I was out on bail, my children and I had been forced to live elsewhere, the house was waiting to go up for sale, the bank was foreclosing and my ex-wife and her real-estate agent were on my case to have the problem resolved. I asked him to talk to Dennis, the technician who'd done the testing, about what the police had supposedly identified as mould; suggested to Dan that the whole thing had been trumped up from the start, "overzealous" policing what my lawyer termed it.

A reasonable guy, thank goodness, Dan said that he'd make it $750 then, but that was the best he could do. He could have someone go back in on Tuesday the 16th, the first available appointment if I wanted it. I said I did, and thanked him for his help.

Over the next few days, I gave the house another full-court cleaning, bleached, vacuumed, left the air conditioning and all the charcoal air-cleaners on for forty-eight hours straight, kept all the windows closed and dehumidified the basement rooms till they were Sahara-dry and spore-free, or so I was hoping.

Callum generously giving me a cheque for $750 to cover the cost of Dennis doing the second test, after three tense days of waiting, everything hanging in the balance, when I got through to Mr. Arulanadam on the 18th, he said he'd been over the results of TH Harrison's new readings carefully, that they appeared to meet health department specifications and so he was pleased to be able to tell me they were now acceptable.

"I can take down the toxic-warning sign then?" I asked, trying not to make my relief and jubilation too obvious.

"No!" Mr. Arulanadam snapped in alarm, practically coming through the phone. "One of my associates and I will need to make an onsite assessment of the premises!"

"What for?"

"To ensure you've complied with the order."

I told him I thought I had.

"You've had the house tested, Mr. Id-leridge," he said. "The bylaws require us to carry out a visual inspection of the property before we can lift the quarantine."

"And when can you do that?"

"Let me see . . ." I heard him rustling through papers, typing on his computer. "We could schedule an onsite inspection next Tuesday," he said coming back on the phone. "The 23rd?"

Julie and Lenny not going to hold out till then, I explained to Mr. Arulanadam that this was an emergency situation. I asked him if there was any possibility he and his associate could come the next day, Friday, so we wouldn't have to wait over the weekend.

He was quiet for a moment. "No," he finally said, "that's

the only date. 10:30 a.m. The 23rd. My associate and I will meet you in front of the house, and we'll take it from there."

"And if it meets your specifications, you'll take the sign down for me?"

"There's a bit of a process involved," he said, "but yes, I think that can happen."

Wise to Mr. Arulanadam's ways by now, I made a point of being at the house by ten o'clock on Tuesday morning. A prudent move, as Mr. Arulanadam and his female associate pulled into the driveway at 10:15.

Mr. Arulanadam introduced me to his colleague, Inspector Hong, an unsmiling Asian woman in her late thirties with medium-length black hair, no makeup, dressed in a dark grey skirt-suit, a white blouse and black high heels.

We went inside, Mr. Arulanadam and Inspector Hong removing their shoes, Ms. Hong taking off her suit-jacket, stepping into the living room and, after folding and placing it on the back of one of the armchairs peering inquisitively around, shooting subtle but probing looks into the dining room as she did so.

Mr. Arulanadam announcing in an official voice that the inspection was now underway, he had me walk them through the house, starting with the second floor: the master bedroom, the kids' bedrooms, the spare room and the bathrooms, Ms. Hong carefully checking the contents of closets, cupboards and drawers, peeking behind shower curtains, into garbage cans and laundry baskets, snooping in every corner of every room with what seemed like a practised forensic eye, while Mr. Arulanadam remained in the doorway of each room and made observations of his own, noting them down in his file folder with a pensive frown on his face yet saying nothing, waiting until Inspector Hong, her search of a particular room done, nodded her head and we proceeded to the next location.

Down to the main floor, they conducted a meticulous search of the cupboards in the kitchen, noted the best-before dates on cereal boxes, did the same thing on food containers in the refrigerator. (No worries here, as I'd bought some basics a couple of days *before* the quarantine order went up so things wouldn't look out of the ordinary when prospective buyers came through the house).

They had me open the dishwasher to see if there were any dishes inside (there weren't), checked under the sink to see if there was anything in the garbage (there wasn't), had me take them down the hall to the laundry room, where Inspector Hong peeked in the washer and dryer (both empty), noted the settings on the control dials, after which she instructed me to take her and Mr. Arulanadam downstairs so they could "search" the basement.

My nerves had had about as much as they could take. Hoping I hadn't overlooked anything, that there was nothing to give me away, I wondered if I should be plotting my exit strategy in the event the police showed up, or stay and bank on them seeing an inspection by health department officials as "routine maintenance." I sat on the second from the bottom basement stair and waited while they went methodically from the furnace room, through the downstairs bedroom, into the DJ booth, the recreation room, the bathroom, into my office, the storage room, the electrical-panel room and the cold cellar, no word from either of them, at least that I could hear, until they returned to the open area at the foot of the basement stairs and Inspector Hong asked me where the grow-operation had been.

"Guess," I said lightly, and stood up.

Puzzled by the response, from the stiff look Ms. Hong gave me, one that I could tell was a little too cheeky for her liking, the three of us went back through the basement rooms, Inspector Hong and Mr. Arulanadam conferring in murmurs at several points, with Ms. Hong announcing their decision as we stood in the bedroom off the furnace room. "Here," she said.

"Ice cold," I said with a playful smile, and asked her to try again. As they returned to the open area by the stairs, I suggested they were getting warmer; said "cold" a moment later when they started for the storage room next to the cold-cellar, then piped, "Red hot" as they came back, turned and, the only place left to go, stepped into my office again. My thousand or so books stood neatly on their shelves, a canvas and pine-frame lounge chair I'd brought from the spare bedroom sat where the grow-unit had been; paintings, posters and other memorabilia were back on the walls, including the museum-framed collage of typewritten letters and doodled self-portraits Kurt Vonnegut had sent me in the 1980s, which I'd decided was just the thing to cover up the "69 PLANTS." Still befuddled as to how the police had arrived at that number, in spite of the two coats of primer and four coats of paint I'd given that side of the room, the black figures had continued to show through, which was the point of doing it in the first place I guess. Everything as normal as could be, Ms. Hong and Mr. Arulanadam met my guardedly amused smile with perplexed looks.

No further questions when we came back upstairs, neither of them even asking about the alleged black mould (and I certainly wasn't about to bring it up), Ms. Hong retrieved her jacket from the chair in the living room, huddling with Mr. Arulanadam by the front door for a few minutes until, by the looks on their faces, it seemed they'd reached their verdict. They put their shoes back on, Ms. Hong slipped into her jacket, Mr. Arulandam noted something down in his file folder then closed it, and turned to me standing across the way in the front hall.

"Despite a few reservations, the clothes in the upstairs closets and the dates on some of the food in the refrigerator, Inspector Hong and I have discussed it and agree that the property meets with Toronto Public Health Department specifications."

"Great," I said, wanting to cheer. "And you'll take the notice down now?"

Mr. Arulanadam handed his file folder to Ms. Hong, the woman still glancing furtively around like there was something wrong with the picture, if she could only figure out what it was.

Opening the front door, Dar took an orange box-cutter from the pocket of his sports-jacket, used his thumb on the button to push the blade out, ran it along the edges of the sign and, lifting it off, carefully removed the second layer of tape, fingered it, with some difficulty, into a ball and shoved it, again with some difficulty because it was so sticky, into a pocket of his sports-jacket.

"Just out of interest," I said, "one of my sons is working on a project at university and was wondering if he could have the sign."

"Absolutely not!" said Mr. Arulanadam, shaking his head, accepted his file-folders from Ms. Hong and slipped the quarantine order inside one of them.

I walked out to the front porch, shook hands with the two of them and made a point of being extra courteous when

I thanked them. Mr. Arulanadam stepped down to the front walk and started toward his car, but Inspector Hong lingered beside me on the porch, a hint of a smile coming into her face as something dawned on her. She turned quickly, stepped over to the brass mailbox and threw the lid open, only to find it completely jammed with mail. Not wanting to take any chances, it was something I'd made sure I attended to before they arrived, just in case.

Giving Ms. Hong an inscrutable, close-lipped smile, pleased with myself for having outwitted someone who'd conducted herself as though she was the Sherlock Holmes of public health order compliance, I shut the front door and locked it. I ran down the drive the moment Dar and Ms. Hong pulled away in his Camry, made my way to the corner and ran along Greybeaver Trail. I dialed Lenny's cellphone as soon as I got in the car. He wasn't available to take the call for some reason (he said he'd be waiting for it with bated breath), so I left him a voicemail message with news of the all-clear: "Ding-dong, the witch is dead . . ."

CHAPTER **THIRTEEN**
THE BLEAKS

While the lifting of the quarantine was a huge relief, I wasn't in the clear quite yet. Two days later I was making another appearance at City Hall court with Larry and Leslie, the crowd noticeably smaller than on previous occasions, maybe twenty of us rising in our pews when the judge breezed in, eight minutes late according to the courtroom clock. A woman in her late forties or early fifties, she mounted the bench with a bright smile and sat down, telling the rest of us we could be seated as well. She produced a pair of reading glasses, cleaned them quickly on the edge of her gown and slipped them on, still a little out of breath as she signaled to the Crown Attorney that she was ready.

Our case was called after about fifteen minutes. I made my way to the front of the room and stood my customary distance back from the bar. Leslie and Larry winding up the conversations they were having with some other lawyers at the side of the room, I was left standing alone for twenty seconds or so before they made their way over.

The Crown Attorney stepped away from her lectern and approached the judge, informing her, in her regular, rather than her courtroom voice, that there was "new information" on this particular file.

"That being?" the judge asked, peering over her glasses at the Crown.

"The initial police report had listed cocaine as one of the substances found during their search of the accused's house, Your Honour. But since that has proved not to be the case, it's now being withdrawn."

"Duly noted," the judge said, and wrote something down in the file folder she had open in front of her. The organized-crime business and the fictitious mould sighting not enough, I guess Officer Val had decided that the mention of hard drugs in her arrest report would add some extra icing to the revenge cake she'd been serving up over the past few months.

He and Leslie standing at the bar in front of me now, Larry begged the court's favour and addressed the issue of police disclosure, asking the judge when they could expect it to be ready, adding that they'd been waiting over three months now; it seemed like a longer time than usual for a case of this nature.

The judge agreed, and looked to the Crown Attorney, who glanced over at the police officer manning the dolly with the case files on it. In a casual gesture he held up two fingers to the Crown attorney, who looked to the judge and told Her Honour that it should be forthcoming in about two weeks, at which point she, the judge, the court clerk, Larry and Leslie gazed up at the cockeyed wall calendar to decide on a date and time for our next appearance.

As we went out to the hall afterwards, Larry hustled up quickly behind me, put a hand on my shoulder and turned me around.

"What was that the Crown was going on about before I got to the bar?" he asked, in some agitation.

"Oh. Sorry, Larry," I said in the same derisive tone he'd used with me on previous occasions, "I'm not at liberty to give you that information," and walked blithely off down the hall.

Lenny had the sign up on the lawn again later that afternoon and held an open house for real-estate agents the next day, which yielded a surprise offer. An agent named Janice Hetherington had taken some clients through the house first thing Saturday morning, a couple with two boys who'd evidently wanted to move into the area for some time. According to Janice they loved the house and were "extremely motivated" to table their offer so as to avoid a bidding war, something that Lenny had told Julie and me we could expect.

As things turned out, however, their "extreme" motivation didn't translate into much of an offer: $420,000, sixty thousand less than our asking price.

Julie was livid, declaring it not even worth considering. Janice, the buyer's agent, was the mother-in-law of Kim Hetherington, an old nursing friend of Julie's from Sick Children's Hospital. According to Julie, Janice would have heard about the drug raid through Kim, obviously hoping to capitalize on the situation and make a fast, easy sale.

Since I was the one who had to move, I told Lenny that I was inclined to accept the lowball offer; Christmas was only a little over six weeks away after all, and these people had agreed to take possession as of December 6. I suggested, as well, that if the two of them were worried about losing the house to the government, holding out for a higher price might not be a good idea. I reminded them I was still out on bail and had taken far too many risks already. Packing up to move within such a short space of time would require me to be inside the house as much if not more than I had been during the fall. I'd come this far without incident, I didn't want to blow it now. "Let's just get rid of the thing and be done with it," I told them. "Jail isn't a good place from which to conduct a real-estate transaction," I said, quoting Malcolm.

The financial implications of delaying the sale were nothing to sneeze at, either. My luck with Joanne at the bank was about to run out, my account off to the Royal Bank's foreclosure team before the end of the month. On top of which, the city revenue department was demanding immediate payment of back property taxes, plus accumulated penalties, or they were going to have the bailiff appear and seize the property. I'd been doing my best to keep up with my half of the installments over the seven years we'd been separated, but Julie's tab had ballooned to about $12,000.

And the gas company was demanding $6,300, about $5,800 more than I actually owed, the result of a dispute that I'd been having with them for several years — a retaliatory move on their part for my having gone to the Ontario Energy Board with a complaint over unfair billing practices.

A week went by after we'd declined Janice Hetherington's client's offer, but no others were forthcoming, not a single inquiry and, of course, no viewings. Julie was convinced that Janice had spread the word to other agents about the grow-op so they wouldn't be interested in a "tainted" listing, something that seemed like a distinct possibility to me too. Lenny disagreed, however, explaining that "blacklisting" wasn't allowed in the Toronto Real Estate Board. Julie suggested that while *he* might care about the Toronto Real Estate Board's rules, "You can bet Janice Hetherington doesn't."

Then, out of the blue, the electric company cut off my hydro one day and demanded $200 on top of the $380 payment on a bill that was about a month and a half overdue, before they'd connect it again. Shortly after that, the gas company added another $800 to my November bill, which sent the amount currently owing to $7,100 — and yet there was still no word from Norm Gardner, the man who headed up Enbridge's "Executive Response Team," but who the lawyer assisting me with my billing issue determined was not a real person. His initials stood for Natural Gas, identifying any matters brought to his attention as complaints that, according to a former gas company employee we talked to, were thrown in the garbage.

I finished the Shakespeare recording project at Simply Audiobooks at the beginning of November, only to be told that Dell Parsons was no longer with the company and no one knew how I could get hold of him. Calvin, the gentleman who'd been left running the accounting department, apologized that he had no knowledge of the cheque for $2,800 that was supposed to have been coming my way.

However, toward the end of October, after six months of waiting I finally received a contract from a publisher in New Delhi, India, who was planning to bring out my Shakespeare novels over there within the next year. He said his cheque for an advance against royalties for the seven books would be forthcoming once I'd signed and returned the contract. The contract offered 20,000 rupees, not exactly big money — about $500 Canadian — however, in his covering letter, the publisher said he felt the books had enormous potential to do well with Indian high-school students.

On November 9, a jubilant Lenny gave us word that a Sri Lankan family had made an offer on the house: $479,000, the full asking price, with a closing date of December 6. The three of us were jubilant — Julie over the moon when she signed the offer accepting the deal. We passed the home inspection with flying colours; the purchasers really liked the place and were itching to move in — but three days later, Lenny shocked us by announcing that the Sri Lankan couple hadn't been able to arrange financing and the deal was off the table. Banks wouldn't put mortgages on houses that had been used as grow-ops, whether you had one plant or a thousand, apparently because there was a risk of mould and accompanying health problems down the road that they could be sued for, or so a friend of mine explained who was a vice president at one of the major banks. He said it was an across-the-board policy and there were no exceptions; the only option available to people interested in buying our house would be private financing.

Perturbed by what my friend said was common knowledge among real-estate agents, I asked Lenny why he wouldn't have known something like this to begin with and made sure any prospective buyers were aware of it. "Didn't you take a course on dealing with this kind of thing?" I asked him.

"I did," he admitted. "But it was over the internet. I don't know how I could have missed something like that, but I guess I must have." Lenny apologized profusely, acknowledged that he'd messed up and, with his inveterate enthusiasm kicking in, declared that he was putting everything else on standby and was going to see that there was a "Sold" sign on the house before we knew it. "Don't worry, Paul," he said, "the chips might look like they're down, but that's when I work best. I promise I'll make something happen."

And, good as his word, he did.

Within twenty-four hours he presented a new offer, from Janice Hetherington (who claimed she heard about the collapse of the deal with the Sri Lankan couple "through the grapevine"). Her clients had now upped their bid to $424,000, an offer that Julie, livid about the loss of the $479,000 bid, flatly refused to accept. Janice persuaded them to go to $430,000 with a December 6 closing date; their final "kick at the can," according to Janice.

Lenny told us this was about as good as it was going to get, that we were already cutting it tight with just three weeks for me to pack up and move into a new place. He reminded Julie that if we went with this deal, she'd have her money in time for Christmas. The message sank in; she relented, the papers were signed and I had a copy of the completed purchase-offer faxed to Joanne at the bank on November 15, as promised.

The small sense of jubilation I felt about selling the house proved to be short-lived. Push had come to shove. And the pressure was on. It was back to my bail-breaking ways for the next three weeks, not enough time for me to be packed up and ready for moving day even if I'd had a team of people helping me, but my bank balance was in the low three figures, my body was run ragged, my nerves not much better, and a decent sleep was something that I could only stew about as I lay awake till three or four every night. I confided to a friend one day that I just couldn't see myself pulling it off, not after what I'd had to cope with in the last five months. He commiserated and in an effort at inspiration reminded me of what

Winston Churchill had said to the British people during the darkest hours of the Battle of Britain: "What do you do when you're going through hell? *Just keep going . . .*"

It was no surprise, when the police released their disclosure at the court hearing on the 16th, to learn that it was, in fact, our neighbours Mary-Ellen and Wes who'd called the police on us. I reminded Malcolm that I wasn't interested in a plea bargain. I said I wanted the case to go to trial, particularly because we were being charged with trafficking and profiting from the proceeds of crime, which was simply untrue. I felt we should tell our story in court and let a judge see that we weren't organized criminals or drug traffickers, that we were certainly not profiting from "the operation" we were supposedly running, and in no way deserved to lose our house to the government of Canada for what was being done in the privacy of our own home, for which the police had already made us pay a pretty hefty price.

I wanted the charges against Carson dropped, since he wasn't involved in any way. I felt that Nicky shouldn't make a plea bargain either, that we should both insist on going to trial. I was fully prepared to take the rap in the end if the judicial process didn't seem to be leaning in our favour, though Malcolm reminded me again it was *my* head the police were after, and the odds were good that, even if it *was* my first offence, a judge could be persuaded by an aggressive Crown to send me to jail for several years, which meant the kids would have to live with Julie. "And that," he said, "won't be good for anybody."

The police weren't the only ones calling for my head. Julie and her new divorce lawyer Victoria Durant were "hankering for my scalp as well," or so Stephen Arkoff informed me, a few days after the house had sold. "The bitches are screaming blue murder!" he hollered into the phone, and told me to get my ass down to his office ASAP.

I made it there within the hour. Tess brought us coffee in the boardroom (Stephen had dispatched her to Starbucks in anticipation of my arrival), and she let me know, as she set one of the cups down in front of me, that she knew exactly what I was going through, since she was in the same boat trying to divorce her husband of twelve years. She didn't say why, but did tell me the whole thing was uglier than she ever imagined it could be.

Stephen let me read over the eighteen-page fax summarizing Julie's position, asking me, when I was finished, what I wanted to do. Minus the legalese, Julie was demanding most of what she had wanted seven years earlier: her share of the house proceeds (by her reckoning $160,000); half my teacher's pension (again, by her reckoning, $220,000, which was $120,000 more than the actuaries had determined she was entitled to); seven years' worth of child support payments ($42,000) plus interest; all outstanding municipal property taxes to be paid by me; repayment of the $150,000 her family had given her for renovations and redecorating when we'd moved into Friendship Avenue in 1997; as well as the $20,000 her family had paid to Nicky's ($15,000) and Carson's ($5,000) lawyers in the drug case, the total coming in at a little over $600,000, almost $200,000 more than we were expecting to receive from the sale of the house, which was our only asset.

At Stephen's request, I dictated my reply, a business letter in which I presented the following points in response: Julie was the one who owed child support to me, rather than the other way around. (About $150,000 worth, as the kids had been in my custody for close to four years.) As to my pension, I'd cashed it out when I left teaching in 2001, paid the required tax and had used the remainder to support myself and the children since then, however the funds were gone now, the account closed. The outstanding property taxes on Friendship Avenue were her responsibility, not mine; and as for the $150,000 from her family, the money was a gift to her so she could pretty up the house to her liking before we moved into it, the transaction one that was never discussed with me, and to which I hadn't been a party. I reminded her that I'd been prepared to hire lawyers for Carson and Nicky who would handle the drug case pro bono and pointed out that in our phone conversation on the August long weekend she had declined the offer. As to her final demand, that henceforward we share custody of the children 50/50, I said I didn't feel that was in their best interest when all indications were she still had a drinking problem, and was known to be taking prescription painkillers on a regular basis. Any agreement on custody would have to take that into consideration.

Tess typed up the one-page letter, had me proofread it (though as I rather expected, it was error-free), and with Stephen giving the okay — quipping that maybe *he* should be the one giving *me* $750 — we faxed it over to Julie's lawyer Victoria.

On my way back to the house I stopped in to meet with Bill Summers, the lawyer who'd agreed to handle the house sale for us. He told me that Julie had been in to see him first thing that morning, and that as far as he could see, things looked to be pretty straightforward and should go smoothly. He did have one small concern, however. Julie had apparently mentioned that Stephen Arkoff was the lawyer I'd retained to look after the settlement agreement for me. Bill wondered if I was "happy with that," asking me if I knew much about Stephen. I said that I didn't, but that he was an associate of a longtime friend of mine, Malcolm Hardy. He said that name wasn't familiar to him, but Arkoff, *well* . . . He raised his hand a few inches above his desk and, with his fingers outspread, made a seesaw motion, tilting his head to one side and wincing, a pained look on his face whose meaning was clear.

"Are you saying Stephen might be a little shifty?" I asked Bill.

He sat forward quickly in his chair and held up his hands. "I'm not saying anything," he protested.

"Right," I said. "Law Society protocols. You're not supposed to malign another member of the bar."

"Exactly," he said, relieved that I seemed to understand his concern.

"Stephen's a bit of a character, I'll say that about him."

"Long as you're happy," Bill said evasively, and got up from his chair.

"He's not big on paperwork, I do know that," I said and stood up, too.

Bill discreetly avoiding further comment about Stephen's approach to the law, he walked me through the reception area where several women were sitting at computers typing, and at the front door told me again that he didn't foresee any wrinkles. "But *get* that settlement agreement done or . . ." Hands in his pockets at this point, he made a face and shrugged.

"Or nobody gets any money," I finished the sentence for him.

"That's about the size of it," Bill said, smiling, and told me he'd give me a call in the event there were any problems.

Mr. Beans was just across the plaza from Bill's office, so I grabbed a decaf and a Morning Glory muffin and headed back to the house. I sat at the kitchen table and made a list of the things that I'd have to take care of by the time the house sale closed in just over three weeks. I stopped writing when I reached the top of the fourth page of the single-spaced list, put down my pen and, hit by a sudden wave of apprehension, looked around.

We'd lived here a little over ten years. It was 3,200 square feet with five bedrooms, a large kitchen and family room, a main-floor office/computer room, the laundry room, a piano in the dining room, a two-car garage, a six-room basement, perhaps a thousand books in my office and several hundred more in the storage and furnace rooms, which were themselves chock-full of cartons, trunks and suitcases, boxes, bags and bins containing the myriad items a family of five accumulates in the course of living in three houses over twenty years.

With no idea where the packing up would even begin, I finished the muffin and my cup of coffee, picked up the pen again and tried continuing with my to-do list, but had to stop when I was partway through the first item, as my right hand had started shaking so badly I couldn't grip the pen. It slipped from my hands and fell to the floor. I looked down at it, stared until my whole upper body was shaking, a sob caught in my throat and I began to cry. I cried for the way I'd messed my life up so badly, how I'd hurt my children, become detestable in the eyes of their mother and her family, of which for fifteen years I'd been a loved member. I cried because I'd let so many people down, because I was frightened, feeling ashamed, worthless and alone, a failure in an uncaring world and thinking that I just wanted to leave it. I just wanted to disappear.

My doctor's receptionist, Jennifer, managed to squeeze me in to see Rae Hayward at 8:15 the next morning, his first appointment of the day. Rae had been my family doctor for fifteen years and, as far as I was concerned, was a good physician and had never let me down. He was a few years older than me, had three children as I did, loved reading, had a great sense of humour (he had cartoons from *The New Yorker* and memorable quotations from eminent writers posted on the wall in his examining room), and was a firm believer in patients advocating for themselves when it came to health issues. We'd exchange a little relaxed banter when he came into the examining room at the beginning of each appointment, often about the author he was currently reading or the latest cartoons and quotations posted on his bulletin board.

Appointments with Rae were somewhat casual affairs, and he kept things light and chatty but at the same time professional. He'd ask me what was up, listen while I told him what I thought the problem was, sometimes agreeing with me, sometimes not. He'd give me capsule reviews of books he was reading while he took my blood pressure, recommending titles he thought I might find interesting, or not as the case might be. He'd mention a movie he might have seen, or an article he'd come across in one of the magazines he read regularly, *Harper's*, *The Atlantic* or *The New Yorker*, ask about my writing, what my kids were up to, and then after notes in my file, he'd let me go. By the end of the appointment I'd leave feeling that I'd had a productive and enjoyable ten-minute conversation with a friend who just happened to be a physician, who would hand me, when we were done talking, the appropriate prescription for whatever was ailing me if he felt I "needed something."

Sitting in his examining room that day, I told him about the shaking hands and said I thought I was coming down with a case of Parkinson's, or having a nervous breakdown because of the worry about being able to pull everything together on the moving front in just three weeks — especially when, because I needed the money, I'd committed to giving an old friend of mine a hand at the One of a Kind Craft Show starting later in the week, an eleven-day event that, with a couple of days off, would only leave me about ten or eleven to pack the house up and have everything ready to go by December 6. Working at the show wasn't something I particularly wanted to do, but Don was an old friend and he was relying on me to help him and, with the cheque I'd been promised by Simply Audiobooks having fallen through, I needed the cash to pay for the cost of the movers and a decent-sized storage unit.

Knowing me as well as he did, I had the impression that Rae, even with the mention of a nervous breakdown, could tell that I was still hedging about something. When he asked if there was "anything else" on my mind, his usual gambit to get me digging a little deeper, I admitted that there was. I confessed that I was finding the prospect of the house-closing more than a little daunting, and decided, on the spur of the moment, to open right up. I told him the pressure I'd been under for the last three months was taking its toll, that I was experiencing bouts of crushing anxiety and debilitating despair as well as panic attacks that were sometimes of terrifying intensity, where I felt I'd had the wind knocked out of me, couldn't catch my breath and was on the verge of suffocating; nightmares from which

I'd wake up at three or four o'clock in the morning, my face, my T-shirt, underwear and the bedclothes soaked through and clammy with sweat. Getting out of bed at my friend Callum's in the morning sometimes took me an hour or more, requiring every ounce of willpower I could muster, though even then it might suddenly peter out and I'd lie down again, slipping under the covers for a little while longer before heading out to face the day.

There were other things, too: out-of-the-blue moments of world-weariness and gloom, fits of despondence that could last for hours, a constant fear that there were more and worse disasters awaiting me around every corner. I was easily distracted, had no ability to concentrate or focus on things for any length of time, had lost my desire to eat, wanted just to be left alone, to the point that nothing I could think of could prompt me to smile. Even whistling, which I'd always done to boost my spirits when I was feeling down, was something I seemed to have forgotten how to do. "I'll put my lips together and try," I explained to Rae, "but nothing comes out."

I mentioned that I'd read *The Unquiet Mind*, Kay Redfield Jamison's book on manic depression, *When Bad Things Happen to Good People* by Harold Kushner, parts of Kierkegaard's *Fear and Trembling*, *The Road Less Traveled* by M. Scott Peck, and though I probably shouldn't have, Franz Kafka's *The Trial*, my point that nothing I turned to for insight seemed to improve the situation: the books were just so many words on the page; nothing alleviated the feelings of despair and hopelessness that had been eating away at me for some time, that of course I'd tried to cover up, in denial that I, too, had succumbed to the "family illness" at last. I told Rae that I thought I'd fallen into the kind of depression my mother and her mother used to — "The Bleaks" they'd called it. "That's the only way I can describe how I'm feeling just now," I said. "That I've come down with a bad case of The Bleaks."

"Hmm . . ." I remember him saying, an almost pained expression coming into his face as he swung his chair around, gazed out the examining room window and reflected for a moment, perplexed, I knew, because he'd never heard me talk like this in the fifteen years I'd been his patient. "I could give you an antidepressant," he said turning back to me.

"Is that my only option?"

He shrugged. "You've got a lot on your plate, Paul. Situations you can't extricate yourself from. Conditions that you can't really control or change. You have little or no money. You're concerned about your kids. You're involved in a criminal proceeding. You're in a legal battle with your ex-wife. So I'd have to say no, that's about it. But antidepressants are a lot better than they used to be," he added, as though that should be some consolation.

"I don't see myself functioning very effectively on pills. I'm not a big fan of pharmaceuticals."

Rae nodded thoughtfully, tapping his pen on my file. "I could put you on one that most people seem to find effective," he said, "though ultimately we might have to give two or three of them a try before we find one that works best for you. That's the trouble with depression — it's a hard thing to pinpoint."

"Doesn't seem that hard to me," I said, light on the sarcasm.

"I just mean there are a lot of grey areas," Rae said with a slightly apologetic smile.

I thought about it for a few seconds, aware that I'd taken up more than my allotted time, probably thrown his appointment schedule off for the rest of the day. "Okay," I finally said. "Bring on the antidepressants. I guess it wouldn't hurt to give them a try."

"I have some doctors' samples in the supply cupboard. Hang on." He got up from his chair and left the examining room, returning in a minute with a small white-and-orange plastic bottle, something called Wellbutrin, which he thought might do the trick. He stressed that the important thing was to take one pill at the same time every morning, the medication would stay in my system for exactly twenty-four hours. He said there were enough pills in the sampler for a month, but told me that I should come back and see him in two weeks. His final instruction, as we were leaving the examining room, was that I stick with the course of treatment, no matter how the pills were making me feel. My system had to accustom itself to the medication, which took a certain amount of time to kick in before the dosage could deliver its optimal effects.

Riding the elevator down, I was already feeling better. Not because of the Wellbutrin though; I knew there was no quick fix for whatever it was that had taken hold of me. No, it was a *New Yorker* cartoon I happened to glance at as I was putting my coat on in Rae's examining room that had perked up my mood: a pilot and a co-pilot are in a search plane, peering down at the beach on a desert island, where footprints have spelled "'*ELP!*" in the sand. In the caption, the co-pilot turns to the pilot and says: "*I expect 'at'll be 'im!*"

The cartoon struck a bright note, and I came out of the elevator laughing, the bottle of Wellbutrin tucked safely away in my coat pocket. "Well, '*ere's 'oping,*" I quipped to myself as I went out to the street.

CHAPTER FOURTEEN
MESSAGE IN THE SAND

It's 5:45 a.m., November 22, and I've just taken my first 100mg dose of the antidepressant Wellbutrin, an orange tablet I washed down with a glass of cranberry juice. It's been six days since Rae gave me the pills; I'm due to go back and see him in a week, at which time he'll be expecting a report on how the drug is working out. I decided it was now or never, readied the cranberry on my night table before I went to bed, popped the pill and swigged the juice the moment I woke up.

Nothing happening yet, as far as I can tell, I've made myself a cup of coffee and a toasted English muffin with peanut butter and banana slices and, though it's the last thing I should be doing with my fear of what may be in store for me, I'm sitting on my bed looking over the medical information that I printed out on Wellbutrin from the manufacturer's and the U.S. Food & Drug Administration's websites.

The words 'Caution,' 'Alert,' 'Warning' and 'Danger' appear frequently in both texts, and in both documents, "Suicidal Thoughts and Behaviors" is noted in bold font and covered more extensively than any of the other side effects or contra-indications. These include arthralgia, myalgia, fever, seizures, extreme thirst, dry mouth, dizziness, dermatitis, worsening depression, manic episodes, severe high blood-pressure, third-degree heart block, completed suicide, hyperglycemia, hepatitis, esophagitis, aggression, coma, delusions, hallucinations, and psychosis.

Both emphasize that in the event of adverse reactions, patients should contact their physician, but under no circumstances should they discontinue medication. The information on Wellbutrin as a treatment for depression is provided in the manufacturer's document, one sentence explaining that its efficacy in treating major depressive episodes was clinically established in two four-week controlled inpatient trials, and one six-week controlled outpatient trial. I'm a little apprehensive about that. Fourteen weeks of testing on a medication that's designed to treat "major" disorders? Doesn't sound like a very rigorous study to me when it's used by millions every day and generates billions of dollars in revenue for its manufacturer. I always thought pharmaceutical companies had to put new drugs through years of R&D and substantial human testing before they were allowed to release them for public use. From what I'm reading about the development of Wellbutrin, apparently this wasn't so.

I don't know whether or not I qualify as a major depressive at this point (as I think about it, I've never really heard of a "minor" one), but if I am, the possible repercussions for those suffering from bipolar (manic) depression and using

Wellbutrin are reported by both the FDA and the manufacturer to be the most potentially dangerous of all. I'm familiar enough with the kind of side-effects and adverse reactions that can occur with pharmaceutical medications to know that even though symptoms vary from person to person, in the coming hours it's likely I'll be dealing with at least a few of those on the FDA list, so I'll have to watch myself accordingly. It's coming up to 6:30, forty-five minutes since I've taken my pill. Definitely experiencing a feeling of light-headedness now, dryness in my mouth and throat, a slight blur in my eyes, my heartbeat accelerating noticeably. The Wellbutrin must be kicking in.

An alert on the bottle warns me "not to drive or operate heavy machinery while using this medication," so rather than take my car downtown to meet Don and help him set up for the craft show, I walk the two blocks to the nearest bus stop, the Wellbutrin really starting to work at about the time the bus pulls into the Coxwell Avenue subway station. As I get up from my seat I seem to keep rising, overcome with a floating feeling. My eyes are unable to look anywhere but straight ahead, and there is a hollow airy sound inside my head like I'm holding seashells up to my ears, a low-level hum that's there — and then not there if I try to listen too closely. I edge my way toward the doors, a feeling now that I'm being ordered not to do anything except stay close to the man who's getting off the bus in front of me. I have no choice in the matter; I'm just supposed to follow him. I hurry to keep up as we proceed along the crowded platform, noticing the man is wearing the same clothes as me, has the same curly hair. He glances back over his shoulder at one point to let me see his face: it's my own.

"All you have to do is stick with me, and everything will

be all right," he says, and leads the way downstairs into the station proper. In a few minutes, in a rising rush of wind, the westbound train bursts into the station, slows, comes to a stop and after the warning chime, opens its doors.

When we enter the car, the Other Me points out an open seat — across the way beside a window — and I jump to take it. The dizziness I've started experiencing eases off once I'm sitting down. The car is about half-full, people averting their eyes, gazing out the windows, swaying with the motion of the train once it gets going again. There's no sound except the clattering of wheels down below as the train speeds along — the Other Me silent beside me, the two of us with our hands on our thighs, staring straight ahead.

At the third stop, a tall thin man in a Toronto Maple Leafs toque jumps into the car the moment the doors open. He checks around with a frantic look on his face then races to take the triple seat directly across from us, which is empty. He yanks the toque off his head, brings the yellow plastic grocery bag he has with him onto his lap, leans back, flings his right arm casually over the top of the seat and crosses his legs, all in a few seconds. With his prominent nose, wavy brown hair swept high on his head, brown sports-jacket and gangly body and energetic manner, you could mistake him for Kramer, Jerry's wacky friend on *Seinfeld*. Like Kramer, he doesn't stop moving. He's jumpy, fidgety, shifting in his seat, crossing and uncrossing his legs as he talks loudly to himself in what sounds like a foreign language. He starts yelping at one point, shooting hostile looks at the other passengers in the car, chuckling, growling, snarling then yelping again several more times before he grabs his plastic grocery bag, opens it and takes out a copy of that morning's *Globe and Mail*. When he finds the section of the newspaper he wants, he glances at a few pages then snaps it closed. He folds it in half then in quarters, and proceeds to tear the quarter-sections into strips several inches wide, which he flings down on the seat beside him. He then does the identical thing with three more sections of the paper he pulls from his bag, jabbering to himself as he continues tearing away: *"Standing-at-the-cupboard-with-a-big-nose-up-his-bum! Standing-at-the-cupboard-with-a-big-nose-up-his-bum!"*

When the next stop comes, he shoots to his feet as the train slows down, takes his grocery bag full of torn newspapers up to the doors, stands there once the train has stopped and waits till they're about to close, then with the loudest yelp he's made so far, throws himself onto the platform, the people in the car around me continuing to stare forward as the train begins moving, wheels clacking again as it accelerates. The Other Me, who has jumped out too, runs along the platform beside the window as we start gaining speed, hands cupped around his mouth and hollering at me over the sound of the train. *"Don't worry! I'll see you later!"* he shouts just before we reach the end of the station platform, and the train plunges into the dark tunnel.

I make it to Union Station, onto the Lakeshore West streetcar and over to the Direct Energy Centre at Exhibition Place without incident. It's booth set-up day for the 800 vendors at the Christmas One of a Kind Craft Show, held in two adjoining exhibition halls, hundred-foot ceilings, high windowless walls, vast as airport hangars.

Sounds magnifying because of the Wellbutrin, I can't tell as I enter Hall B if the roaring in my ears is being caused by the drug, or just the noise level in the busy hall. There are fans rumbling high above, though they sound like they're thundering right over my head; forklift engines are revving, back-up signals beeping, loaded dollies rolling by, hundreds of hammers banging away, drills whirring, vacuums whining — it seems to me, as I wander through the aisles, like the Greatest Show on Earth is getting underway.

I link up with Don at the security desk. Laughs, hugs and slaps on the back — we're happy to see each other for the first time in about five years. We buy muffins and coffee at the snack bar while we wait for the shipping crate with his cutting boards in it to arrive at our booth space.

A friend of mine since childhood, Don has been living in East Margaree, Cape Breton Island, for the past twenty years, drawn there by a Tibetan monk, Chögyam Trungpa Rinpoche, who had established an abbey at the northwestern tip of the island in the mid-1980s. A student of Rinpoche's, Don was one of the main builders of the abbey and its *stupa* shrine. He'd had his own construction business in East Margaree for a number of years, but was now managing a small wood-products company on the Margaree River about a mile from the ocean. The company makes end-grain cutting boards from Eastern Canadian larch trees, which Don tells me are plentiful in the valleys along the Margaree River basin.

"They're unique boards, Sledge," says Don with peppy enthusiasm as we start to work, "and they're really catching on." Apparently this is the first time he's done the One of a Kind show, however if all goes well he's been told he can expect to make $20,000 to $30,000 during the eleven-day event. He fills me in on the schedule for the day while we take our first break: put the booth together (walls, display tables, racks and stands), erect the lighting grid, install the cushioned-rubber floor tiles, unpack the cutting boards, hang the drapes, pictures of the boards and the two Larch Wood company posters across the rear of the booth, then we'll head over to a restaurant on King Street called the Bank Note to have dinner with some vendors on the trade-show circuit that Don's become friends with in the last few years.

We catch up on what some of our mutual friends from high school have been doing lately, and talk about trying to get a group of them together at some point while he's in town. And as is always the case when I'm with Don, there's no shortage of laughter, kibitzing and joking around, though as the effects of the Wellbutrin continue to intensify, it's Don who does most of the talking.

The drug seems to have pulled the plug on my sense of humour too. I manage a few chuckles and the odd smile — when it seems like it's appropriate — but I drift in and out of understanding what it is I'm supposed to find funny in the jokes he's cracking . . . and these are old ones I've heard before, lines and comedy bits that Don and our other friends picked up when we were teenagers and have been entertaining each other with ever since: Firesign Theatre, Monty Python, The Bonzo Dog Band. Today, though, I can't recall a single routine. A *dog band*?

It's so bad that sometimes when I try to force a laugh — because I notice Don is laughing — I can barely manage a weak smile. It's like I've been given a strong sedative, or Botox, all the muscles in my cheeks and jaw frozen solid, my lips pressed together, my mouth dry, my mind drawing a blank every few seconds as to where I am and what I'm doing, the only thing I'm conscious of the steady hum of the heating fans high above.

If Don notices that I seem out of it, he doesn't say anything, there being more than enough to do. And as is usually the case on the day before a show opens, there are mix-ups, hold-ups and screw-ups, some of which have Don heading to show headquarters somewhere in the far reaches of the exhibition hall, leaving me sitting on an IKEA folding chair, watching, in my altered state, as vendors in the surrounding aisles work on assembling their booths, displaying their wares . . . talking in what sounds to me like Japanese, or backwards English, the air in the hall heavily tinged with exhaust fumes from the forklifts, and so dust-dry I have real trouble swallowing, my contact lenses smarting, my eyes unable to focus on anything for very long before I feel I have to look away.

Any time I try to get down from the folding chair, I can't. It's like I'm fixed to the spot, a strong set of hands pressing down on my shoulders keeping me right where I am . . . my eyes drifting over to the photographer's booth across the aisle, a framed, close-up shot of a bald eagle, piercing yellow eyes looking into mine . . . to the right of this a booth displaying Inuit art, an array of white walls, black shelves on chrome racks and track-spotlights trained on green, brown, black and grey carvings: soapstone, marble, quartz; bears, birds, wolves and whales . . . to the left a booth that sells shortbread cookies in two dozen different flavours, sweet and savoury aromas wafting my way and mixing, somewhere in the vicinity of my nose, with the scents permeating the curtains from the booth behind ours: soaps, exotic oils and candles . . . jams and jellies further on; handmade silver jewelry; mohair scarves, hats and mitts, barley husk-filled pillows.

The fire alarm sounds over the PA every five minutes or so, a system test, according to a man's very British voice. "Please make your way to the nearest fire exit," he intones. Some do, though most continue to work, the power-tool cacophony resuming, at which point I notice five or six pigeons that have got in the building, flapping their wings in some distress up near the ceiling. When the fire-alarm tests conclude, music plays over the PA system again: Christmas favourites that I know like the back of my hand, but which spark not the slightest urge to sing, hum or whistle today . . . the Wellbutrin is seeing to that.

"Earth to Sledge," Don quips when he returns from his third trip to the administration office. "Everything all right, b'y?"

"Everything's all right," I reply, not letting on that it most definitely isn't.

Once we have the rubber floor tiles down, the lights, tables and display counters put together, we get to work unloading the hundred-pound boxes of cutting boards from the shipping crate, going over product information, Larch Wood's company background, facts about the way the boards are made, prices, tax, the processing of payments with the debit- and credit-card machines, what to do with cash, storage-room procedures, discounts and online sales. Don might as well be talking to himself, though, because by the time he's finished, about the only thing I remember is that in Ontario we call larch trees "tamarack," while in Newfoundland they call them "Hack-ma-tack" or more strangely, "snotty var."

With the booth built and the cutting boards in place by a little after 4, the air in the hall so dry now that neither of us is even close to cracking a sweat in spite of the heavy lifting we've been doing, we drive over to the Bank Note pub at the corner of King and Bathurst in Don's rental car, a glossy silver-grey Dodge Magnum, "with 450 cubic inches under the hood," he informs me on the way. Even though the radio is playing a Creedence Clearwater Revival tune, what I hear mostly is the thrumming of the Magnum's turbo-charged 450 cubic inches, a rumbling in my ears that makes it impossible to concentrate on very much else. As we enter the pub, Don tells me I can stay with him in the hotel for the week if I want to take a break from our mutual friend the "Doctor."

The Note, as it's called, is a large, square room with high ceilings, low-hanging 1920s-era lights, period tables and chairs and dark oak booths divided by the original frosted-glass teller's cages. The place isn't too crowded, but it's noisy with wall-mounted TVs around the room showing different sports — hockey, basketball, soccer — rock music blasting, voices raised to talk over it — a dozen or so vendors with booths in the craft show rolling in just as we do. Don makes introductions as we take seats around a long table for twelve, me somewhere in the middle, next to a three-hundred-pound man by the name of Bob. With a wild mane of grey hair, a bristling grey beard and spectacles, Bob paints oil canvases, landscapes and wildlife mostly, on Salt Spring Island, British Columbia. He's a man who, according to the woman on the other side of him, is beginning to "look more like Claude Monnay every year." Someone sitting across the table laughingly corrects her: "It's *Moan*-ay, isn't it?" "Monnay, Moan-ay," the woman comes back. Bob strokes his beard and with a benign smile pipes up: "Maybe *that's* my problem, I need a name change." To the left of me is a thin, small-framed, timid-looking man with a voice so high-pitched and soft I can't hear much of what he's saying — named Graham I think, a musician who makes CDs of children's songs — who suggests that what Bob really *should do* . . . however his voice gets lost in the din of conversation . . . the people around me talking up a storm, voices raised and shouting over the music, everyone at the table laughing, or at least smiling, except me, but hard as I try, I can't make the muscles in my face work. I can't smile.

I pass on the offer of free drinks and order ginger ale instead, taking in snippets of what people around me are talking about, answering the questions that are put to me with a nod or a shake of my head, it doesn't seem to make much difference, since everyone is having such a good time . . . Don's friends slapping me on the back, happy to shake my hand, telling me I'm going to enjoy doing the One of a Kind show for the first time, then someone else warns me that at eleven days, it can be a *real killer*, you have to pace yourself . . . More drinks are called for as soon as the waitress finishes setting the fresh ones on our table, and then the food starts arriving and everyone digs in, the waitress plopping a plate with an Angus steak shish-kebab skewer, rice and vegetables in front of me, a dish I don't remember ordering and have no interest in eating . . . too anxious now, agitated, nervous and shifting in my seat somewhat like the weird guy on the subway this morning, his bizarre chant all that I can hear in my head: "*Standing-at-the-cupboard-with-a-big-nose-up-his-bum! Standing-at-the-cupboard with —*"

A young guy in his late twenties, who's been making me paranoid with the looks he's been giving me from a nearby table, stands up suddenly, walks over, comes up beside me and, leaning down, puts his mouth close to my ear and says he's on his way out, but he wanted to say hello. He introduces himself as Brandon, telling me I was his grade 12 English teacher at Thornlea Secondary School in 1999. I think I remember him, but I'm not really sure. I make like I do though, and ask him what he's up to these days. He's single, in financial services, lives in a condo nearby . . . I pick at the vegetables and rice on my plate after he's gone, thinking I haven't eaten all day except for the muffin I had with Don before we started assembling the booth around 10:30, plus I'm experiencing the floating feeling again, my thoughts running in circles, the fork shaking rather obviously in my hand so I put it down before anyone notices . . . Shaking off the dizziness feels like it will take more effort than I've got at the moment, I'm sweating I'm so hot, yet when I put my hand to my forehead it's dry and perfectly cool, and I have to use both hands to hold the glass when I take a drink of the ice-water the waitress has finally brought me . . . A young woman named Heidi, sitting two seats away, leans in front of Graham and asks if I'm feeling all right. I want to say "I don't know," but we've just met so I tell her I'm "right as rain, Heidi," the expression one that has just popped into my head, one I don't ever remember using before. But Heidi has never heard it; she starts shouting it around the table she likes it so much: "Right as rain, Donny!" "Right as rain, Roger!" "Right as rain, everybody!" she hollers up and down the table and, hoisting her drink, tells the group to raise their glasses in a toast to us all having not just a good show this year, but a *great* show!

I'm far from right as rain, though. Things inside are out of control, my only thought is that I have to get out of the building as quickly as I can or something terrible is going to happen to me . . . but again the hands from above are holding me fast to my seat. I put both my own hands on the edge of the table and force myself to a standing position. The chair tips over behind me. I step behind Don's chair, lean down and shout in his ear that I have to be leaving, thanking him for the dinner, telling him I'll see him tomorrow, and then make my way over to the door, gasping for air as I come out to the street, my heart racing, the traffic, the shivering cold. I've left my coat in the restaurant. I run back and retrieve it. Outside once more, I rush for the corner to make the yellow light at the intersection, crossing as it turns red, desperate to catch the streetcar I can see further along King Street, heading my way.

On the ride to the subway, I sit hunched in my seat, head down, wringing my hands, chewing my lips, my throat drier than it's been all day . . . a sensation that I'm being held in my seat as before, but it comes from below this time . . . something is gripping me firmly by the ankles and won't let go. A bleakness deeper than I've ever felt, even at the worst of times, envelops me in sadness, helplessness, hopelessness that I'm too weak to fight off. All I want to do is lie down and rest, hide from the darkness that's spreading across my eyes . . . hoping sadness will close them for me when there's a choking sob, tears start streaming down my cheeks, yet when I use the back of my hand to wipe them away, nothing's there, and this makes me even sadder, and still the non-tears course down my cheeks . . . a hand suddenly clutches at my throat and begins shaking me, hard, laughter and a voice from somewhere daring me to cry, to go ahead and cry, and that's the only thing I want to do. *Just let me cry!* I hear myself pleading. *Just let me cry!*

"*University Avenue,*" the streetcar's computerized voice announces. Wobbly going down stairs into the subway, I pay my fare and take the escalator down one more level to the platform. I pass two other people standing together talking, but keep my head lowered, eyes on the platform floor, holding the sadness within, the lights buzzing overhead, the dark mouth of the tunnel toward which I'm walking — when I see, on the island between the two sets of tracks, the Other Me leaning against an advertising billboard with an I-told-you-so smile on his face. I stop and stare at him. He says nothing, but continues smiling, the low moan of wind and the sound of an approaching train mounting in the tunnel, green and red signal lights twinkling in the far darkness, the Other Me nodding now, as if to say, "That's the way." And I think to myself: *it is*. To stop the sadness, it's what I'll have to do, there's nothing else, *nothing* . . . my feet move, the wind moans, the noise of the train grows louder, my toes touch the yellow line at the edge of the platform, the Other Me smiling over, nodding slowly as he leans against a billboard with a beautiful smiling woman on it, arms crossed, his lips mouthing the words "Come over here and I'll tell you . . ." The wind surges stronger and the roar in the tunnel deepens till there's rumbling under my feet. "Quick!" the Other Me shouts. "Come *over* here and I'll *tell* you!" Yet my eyes are planted on the yellow line, my feet sliding forward the final few inches, the shining steel tracks, my hands in my coat pockets, the rushing wind into which I now lean, end of the line, so long, my lips together as I lean out further for a kiss before — the train bursts from the tunnel and hurtles into the station, I hear whistling in with the roar, growing louder as the train slows, then stops, the doors open, and I realize that it's me who's whistling, it's *me* . . .

No one is home when I arrive back at Callum's, so without taking my coat off I run to my room, grab the bottle of Wellbutrin off the radiator where I've left it, run into the bathroom and flush the rest of the pills down the toilet. I then wrap the empty container in a plastic grocery bag and tuck it under the pizza boxes, cans and pop bottles in the recycling bin at the side of the house. I take a long hot shower, climb into sweatpants and a clean T-shirt then turn out the lights and lie down on my bed, The Bleaks still hovering around but, breathing slowly in the darkness, my arms at my side, my mouth slightly open, my ears listening to the air when I slowly breathe out, I'm not frightened of them. The feelings of sadness creeping into my thoughts now seem more like embers in a dying fire that will flame up if I blow on them, so I don't, I just lie there calmly with my eyes closed and breathe, smiling to myself, after a few minutes, when the *New Yorker* cartoon I saw in Rae Hayward's examining room a week ago pops into my head: the desert island, the search plane, the pilot circling around and coming in for a landing — like 'e and 'is co-pilot 'ave spotted my message in the sand.

CHAPTER **FIFTEEN**
CATCH-23

The trip to Wellbutrin Land mercifully behind me, I packed my suitcase the next morning, kidded Callum and Angus that The Stooges would have to get by without Curly for the next eleven days and, taking advantage of Don's offer, drove downtown and moved into his double room at the Travelodge Motel, then headed over to the Direct Energy Centre for day one of the craft show.

Much of what Don had explained to me during set-up about the uniqueness of his cutting boards, how to handle debit and credit card sales, the phenomenal properties of the larch tree and so forth, turned out to have sunk in after all. I quickly developed a snappy but informative patter that translated into a few good sales early on, many people assuming, when they stopped by the booth, that because my nametag read "*Larch Wood*, East Margaree, Cape Breton Island," my name was, in fact, Larch, that I was the maker of the boards, and hailed from the town of East Margaree. Not wanting to disappoint them, and seeing what my East Coast identity was doing for sales, I stuck with it and began talking in the clipped tones of an islander, pronouncing my Ds like Ts, imitating the broad As and quick intakes of breath that I knew Cape Bretoners were known for. In the event anyone called my bluff, and a number did, I'd fess up and explain that Don was the one who made the boards, he and I were childhood friends here in Toronto, where I still lived, and I was just helping him out. Whether it was my honesty or my entertaining persona, I couldn't be sure, but people usually ended up buying cutting boards and shook my hand when we completed the sale, one couple joking that I wasn't to worry. My secret was "safe with them."

Having been out of the teaching profession for six years now, working on my own in my basement office on speculative and mostly un-remunerative publishing projects, I found that hawking high-end cutting boards and bantering jovially with the passing crowd was like stepping back on stage again. My acting chops were good after the Shakespeare recordings at Simply Audiobooks, and even if my sales pitch didn't always have people reaching for their wallets, I think they walked away with *Hamlet* on their minds: "To buy, or not to buy," I sometimes joked with them when they moved off to the next booth, "that is the question," adding a little mock–Arnold Schwarzenegger just for fun: "You'll be back . . ."

My spirits received a surprise boost on the second day of the show, when Dell Parsons at Simply Audiobooks called to say he hadn't forgotten me and they were cutting me a cheque for $2,800. It was going to be ready early the following week if I wanted to drive out to Oakville and pick it up. I jokingly asked if it was going to bounce. "Like rubber," he kidded, then told me the cheque should be at reception by Wednesday.

Malcolm, who had been part of the same group of friends from high school as Callum, Don and me, stopped by on Saturday afternoon to say hello. He brought a friend along with him by the name of Joe Lukacewicz who, it turned out, had known Don at the Toronto Buddhist Centre back in the early 1980s before he went east. While the two of them had a short catch-up chat, Malcolm took me aside and let me know he'd had his case-conference with the Crown Attorney the previous Thursday and told her that I wouldn't be pleading out.

I asked him if he'd heard what Nicky was doing.

"Not really sure," Malcolm said. "Larry made his own appointment with the Crown, but apparently missed the conference. Got his dates mixed up or something."

"Tell me you're kidding," I said.

"I'm not. It slipped his mind I guess."

"Fifteen-grand, and he forgets to show up?"

"Like I told you, nice work if you can get it."

"So where does that leave Nicky?"

He shrugged. "Larry'll have to make another appointment."

"Do you think he'll go for a plea bargain?"

"What choice does he have? The family's given him fifteen-grand already. They're not gonna cough up another forty or fifty for a trial."

"Stranger things have happened," I said.

"I'm sure," said Malcolm and, noticing my name tag, threw me one of his cockeyed grins. "Who the hell's *Larch Wood*?"

"Funny," I said, "a lot of people have been asking me that."

"I'll bet," he said, winking.

After a strong opening weekend (sales for the first four

days had paid for the rental of his booth, according to Don), on Monday morning, the show having been open for maybe half an hour, I was closing a transaction on one of our most expensive boards with an interesting couple from Anchorage, Alaska, when my cellphone rang. This surprised me, because I was on a pay-as-you-go plan and thought I had run out of minutes a couple of days earlier.

I excused myself with the customers and took the call. It was a woman named Martha, from Bill Summers's law office, letting me know a few things had turned up when they'd done the legal search on my name. Bill was wondering if I'd pop into the office and see him as soon as possible.

Talking fast, I told her I wouldn't be able to do that. I asked if maybe she could give me some of the details over the phone — at which point Fido cut me off, and the line went dead.

Since Don wasn't scheduled to come on duty for several hours, I finished the sale with the Alaskan couple and asked Cleo, the woman selling jewelry in the booth across from ours, to tell anyone checking out the boards that I'd be back in about five minutes. I grabbed the money pouch, as Don had told me to do anytime I left the booth, and went looking for a payphone.

The only one I could find was located beside the show's busy main entrance. A steady stream of chatty Christmas shoppers passed by as I spoke to Martha, whom I'd called back for details on what the search had turned up. The gist of it was that there were several judgements registered against my name: $6,200 to a Capital One MasterCard, $18,000 to Revenue Canada, and $67,000 to the bankruptcy trustee for a Mr. John James Illidge. According to Martha, Bill wouldn't be able to close the sale of the house till all three judgements were removed. I'd have to contact the various parties and work something out. If not, I could agree to let the money be taken from my share of the proceeds of the house sale — though to do that, she pointed out, I'd have to get Julie's agreement, since she was co-titleholder on the house. Martha said I should resolve matters as quickly as I could; the lawyer handling the sale for the buyers was quite concerned. She repeated that my first step was to call the parties and see if any of them would be willing to take less. "Are you related in some way to this John James Illidge?" she asked.

"He's a younger brother of mine," I said, adding quickly that I couldn't really talk just then. I told her I'd come in to see Bill the following day.

"Not a problem," said Martha, and let me go.

I hadn't had a MasterCard since 2000, and as far as I knew my credit rating was still good. The $18,000 to Revenue Canada must have had something to do with income tax, but again, as far as I knew, things were in order. No, it was the money being claimed by Howie Gertz, my brother's bankruptcy trustee that had me slamming the receiver back on its hook after the call. "A vengeful little prick," John used to say about Howie, the kind of comment my brother freely dispensed about people who rubbed him the wrong way, characterizations that I usually took with a grain of salt. But in dumping what I knew was a fraudulent $67,000 judgement against me, it was clear that, at least in Howie's case, my brother's assessment had been quite astute.

I took a few slow breaths to calm myself down, watched the passing crowd until I spotted an opening then made my way back to the booth. I thanked Cleo for keeping an eye out, had a seat on the IKEA folding chair behind the display counter, a lull in the crowd giving me a moment to think about what losing ninety grand was going to mean.

Even if Julie relented and let me keep my half of the proceeds of the house sale, after real estate commission, closing costs and the unpaid property taxes, I'd be lucky to net $100,000 when all was said and done. Yet here I'd been told that $91,200 of it was to be paid to other people; that everything I'd done to get the house sold had pretty well been for nothing; that the most I could expect to walk away from Friendship Avenue with was somewhere in the neighbourhood of $7,500, enough to rent a basement apartment for six months, if that —

I guess I'd started whistling along with the Christmas carol that was playing on the hall's PA while I was ruminating. A woman, maybe in her fifties, wearing a coat, scarf and toque in seasonal reds and greens, sauntered up to the booth and with a cheery smile said: "*You're* a happy guy!"

"I am," I said, managing a smile, waiting while she appraised the different boards.

"So," she said, having a glance at my nametag. "What can you tell me about these cutting boards of yours . . . Larch?"

I drove out to Oakville the following Wednesday morning and picked up my cheque from Dell Parsons at Simply Audiobooks. Back in the city by about eleven, I went to the bank, my home branch, where the manager knew me and waived the usual hold when I made the deposit so that I could have the whole $2,800.

I then headed downtown to Stephen's office for an emergency meeting with him and two "associates" who were going to help me brainstorm a solution to the $67,000 bombshell which, Stephen informed me as we walked toward the boardroom, had "Pearl Harbored the chicks. They were still on about the other shit," he said, "but it was the sixty-seven K that knocked them into the hysterisphere. 'Your client failed to disclose information,'" he said, mimicking Victoria. "'Why wouldn't you and your client have told us about the liens?' I said we would have, if we'd fucking well *known* about them. 'Course Victoria is absolutely sure we did and," he shrieked, "''You and your client are just fucking us around!'"

"Victoria used the word 'fucking'?"

"Not in so many words," Stephen said. "But how am I supposed to deal with that kind of shit? What am I supposed to say for fuck sakes? Hey," he changed the subject, "did you give Angelo a call yet?" but before I could answer, he showed me into the boardroom where his two associates were waiting.

Stephen introduced me to Al, a guy in his early seventies wearing a nut-brown sports-jacket and brownish plaid flannel shirt, thin-faced, glasses and a raspy voice, and Denny, early forties my guess, a squat, pug-faced bulldog of a guy with brush-cut hair in a black leather jacket over a black, western-style shirt with pearl buttons. He was sitting with his hands turned inward on his knees in a chair beside Al, a few feet back from the table. Stephen and I taking seats across from them, he explained that Al was an accountant who did a lot of bankruptcy work — a friend of Angelo's too, apparently — and asked me again if I'd given "Ange" a call yet, which I said I hadn't but was planning to.

I didn't know what Denny's background was; he looked on with his lips pressed together, the bottom one jutting out a little, his face set in a thoughtful frown. Stephen was sitting back in his chair with his legs crossed, turning his burgundy cellphone this way and that on the table as Al went through the pros and cons of declaring personal bankruptcy, which he said was something that I might consider doing. I quickly picked up, at least from the way Al explained it, that there really weren't many advantages to declaring insolvency. "Doesn't it cost me to go bankrupt, too?" I asked him. "I seem to remember my brother telling me it did."

"Oh sure," Al said. "You have to pay a bankruptcy trustee to protect you from your creditors."

"How much in his case?" Stephen asked. "Ballpark."

"Twenty-five hundred would probably do it," said Al, looking over at me. "But that way you'd be off the hook for the judgements. That's the thing you've got to consider first, right?"

"But if I declare bankruptcy, I can't have any assets, isn't that the way it works?"

"Right."

"In other words, I won't be able to collect any money from the house sale even if I can get it."

"You might be able to put it in trust for your kids," Denny piped up helpfully.

"But who administers the trust?"

"Your ex-wife," said Al, not so helpfully.

"And if the judgements aren't lifted," I said, "we can't close the real-estate deal, there's no money for anybody, and the bank takes the house?"

"It's a Catch-23," said Al, nodding.

"Twenty-two," I corrected him.

"What?"

"It's Catch-22, not 23, Al!" said Stephen, raising his voice like maybe Al was hard of hearing.

We sat in silence for a few moments, Denny with his hands on his knees, frowning, Stephen spinning his cellphone one way then the other, Al pondering things with knitted brow — until his face brightened like he might have come up with an idea. He said he *did* know a couple of the guys over at the firm handling my brother's bankruptcy, maybe he could fax them a note and get them to drop the amount by ten, fifteen thousand or so. "Let you have a little something to keep you on your feet afterwards." He took a beaten-up address book and a blank piece of notepaper out of an old brown-leather briefcase he had with him, got up, came around the table and went out to the office, presumably to send the fax.

Stephen reminded me again about calling Angelo, said he was waiting to hear from me, that I was gonna like him, he was a good guy. "Isn't that right, Denny?"

Still with his hands turned inward on his knees, Denny put his bottom lip out further and nodded. "Angelo's a real good guy," he said, almost smiling.

Stephen asked how the court case was going with my son.

I told him about Larry Heffernan missing his appointment with the Crown.

"Guy's a fucking nincompoop," he said, shaking his head. "What's Malcolm say?"

"Just that he hopes Larry shows up next time."

"And the guy's making what, fifteen grand?"

"So they say."

"What a fuckwit," said Stephen.

Al returned to the room. Closed the door and made his way around the table back to his seat. He said we should be hearing back soon; these guys at the bankruptcy trustee's office weren't the type to pussyfoot around. Once he'd sat down and tucked his address book away in his briefcase, he leaned back in his chair and asked what exactly the beef was between my brother and me, said maybe we should take a look at that first.

I gave him a précis version of the story, explaining that the beef wasn't so much between my brother and me, though we certainly had our issues. In the autumn of 2001, the Ontario Securities Commission shut down the investment firm he was running because it was severely undercapitalized and because, having been disciplined and fined by the Investment Dealers Association of Canada for a dozen securities infractions several years earlier, it looked like John could be up to his old tricks again, treating investor money as his own, making unauthorized trades and creating phony accounts into which he dumped the proceeds of his sales. He declared personal bankruptcy immediately, so he wouldn't have to make good on accounts where investors had lost money, of which there were quite a few, as it turned out, to the tune of four or five million in some cases. My sister-in-law told me that after the first meeting of his creditors about $70 million was being claimed. Swearing that he had nowhere else to go, John and his soon-to-be new wife moved in with my children and me out in West Rouge until the furor died down. I took him at his word that it was equity problems at his firm (i.e., because somebody had been "taking money out the back door") that had prompted the Ontario Securities Commission to open an investigation into his activities. He conveniently never told me about any financial irregularities, or that he himself, as I discovered later, was the one who'd been "taking money out the back door," and though sometimes, after he'd had a few drinks, he'd allude vaguely to the possibility that he might have "mingled" some of his clients' money in with his own once in a while, in the nine months he lived at my house he maintained, and fervently so, that he was innocent of all the charges and accusations everyone was leveling against him.

"Any beef I had was with my brother's bankruptcy trustee," I told Al.

"Who was that?"

"Howie Gertz."

"Yeah, I know Howie."

"Once he heard that John was living with me — 'holed up,' as he later referred to it — he became convinced I was in on the fraud and must have known where my brother had squirreled his loot away. I had a slight idea where some of it was; John and I had talked about it a few times when he'd been drinking, about who could go to the Caymans, the Isle of Man or Barbados for him and bring two or three million back. Take maybe five hundred grand for doing so. But I didn't have anything like what Howie needed as evidence to take John to court and have the embezzled funds seized, which was what he wanted to happen. I was supposed to pry key information out of John and report it back to him. Either that or, as Howie warned, I could decide not to play ball, in which case, according to him, he could do things that would 'really fuck my life up.'

"After about six months of pestering, he said he'd had enough of my bullshit, he was tired of the runaround I was giving him; told me he was only going to let me off the hook if I cut the crap and delivered him some juicier goods for a change, stuff he could work with 'to recoup his losses,' as he phrased it. In our initial conversation I asked him what he meant by 'off the hook' and said I wasn't aware that I was *on* the hook.

Howie saw it differently, announced that the jig was up and I was going to help him out or pay for my 'involvement' one way or another. After that I pretended I knew exactly what was going on and fed him information, some of it true, culled from different documents John had left lying around; the rest, pure speculation. It was a kind of silly game that I thought he'd just stop playing after a while. With the time and energy Howie spent harassing me, I figured he couldn't be getting back too much money for my brother's other creditors, of which I was one myself, ironically enough: John pocketed $1.3 million of my mother's money, our inheritance, between 1991 and 2000 when he was her power of attorney.

"Following the third of our clandestine lunch meetings to 'discuss the ongoing situation' (at which Howie always arrived in a Clouseau-style, belted khaki trenchcoat, dark glasses and a green fedora with a feather in it, inviting me to frisk him before we got down to business to see if he was 'wearing a wire'), he broke the news that he was still finding my information 'totally lacking,' and threatened that if I didn't provide him with more incriminating material, and soon, he'd slap a lien on my house for fifty or sixty thousand, which is about what he considered my information to be worth to him. I told him he should do whatever he had to do, but thought it might interest him to know that, according to John, he was turning over $5,000 a month, cash, under the table, so Howie would back off on his recouping efforts with the more aggressive creditors; and that just in case it hadn't yet come to his attention, to protect myself I'd made a point of recording all our lunchtime conversations, this one no exception, as well as most of our phone calls. I told Howie that as far as I was concerned he could go fuck himself with his fifty or sixty thousand dollar lien. I had enough to get him into as much trouble as John was in.

"It was a pre-emptive strike as I saw it. My brother had bought a company called Oakville Movers just before he went bankrupt and moved in with me. It was a cash business, I explained to Howie a few weeks after the conversation in which I'd told him to fuck off. He'd continued calling me, leaving indignant voicemail messages to let me know that the jig was up, that although I might have thought my brother and I were 'pulling the wool over his eyes,' he knew exactly what was going on. I picked up one day while he was leaving a message, asking him why, if he was so smart, he didn't know that on Fridays John was bringing home ten to fifteen grand in cash from Oakville Movers. I told him I knew this because he counted the money at my kitchen table, gave his fiancée five grand to take to Howie's office the following Monday before she went back to Ottawa, where she and John had rented a house. I gave him the gist of the Oakville arrangement, pointing out that *that's* where his generous monthly stipend was actually coming from. Howie said the whole thing sounded like a typical load of Illidge bullshit. It couldn't be proven; it was just my word and John's against his. Any money John made was supposed to go through him. He received copies of all John's transactions, he'd never heard a thing about any moving company in Oakville. As far as kickbacks went, Howie said they must have been a figment of my brother's imagination. 'So his fiancée *isn't* dropping off five grand a month under the table?' I asked him. As expected, he almost came through the phone, told me to fuck right off, called me a 'goddamn fucking cocksucker' for trying to fuck him over with such bullshit. At which point I said that he was right, the jig *was* up, but on him, not me. I held my tape recorder up to the receiver so he'd be sure to hear me clicking it off. That was the last time I had the pleasure of talking to Howie Gertz."

"Phew!" said Al, flabbergasted.

"Phew is right," said Denny, putting out his bottom lip, his frown deepening.

"You gotta write a *book* about that, Paul!" Stephen erupted. "What a fucking *story*!"

"I thought I'd heard it all until now," Al said, still a little shaken.

"Can you talk to your brother?" Denny spoke up. "Maybe he can call off this bankruptcy trustee?"

"*Nah*," said Al. "Doesn't work that way." He thought about it for a moment. "Do you have anything on him?"

"On Howie?"

"No, on your brother. Papers, documents, emails, maybe from when he was living with you."

"That was seven years ago. Even if I did, I don't think it would stand up in court."

Stephen shook his head. "Not if he was living with you. They'd figure the two of you were in cahoots and you turned on him. He'd probably marry the fiancée before the case went to trial so she wouldn't be able to testify against him."

"How much do you figure she knows?" Denny asked.

"Not a lot. John said that was one of the reasons he'd hooked up with her in the first place. She wasn't too bright, and she'd do just about anything for cash."

"Does she know the judgement against you was cooked up?"

"I doubt it."

"If you *had* something on him," Al said, "there's a chance we could show that the judgement was obtained under false pretenses."

"You never heard anything about it?" Stephen said. "Nobody ever came to your door with court papers or anything like that?"

"Nobody."

"Could be worth a shot if we had something," Al repeated.

"I don't know," said Stephen, giving me a look. "You want to spend four large going to court to try to have a judgement lifted?"

"I don't *have* four large, if that makes any difference. And if I did, I wouldn't waste it on a worm like Howie Gertz."

"So your brother's still in bankruptcy after how long?" Al asked.

"Six years and counting."

"Three years is supposed to be the maximum."

"And it was seventy million he got his hands on?"

"Five million, either way, from what I was told."

"Shit," said Al, "no *wonder* Howie's pissed."

After a rap at the boardroom door, Tess stuck her head in and handed Stephen a fax, a reply to Al from his friends at the firm handling my brother's bankruptcy.

Al read the fax over. "Shit," he said, looking up. "Goyer, one of the partners, says the payout's gone to $78,000 now with legal fees and costs. And it's gonna go higher still. He sees no reason there should be a lower settlement when they've got documents proving your brother loaned you the money."

"Whatever they have will be forgeries, my brother's stock-in-trade. Gertz wouldn't know the difference."

Al thought for a moment, then gave a troubled shake of

his head. "$7,500 won't take you very far these days," he said. "Maybe declaring personal bankruptcy is your best option here, Paul . . ."

"Maybe, maybe not," Stephen interjected, tapping his pen lightly on the table in front of him. "He could always walk. Nobody gets a shekel until he signs, right?" He looked at me. "And why would you even bother doing that when you're gonna be left with fuck-all in the end? *Nah*," he said, shaking his head. "Why not leave the whole bunch of them standing at the altar with their dicks in their hands," Stephen delivering his pointed mixed-metaphor with a gloating smile, tossing his pen in the air and casually catching it when it came down. "See how they like *them* fuckin' apples!"

Al made a face and let out a breath. "Yeah, but what's he gonna do for money, Stephen? The guy's gotta live."

"He'll think of something — the guy translates Shake-speare, Al."

"You do?" Al said.

"I do," I said, noticing Denny with his bottom lip out, nodding like he was impressed too.

The meeting over, the question of what I should do still unresolved, we stood up. Stephen suggested I give Al three-fifty, said he'd take care of Denny, and I could give him two-fifty for setting things up.

"Sorry we couldn't be more help," Al said when we shook hands.

"Food for thought, anyway," said Denny.

"What can you do?" I said, and distributed the cash.

Sensing my frustration after what was clearly a pointless meeting, Stephen walked me out to the elevator, clutched my hand for a second after shaking it. "Just remember," he said.

"*You* have the power here, Paul. Nobody gets a cent without your say-so. Like I said in the meeting, any time you want to, you can tell them all to go fuck themselves, and walk away. Bankruptcy or not, going broke ain't the end of the world, believe me. I see it all the time. Think about it!" he said, winked, cocked his thumb and pointed his index finger at me as the elevator doors were closing.

CHAPTER **SIXTEEN**
THE D-WORD

By Friday I'd lined up a mover, a former client of Malcolm's named Deshaun who had a half-ton truck, a couple of helpers, was fairly reliable and wouldn't charge me an arm and a leg for his services. I rented a ten-by-twenty-foot storage locker where anything I wanted to keep would have to go until I could find another place to live. I also contacted the credit card people, who weren't budging on their six thousand; got nowhere in my search for someone at Revenue Canada who could help me out with my tax problem; and exchanged emails with a lawyer named Skolnik who was representing Howie Gertz and his bankruptcy firm. Skolnik dismissing my contention that the judgement against me was out-and-out fraud, he not only wouldn't agree to lower the amount payable, but warned me that the longer my ex-wife withheld her agreement to have the money come from the house sale, the more it was going to cost me in additional legal fees. He let me know that he could "drill" the account from seventy-eight thousand up to a hundred grand with no problem at all. I wanted to ask him just why he would do something like that, but all I could say, a little too emotionally perhaps, was that I was happy with my wife's disagreement if it was keeping a greasy scumbag like him from getting his hands on any of our money. No skin off his nose, Skolnik said, but it was still going to cost me.

Stephen said Victoria Durant was in full meltdown mode; Bill Summers told me that the people buying our house, along with their lawyer and real-estate agent, were panicking at the undue delay in resolving matters with the bankruptcy trustee. Lenny, in desperate straits because I hadn't already done so, said he needed me to fax him copies of all property tax payments that I'd made in the last seven years so he could show them to the city. A woman from Enbridge collections phoned to ask who would be looking after the $7,100 gas bill at closing. "Haven't a clue," I said matter-of-factly, and hung up.

Late in the afternoon on Friday, a woman from Revenue Canada returned my phone call and gave me the name of a person who might be the one assigned to my tax file, and who could explain what the $18,000 was all about, a man whose name I didn't catch, though I memorized the number. He was going to be out of the office on Monday, the woman said, so I should call first thing Tuesday morning, the 4th. I told her there was some urgency here, with the deal on our house set to close two days later. I said I sure hoped it was the right number she was giving me. "I do too," she said pleasantly before she rang off.

My shift over at six o'clock on Saturday night, I considered driving back to the house to do some packing, but after nine hours on my feet flogging boards, I was pretty beat, so I decided to stay downtown and head over first thing in the morning. Sunday was the last day of the show and Don wouldn't need me until four o'clock to help take the booth down. I'd have the better part of the day to spend at the house, and I was getting some much-needed help from my friend Curtis Harvey and his wife Suzanne, who were coming over with a carload of moving supplies and, according to Curtis when he made his offer, weren't leaving until the kitchen had been packed up and cleaned within an inch of its life.

I had a leisurely steak dinner at the Bank Note, courtesy of the Larch Wood Enterprises credit card that Don had loaned me, then, rather than return to the hotel room, I thought I'd take a stroll along King Street and clear my head after a day of hot, dry, exhibition-hall air. There weren't many other pedestrians out, if you didn't count the homeless types and assorted panhandlers, who seemed to be a pesky lot that night. I gave a couple of the more entertaining ones some change, though my cheery "Good luck!" was tinged with more fellow feeling than usual that night since, from the way things were looking, in a week's time, I could very well be out here with them.

As I walked past one of the tonier restaurants coming back along Richmond Street, I realized a man standing out front with his wife and a few friends was none other than Eddie Greenspan, the legendary Toronto criminal lawyer who'd been in the news most recently for defending Conrad Black at his fraud trial in Chicago. I found myself thinking about Black and his much-publicized legal battles while I made my way home to the hotel. The man was reviled by just about everyone in Canada, his international reputation was in tatters, he'd been pilloried in the media, ousted from the boards of all his companies, had all his holdings, bank accounts and personal assets frozen, and he was doing a six-year stretch in a Florida prison . . . all because he'd allegedly treated six million dollars of shareholder money as his own, and lied about it. Yet there was my brother John, who was said to have pilfered more than ten times the amount Conrad had, treated the money as his own and lied about it, yet was currently living in an elegant rented townhouse overlooking Lake Ontario with his wife Mandy, squiring her around in one of the three high-end cars that he still drove, lunching and doing business at the exclusive Granite Club during the day, then making the rounds of his favourite restaurants at night, leading, to hear him tell it, a life of pleasure, comfort and ease.

Maybe Conrad should have used John's lawyer, I thought wryly as I entered the Travelodge and took the elevator up to what Don and I were calling the "Larch Suite." I grabbed a beer from the mini-fridge, lay down on the bed and caught the tail end of the Toronto–Montreal hockey game on TV. Though the Leafs were on a much-talked-about losing streak, I remember they ended up beating the Canadiens that night on a late-in-the-third-period goal by Mats Sundin.

While the gods might have been smiling on Mats and the Leafs Saturday night, they certainly weren't for me come Sunday morning. I was awoken about 7:30 by a phone call from my friend Curtis. He apologized profusely, but said he and Suzanne probably wouldn't be able to make it over to the house to help with the packing, what with the ten inches of snow that had been dumped on the city overnight. Curtis said he hoped I'd understand: the roads were treacherous, their car didn't have winter tires on it and he and Suzanne just didn't want to chance it with driving conditions being what they were. He told me by all means to come by the house and pick up the moving supplies. He'd taken them out of his car and left them in the lobby, and he'd told the concierge to let me pull up to the front door whenever I arrived.

I understood completely, said not to worry about it. I was tired from my two-week stint at the show and didn't know how much packing was going to get done anyway. I told him I was more disappointed because I'd been looking forward to spending some time with him and Suzanne. I could have added, but decided not to, that working alone in the house dodging the authorities for more than six months now had worn me down. With somebody else on the premises, I wouldn't have had to put on the paint can bluff, worry that the dreaded doorbell was going to ring any minute, my luck with the police having finally run out.

After a bacon-and-egg breakfast in the hotel café, I went out to my car, spent about fifteen minutes cleaning off the snow before starting up and, tires spinning until they got traction, skidded my way over to the exit, crashed through a three-foot bank of snow that the ploughs had left behind and fish-tailed out of the hotel parking lot onto King Street, where, because of the heavy snow, there was little traffic to speak of. No one was getting anywhere that Sunday morning.

I made it to Curtis and Suzanne's uptown condominium without calamity in a little over an hour, pulled up at the front door, where the concierge was expecting me. He buzzed Curtis, who came down and helped load the moving supplies into my car. He thrust $200 cash in my hand "to help with expenses" as I was preparing to leave, scooting back inside the building before I could protest or try to give it back.

The snow was still falling hard. Even with my high-beams on, visibility was reduced to about twenty feet ahead and the driving was touch-and-go on the hills leading up the Don Valley Expressway, where more than a few people stood beside their stuck or stalled vehicles talking on their cellphones. The good news though, was that when I turned onto the 401 there were only a few cars heading east, motoring at slow speed behind the four snowploughs ten yards in front of us, the big trucks running in a flying-wedge that stretched across the highway — not a problem for most of us on the road at the time, though it meant the in-a-hurry-to-get-somewhere types that hurtled past in invincible-looking SUVs doing 120 kilometres per hour had to do some pretty fancy braking when they realized there was no way of slipping past the ploughs. After some frantic and flurried white-knuckle swerving, they always ended up falling back in line with those of us putting along at a cautious twenty kilometres per hour, a speed that was just fine with me, as I was in no particular hurry to start packing.

The jazz program that I'd been listening to wrapped up, and I found a program on the University of Toronto radio station that seemed more than a little à propos for the bleakish mood I was in — the one I fell into almost every time I headed over to Friendship Avenue now. The glum mood had been exacerbated by the snowstorm and the letdown with Curtis and Suzanne, as well as mounting anxiety about what lay in store for me starting first thing the next morning; when the craft show closed, I shed my Larch Wood persona of the last eleven days and reverted to being Paul Illidge again.

As it turned out, the host of the university radio program was interviewing a psychologist, a Dr. DeSerres who, among other things, trained the people who handled calls on the university's distress/help line. He said depression is too often taken to be a mental illness, when it's no more than a strong emotional reaction to common life events and situations. The more extreme situations, to one extent or another, were sure to cause depressive feelings in all of us. He said the mental illness stigma was one of the biggest misconceptions about depression and a major reason why treating people for it was so problematic. According to studies, depression was the least-talked-about subject of conversation between people, after death. Medication for it was soon to be the one most-prescribed by physicians, the dispensing of antidepressants reaching epidemic proportions. In the cultural realm, he said, depression as a theme in movies spelled box office disaster, and for publishers, writing was dead on the page any time the word *depression* made its appearance. People not only didn't want to read about it, they didn't even want to see the word. So here we had a condition, the solution to which lay in communicating about it, and yet doing so had become one of our most entrenched taboos. Even in economics, he pointed out, governments, banks and business leaders have coined the euphemism "recession" to avoid the negative impact the D-word has on global financial markets.

Explaining what to look for as symptoms, he talked about the kinds of events, experiences and life incidents that could bring depression on (some that involved trauma, but many that didn't); the age range in which it was most commonly found (men and women between forty-five and seventy-five, a surprise to me, as he said it was to most people); that both sexes were equally susceptible to it, though because it was less acceptable for men to reveal their "depressive side" they were generally better at "masking," something which, as he talked, I realized was exactly what I'd been doing ever since the night of the raid: keeping up an appearance of strength, competence and capability in trying circumstances, just as Dr. DeSerres described. "Performing beyond most other people's limits and abilities. Pretending excitement over things you're indifferent to. Putting on a face that has you looking and sounding the way you think other people want you to, when all the while you're angry at their failure to recognize, appreciate, understand or respond in any way to the hurt, the guilt, the shame, the fear you feel they've inflicted upon you."

"Depressives," he said, "feel they've failed . . . that no matter what they accomplish they're not good enough, not worthwhile, their concerns of no interest or importance to anyone else. They can experience recurrent feelings that they're empty, lifeless and dead inside, what writer Hugo Wolf called 'the sleep of a thousand wounds'. Suicidal in their thinking, perhaps." But as the doctor reminded the host, "the desire to kill oneself is not a medical symptom in any diagnostic manual of disorders. If it were," he said, "we'd have to include sadness, loneliness, resentment and anger as diseases, too. Having emotions is not an illness. Any more than not being able to express them is."

He said the thing he emphasizes with his distress-line volunteers is that their main task is to help callers understand that depression has to do with unexpressed angry feelings, about what they see as their inadequacies, their badness, their worthlessness, that they have failed. "We don't try to help them understand those feelings," he said. "We just try to have them understand why it is they can't express them."

In one of his final points, he drew the host's attention to the difference between *understanding* and *treating* depression, his contention that the focus should be shifted from the latter to the former since treatment for depression consists mainly of prescription pharmaceuticals. Antidepressants were not only harmful physically, he explained, but the very idea of them was one that had contributed significantly to a view that depression is somehow the enemy, something bad, which has to be overcome and got rid of ("they're not called *anti*depressants for nothing"), rather than appreciated and accepted as what, again in his view, was actually an intelligent person's guide to better health, a wake-up call to yourself. The comment floored me, I remember, since it was the first time I'd ever heard depression described in such a positive light. "Don't get even, just get angry," I remember the host putting in rather obliquely. "No," the psychologist corrected him. "The thing we *want* to do is acknowledge this anger in ourselves, make friends with it and, more than anything else, try to stop being so afraid of it."

The host provided listeners with the university's help-line phone number, which was available twenty-four hours a day, seven days a week, thanked the doctor for his informative insights then broke for a commercial. I turned the radio off and drove the rest of the way in silence, my spirits, despite the blizzard, the tricky driving and the packing that awaited me, much brighter than they'd been for quite some time.

I reached the house in one piece a little before noon. Unable to park on the street because of the snow banks, I drove past it twice to make sure the coast was clear, then, as I turned in, hit the gas and launched the Honda at the two-foot ridge of snow the ploughs had left at the foot of the driveway. With the rear wheels still partially on the street, I turned the engine off and got out of the car. Mary-Ellen and Wes, having cleared their driveway, were just starting in on the snowplough bank, neither of them looking up from their shoveling when I ran up the walk to the front door, the two of them pretending they hadn't noticed my arrival, I was sure, which was perfectly fine with me.

I donned my painting-clothes, brought Curtis's moving supplies in from the car (Wes and Mary-Ellen still not glancing over during my three sorties) and put them in the living room. With the open can, stir-stick and paintbrush in position by the hall closet, I slapped on my Benjamin Moore cap and went to work with the tape-gun assembling moving boxes. When I had a dozen ready to go, I ran them upstairs two at a time, tossed a few items in each box, did the same in the computer room, the family room, the laundry room, and after checking the front of the house through the living-room window, booted it downstairs and put a couple in my office.

My thousand or so books still on the shelves, I went to the box where I'd put the fifty-six (one for each year of my age) that I wouldn't be consigning to the shredder at the recycling station on moving day, and dug out Charles Dickens' *Bleak House*. An old, leather-bound hardcover copy of the novel, it was the last of a collection of six Dickens works that my Grandma Illidge had given me as a birthday present when I was a boy, the gift of special significance, it seemed to me at the time, since the books had been bequeathed to her by her own grandmother when she was a girl.

My stopwatch alarm sounded as I slipped the book in a plastic grocery bag: time for my security break. I hustled upstairs and changed out of my paint clothes, threw my coat and boots on and went out to the car, Wes and Mary-Ellen still working too hard on their snow to notice me.

I opened the trunk, put the bag with *Bleak House* in it into the suitcase where I was keeping my clothes and other personal belongings, backed out of the drive and decided to hit my horn a couple of times at Mary-Ellen and Wes as I drove away, just to let them know there weren't any hard feelings.

After a quick coffee and a Danish pastry at Mr. Beans, I left my car in the plaza parking lot and hiked through the snow down Port Union Road to the lake. I stood under the open-sided gazebo the parks department had put in last summer, looking out at the grey lake and sky, no one else around, everything still and snow-silent. It might have been what the psychologists call avoidance behaviour, but the fact was, I was feeling happier than I had in a long time.

I returned to the house a little after two, and in a burst of activity cleared out the cupboards above and below the counter along one side of the kitchen, threw most of the clothes from the kids' closets in garbage bags, hangers and all, made some inroads with the spare room in the basement, with the furnace and the recreation rooms, from which I carted about twenty boxes of stuff destined for the garbage out to the garage.

Before I knew it, it was after three and time to be leaving if I hoped to make it back to the craft show by four o'clock. I changed into my street attire, closed up the paint can, put my coat on and was in the living room turning the thermostat down a few degrees, as I always did prior to leaving, when I noticed the humidifier that I kept in the dining room beside the piano had run dry. The movers were coming the next morning to take the piano over to Julie's, who was allowing me to leave it at her house "temporarily" as part of a deal that Nicky had worked out with her. I'd made up my mind during the craft show that the instrument had to go; it was a good make, a Baldwin, in excellent condition and liable to fetch upwards of four or five thousand dollars, cash that would come in handy as it wasn't likely that I'd be moving to a place where I could keep a piano, at least any time soon. Nicky had been adamant that we hang onto it, however. He'd taught himself to play over the last few years and wanted to be able to keep doing so while he was living at Julie's. He wanted to continue with his "time outs" as he called the sessions, when he'd sit down at the keyboard and riff on Pink Floyd, the Doors, Lynyrd Skynyrd, Neil Young or his own rock-inspired creations for an hour or two at a time. "Just letting the music take me places I want to go," as he described it. He said we'd find a spot for the piano somewhere down the line; that his mom would just have to get used to his playing. He felt that we'd only regret the decision if we got rid of it now.

With this the last opportunity I'd have to play, maybe for quite some time, after I refilled the humidifier, I went over, pulled the bench out and sat down at the piano. Dozens of song possibilities tumbling through my head, I found myself with a sudden case of cocktail-pianist's block: so used to performing music other people want to hear that when it comes to playing something for yourself, your mind draws a blank.

I spread my fingers above the keys anyway, wiggled them to limber them up and let my thoughts drift wherever they might for a minute . . . until inspiration kicked in and, laughing to myself, I swept into the final, *presto agitato* movement of Beethoven's "Moonlight Sonata," watching my hands race over the keys almost as fast as they had when I was twelve and playing the piece for my piano teacher at the time, May Barclay-King, in her basement studio during my weekly lesson. May would lean in over my right shoulder, her face close to mine, bobbing her head vigorously and humming in time to the music, a cup of triple-triple instant coffee in the hand she had over my left shoulder, the Cameo Menthol she was smoking tucked in a corner of her mouth, a few inches from my face. Nodding her head, humming loudly and her right hand beating the air in time to the music's blistering pace, she was oblivious to the fact that the ash at the end of her cigarette was growing longer by the second. Naturally most of my attention was on what my fingers were doing, but with a boy's fascination, I often wondered if, in all the frenetic activity, the lengthening column of ash on her cigarette was going to break off and land on my fingers. I marveled at the way she always managed to keep that ash from dropping, and was still marveling about it that afternoon as I charged through the *presto agitato*, smiling to myself because in the many times I played the third movement of the "Moonlight" for May, I don't remember that it ever did.

Red-faced, breathing hard and looking none too happy, Mary-Ellen and Wes were still shoveling like there was no tomorrow when I came outside, pitching the snow well out onto the road so that a foot-high mound was building up in the middle. I watched as a red Chevy Cavalier, spinning its wheels mightily and fishtailing badly as it struggled up the hill from the lower part of the street had to swerve around the snow-mound or risk getting stuck in it. The driver shot them an angry look, took his hand off the wheel and gave them the finger. But Mary-Ellen and Wes remained oblivious to the gesture, kept their heads down and continued clearing the snow off their driveway, like there was a whole lot riding on them being the first ones on the block to have done so.

The wind having died, but the snow falling hard again, I drove down Starspray Boulevard, turned onto Lawrence Avenue and, flicking on my windshield wipers to maximum, switched on the radio and headed up to the highway for what I figured would be a slow drive back to the craft show.

With the traffic hold-ups and several minor accidents on Lakeshore Boulevard, it was almost six o'clock by the time I reached the Direct Energy Centre. I parked my car, ran back across the lot and pressed my way through the crowd streaming out of the hall, slipped my Larch Wood nametag around my neck for the last time and raced inside: the eight hundred or so vendors in the hall cheering, whistling and applauding wildly, not at my entrance of course, but because the announcement had just come over the PA that the 2007 One of a Kind Craft Show was now officially over.

Don was standing in the aisle in front of our booth fitting the battery to his Ryobi rechargeable drill when I ran up. "You made it," he grinned as he held up the Ryobi and zoomed it a couple of times to make sure it was working.

"I did," I said, catching my breath and throwing off my coat.

"So, you ready to do some packin', b'y?" he said.

"Ready and rarin' to go," I said.

"Well, b'y," he said, a reassuring glint in his eye because he knew I'd been working at the house all day, "it doesn't get any better than that now, does it?"

"No it doesn't, b'y," I said in my best Larch Wood voice, and chuckled as I accepted the tape gun from him and started assembling packing boxes, which, I have to say, I was getting pretty good at by then.

CHAPTER SEVENTEEN
"HANG IN THERE, DADDIO"

I cashed Don's cheque on the way back to the house Monday morning, met the movers who were taking the piano over to Julie's at 11, then started in on the packing. I created three piles in each room: Storage Unit, Charity and, the biggest of the three, Garbage. In the computer room I found the contract from my Shakespeare Novels publisher in India that I had yet to sign — a pleasant surprise. I did so, dated it and put it with the change-of-address form I was taking over to the post office later. When Anuj received it, he was going to send me the stipulated 20,000 rupee advance, about $500 in Canadian funds for the seven books — chump change as they say, but with the more easy-going way I'd discovered Indians conduct business, not to mention the vagaries of the mail service between Toronto and New Delhi, by the time the cheque arrived, probably in February or March, I knew $500 might seem like a small fortune.

The usual distressed and angry phone calls continued to flood in while I was working: Lenny on about the lawyer for the buyers, who was hitting the roof because it was only three days till closing and his clients didn't know where they stood; Stephen at his wit's end with Julie's lawyer Victoria who, according to him, was screaming for blood because I wasn't being "collaborative enough" in the whole process. He'd apparently told her my life was being turned upside down, that I was going to be broke and on the street in three days' time and that it was pretty hard to be "fucking collaborative" about something like that; Bill Summers lambasting me for not having attended to all of this sooner, telling me we had the makings of a disaster on our hands; Joanne at the Royal Bank collections department wondering why she hadn't heard from me all last week. I was supposed to have checked in with her. She was hoping things were still moving ahead, but wanted to make sure that everything was good for the house-deal to close on Thursday, reminding me once more how foreclosure litigation would work in the event that it wasn't. I lied and told her there was nothing to worry about; I wasn't anticipating any problems. I apologized for being out of touch, explained to her that I'd been working at a craft show for the past eleven days and hadn't had time to call. I told her that things were right on track and proceeding as planned, promised that my lawyer would fax the necessary paperwork to her the moment the deal closed Thursday afternoon. My confident assurances appearing to allay her concerns, she let me go.

I spent the first hour cleaning up my office, working like the proverbial fiend crating books, clearing out my desk, disconnecting my PC, screen and printer and swathing them in bubble wrap until such time as I could use them again. Next came my filing cabinet, the top two drawers filled with elastic-bundled bills, household receipts and bank records going back to 1997, the year Julie, the kids and I moved into the house; buried beneath more papers and bill bundles in the bottom one, I discovered the four large manila envelopes containing all the material which, at one time, I had thought might be useful in the event my brother were ever to go on trial for fraud. According to a police detective named Les Bucyk, whom I'd got to know in 2003 when I was trying to recover the $1.3 million John had embezzled from my mother, the problem with prosecuting him for fraud, or even for theft, was that there was no paper trail to speak of, and if there was one, as far as Les saw it, there was a strong likelihood that many of the documents would turn out to be forged, tainted or inconsequential from an evidentiary standpoint. In a fraud trial, as Les explained it, you have to prove clear, premeditated intent on the part of the accused to commit it, "Pretty much like asking a murder victim how their killer had gone about planning the job," was how Les put it.

I told him that I did have a paper trail of sorts, a 468-page novel I'd written called *Lost in Paradise*, a fictional thriller that my agent at the time thought we had a good chance of selling to a publisher, but as I explained to Les, it was based almost entirely on material I'd gathered during the time when John declared bankruptcy and came to live with my children and me. I had printouts of email correspondence, conversations with my brother and his girlfriend Mandy, some of them tape recorded, some anecdotal; legal documents, registered letters, business contracts of various kinds, promissory notes, faxes, phone records, account ledgers. There were even copies of investment deals he'd had Mandy (who was back and forth from their house in Ottawa) type up on my computer when she was in Toronto: stock swindles, as I came to learn, most involving tech companies on the venture exchange hoping to increase their capitalization and jump to "one of the big boards." When, in the normal course of things, prices rose ten or fifteen cents a share, John would sell the two or three million he'd been given for free for his "investment services" and come away with a tidy two- or three-hundred thousand dollars, on top of his original $50,000 "promotion fee" of course, squirreling the money away in the Cayman Islands, a short plane trip, as John liked to point out, from his house at the Palm Beach Polo Club not far from Miami.

There were chequebooks from a variety of banks in one of the envelopes, perhaps twenty different accounts, none of them in John's name, along with several dozen sheets of paper on which he'd practised writing signatures, none of them his own. There was information from the Investment Dealers Association of Canada detailing a litany of regulatory concerns they had about the way he was directing his companies: multiple instances of identity theft, bank and investment accounts that he'd set up using the names of dead people, secret trades, bogus press-releases; documents with forged signatures; buying and selling client stocks without their knowledge or consent among the different "unprofessional practices" the Association had been alerted to.

I had business cards as well, a dozen boxes of them, which I'd found in the back seat of his Jaguar the night in November 2001 that a tall black gentleman with a football player's build, wearing a black leather coat and a gold earring, showed up at my house at 1 a.m. to repossess the car, John's ex-wife

Nancy having apparently given him my address. I told the repo man John wasn't there (he was, but he was asleep and I didn't know what the repercussions might be if I woke him up). The man said he was only asking because he was taking the car away and wanted to allow John the opportunity of getting anything he wanted out of it. I went out and, the doors standing open and the cab-light on, gathered up the boxes of business cards, file folders stuffed with documents, two attaché cases, some clothes, shoes and sports equipment, handed the keys to the repo man and went back inside, pilfering two or three cards from each of the boxes, noticing the names of what I had a pretty good hunch were phony companies, "capital corporations" according to the business cards, of which "John J. Illidge" was president, chief executive officer or both. Doing business in places like Toronto, New York, Paris, Tokyo and Dubai, all the company names were designed to convey strength, security and stability, as had the name of the securities firm he was in fact running at the time he declared bankruptcy: Rampart.

There were details about calls to my home phone number from an assortment of individuals, most of them checking to see if sums of money in the mid-six figures had been deposited in their companies' bank accounts yet, many of the callers alarmed and confused when I told them I was not "Candy," or "Sandy" or "Brandy" (the names he'd apparently left, along with my number), letting them know that this was a family residence, not a place of business. I had calls, too, from financial institutions in the United States, many of them from south Florida regarding various six-figure transactions, a number coming in regularly from the bank that was holding the mortgage on his Palm Beach house. Assuming I was John

Illidge, they informed me that my account was six months in arrears, the different representatives I talked to demanding to know exactly when I was proposing to bring the account up to date, none of them inclined to believe me when I told them that I was in fact not John Illidge, but his brother Paul, and I had absolutely no idea what they were talking about.

While some of the phone calls had a certain humour to them (why would they expect someone named Candy to have a man's voice?), the ones from the husbands of women John had been "running around with" (my mother's term for his philandering) were utterly distressing. These men were distraught because John was wining and dining their wives and whisking them off to places like New York, Miami, London or Paris for weekend shopping sprees. They claimed John was jeopardizing their wives' careers, destroying their marriages, hurting their children; that there was no way they could ever hope to compete with someone who threw money around like he did. The husbands said they knew he was going to drop their wives as soon as the fling was over and he'd got what he wanted from them; they pleaded with me, often in tears, to talk to John and make him stop before any more damage was done. I felt horrible, of course, but I never spoke to my brother about the calls; it wouldn't have done any good if I had. As I learned later, he did drop the women, though not without pocketing loans for several hundred thousand dollars or so in the process, the funds drawn on commercial accounts of which, not surprisingly, the women he was carrying on with always turned out to be the managers.

I'd sent Detective Bucyk a copy of the manuscript to see whether he thought the first half of the book, about 240 pages, as well as the four-envelope dossier of "hard evidence" that I'd put together to back up the story, would demonstrate a "clear intent" on John's part to commit fraud. Les said the book made for compelling reading, no question; he didn't see how a publisher in his or her right mind could turn it down. However on the legal side, the problem would be that my brother was living with me at the time he was doing some of the things I was writing about. I could be construed, in some ways, as having been complicit in his activities, my hard evidence, good as it was, considered by the judge as tainted. "And even if it wasn't," Les had said, "it'll take a hell of a lot more than what you've got to nail someone who can cover his tracks like your brother John can."

The material no more good to me now than it had been then, I stepped over to the three packing piles that I'd created on the floor of my office and, with surprisingly little compunction, tossed the four manila envelopes and the manuscript and computer files of *Lost in Paradise* onto the one labeled "Garbage."

I changed out of my painting gear and left the house on my security break around two o'clock. I went to Mr. Beans for a coffee, drank half of it there while I was talking to André then took a run down to the beach and, walking along the snowy shoreline, plotted my packing strategy for the rest of the afternoon.

I skipped dinner at Kelsey's and, with time out every hour or so for a coffee at McDonald's (since Mr. Beans was closed), packed until after 2 a.m. I took a couple of Advil with a glass of cranberry juice when I got back to Callum's, limped into bed at a little before 3 and lay there until about 5:30 when, still wide awake, I gave up on sleep, hopped out of bed, showered and got dressed and drove back over to the house.

I spent a few hours in the kids' bedrooms, went through most of the above-the-counter cupboards in the kitchen then loaded the bags filled with charity items into my car and dropped them off at several used-clothing stores. I bought another twenty-four boxes at Staples Business Depot, assembled them in the living room then, to be on the safe side, brought my "routine maintenance" can of paint, brush, tray and roller with me when I went downstairs to work in my office. I cleared the books off the shelves on the wall below where I'd removed the framed collage of Kurt Vonnegut letters covering up the "69 PLANTS" Officer Val's crew had written there. Despite four coats of paint, it was still the first thing that caught your eye when you stepped into the room: 69 PLANTS. The couple buying the house knew all about the grow-op of course; but the police graffiti put forward specifics I didn't want them or their children to have to see or wonder about, the myths and misconceptions most people had about cannabis liable to make them think that sixty-nine was an alarming number of plants to have growing in this, a family home. The truth was there had only been eight twelve-inch plants under a 600-watt light in the hydroponic unit the night of the raid, two "mother" plants about thirty inches high in soil pots beside it, from which Nicky had taken about three dozen clones that he'd placed in rock wool cubes in a garden tray under a small fluorescent light in the corner. Only about four inches tall at that point, "babies" as Nicky referred to them, even if they all survived until harvest time in about four months, the amount of pot they produced would hardly be considered a trafficking motherlode. Why write anything on the wall in the first place, was my question. After all, Val and her team had made a point of informing us repeatedly during the raid that the house was "gone baby, gone." By whom was 69 PLANTS even supposed to be seen, the demolition crew? A reminder from the police that they shouldn't feel bad that, family home or not, the place had to be torn down because marijuana plants had been found growing there?

Sixteen boxes of books done, maybe twenty more still to go, I put in a call to the gentleman at Revenue Canada whose name and number I'd been given on Friday, left my contact information in a voicemail message, and closed off with a polite plea for a return phone call, adding, without trying to sound pushy, that there was some urgency to the matter.

I managed to get an appointment at 1:30 with Heather, the physiotherapist who'd been treating my knees for "heavy-lifting strain" since September, the time when I was cleaning the house after the raid. It was to the point that going up and down stairs was an agony now, even if I wasn't carrying anything, and because I could only keep my right knee bent and my foot on the gas pedal for a few minutes at a time, I'd resorted to driving with the cruise-control on all the time. To top things off, the staple in my left-shoulder was acting up again; it had never fully recovered from the handcuffs the night of the raid, but because of all the lifting I was doing, there was a constant piercing pain where the staple was pressing against my shoulder socket. The pain was not helped by the fact that lately I'd been leaving the thermostat at 62° to keep the gas bill down. The house was always cold.

On Heather's firm warning, when I came back to the house around 2:30, I turned the heat up to 75. A few minutes later, however, when I crouched to pick up a screwdriver I'd dropped while disassembling the wall-unit in the computer room, I noticed that there was a noticeable squeaking sound coming from the heating vent, originating in the furnace from the sounds of it. My regular "gas guy" Norm Hopper had retired the year before and I hadn't had time to call someone new about doing a cleaning. I was hoping that was the problem.

I headed downstairs to check things out in the furnace room, realizing as I stood there listening, that the squeak from the fan belt on the blower was quickly turning into a high-pitched whine. I switched it off, went back upstairs and, in the classified ads at the back of the community newspaper, found a number for a gas-service technician named Dirk. Once he heard about the predicament I was in — the house-deal closing in two days and the furnace making noises like it needed a cleaning, the people buying the house having two small children and I didn't want them moving into a place without heat — he agreed it was something that needed looking at and said he'd be right over.

Good as his word, Dirk showed up about half an hour later, parked his beaten-up and slightly rusty white panel van in front of the house, hopped out, along with a young helper, hustled into the house and, after quickly shaking my hand, headed straight for the basement, his helper right behind him like they knew exactly where they were going and precisely what they were going to find. I stepped into the furnace room a few seconds behind them, saw Dirk crouching by the main gas valve, turning it with his wrench and putting a red-tagged wire tie on the closed valve, pulling a piece of lead the size of a dime from his shirt pocket and, with a set of pliers, sealing the wire tag so it couldn't be removed.

"What'd you do that for?" I asked him.

"Had to," he said.

"Look, buddy, take the red tag off, turn the furnace on and let's have a listen to it."

"Don't need to."

I made a move for the gas valve. Dirk blocked my way.

"No can do, mister!" he said, putting an aggressive hand on my chest. "Government regulations. I could lose my gas-fitter's licence if I did. Your furnace is a safety hazard. You need a new one."

"You didn't even look at it."

"Like I said, I didn't have to. It's toast."

"So why wouldn't I just ask you to get the fuck out of my house before I called the cops?"

"Call whoever you want, sir. You don't get the red tag removed without a new furnace." He shrugged and shook his head, said: "Suit yourself," handed me his business card and led his helper out of the furnace room to go back upstairs.

I argued with him in the front hall, asked him why the fuck he would have done something like that to me, taking advantage of the situation I was in to extort a new furnace out of me. He took in a breath, shook his head again, as did the helper, and said he would level with me. He knew from what I'd said on the phone the furnace was history. He gave me a garbled explanation that, except for the words "compressor" and "regulator" I couldn't understand, though I was pretty sure it was a load of bullshit. The good news, he said, was that he could put in a brand new Goodman unit for $1,500, a steal at that price since they normally retailed for $2,300. It would take him a half hour to go and pick it up, half an hour to install. Full guarantee. No tax.

I'd been onto him from the moment he arrived and had shot down the stairs ahead of me; knew full well that his purpose, from the beginning, was to shake me down for a new furnace, so I told him to hold on while I called a friend of mine who knew something about them, the friend who'd be paying for the new one, as I was completely out of money.

I stepped away from him and pretended to make the call. Asked Dirk (as though my friend wanted to know) a couple of questions about BTUs and energy-efficiency (things that I'd picked up over the years from my old gas-man Norm Hopper), telling him my friend didn't have cash on him, but could give him a cheque if that was all right. Impatient to get going on the job, Dirk said that was okay by him; it would take him half an hour or so to pick up the new furnace anyway. I told him that would work out well, since that's about what I'd need to drive over to my friend's and get the cheque. We agreed to meet back at the house in about forty-five minutes.

I watched him drive off in his panel-van, went inside and downstairs to my office, over to the garbage pile where I'd tossed the evidence envelopes, and selected a chequebook from John's collection of forgery materials that I thought would do. With some time to spare, I took a trip over to Mr. Beans and had a quick coffee and a muffin, chatted with André about the Leafs then zipped back to the house to let Dirk and his helper go to work installing the new furnace.

Done, as he'd said, in about half an hour, Dirk pointed out to me, as though it should take some of the sting out of getting stung, that Goodman was a top make when it came to furnaces, and I was getting it at a *real* bargain price; something that I said I was glad to hear, and would pass on to the friend who was loaning me the $1,500.

Though it may well have been one of the top makes, the information didn't matter to me in the least since I'd actually had the furnace installed for free, as Dirk the wily gas man would discover when he saw how high the cheque from "Mr. Charles M. Rounthwaite" bounced when he went to cash it. All I hoped was that Mr. Rounthwaite, of 116 Rosedale Gardens Road in Toronto, had got himself a new bank account some time in the past five years. With the trouble my brother might already have caused him, I'd have hated for the poor man to find out that someone with the name Illidge was kiting his cheques again.

As I hadn't eaten a proper dinner since Sunday night at the Bank Note, I decided to drive over to Kelsey's. I thanked Monroe, the manager, for his kindness, good humour and hospitality — and for that of his staff — over the past five months. I told him it was probably the last time I'd be in for quite a while, that I was "changing income brackets." He laughed at that and said he sure knew what that was like; said, too, that it was quite the coincidence because, in two weeks, he was being transferred to a new Kelsey's that was opening up in north Mississauga. As he lived not far from the restaurant and walked to work every day, I kidded him about a move to such a distant location being because of the money Kelsey's was losing due to the generous employee discounts he was giving to non-employees. He laughed, louder this time, and joked that that was *why* they were moving him — it was a new "marketing strategy" that he'd come up with. He told me to order whatever I wanted from the menu — dinner and wine were on him that night.

Hannah had phoned early in the afternoon and invited

me to her Christmas concert at the high school, if I wasn't too busy packing, and of course if I felt up to it. The senior orchestra, in which she played the cello, was performing several numbers, their segment of the concert scheduled for about eight o'clock, she said. She felt a few of the pieces were on the "dud" side, but there were a couple of others more in the Christmas vein that she had a feeling I might enjoy hearing. I reminded her that I hadn't missed one of her concerts yet, and wasn't about to start now. I added that I'd be happy to drive her home afterwards as well, if she wanted.

The concert underway when I got to the school, I squeezed into a standing-room spot just inside the side door of the auditorium. I stayed for the concert's full two hours, the first truly relaxing and enjoyable evening I'd had in a while, the music, in a few cases, of what I'd call professional par. I chatted with the parents of some of her friends and several of her teachers at intermission, met her at the back doors of the school afterwards and drove her home to Julie's.

I gave the concert a rave review, singled out the work of the senior orchestra, in particular the performance of the girl closest to the audience in the second-cello chair. "Oh, wait a minute," I said, "I guess that was you!"

"You're too kind, faw-ya," she chuckled in mock modesty, explained that they could have sounded *so* much better except the second violins, and half the viola section, had been out of tune the whole time they were playing. Ms. Fish, their conductor, had snapped her baton she was so angry with them, so their timing ended up being off as well.

I suggested that there probably weren't that many in the audience who would have noticed, and that the out-of-tune playing brought some character to the music. I said it was about time somebody gave Leroy Anderson's "Sleigh Ride" more of a Stravinsky touch.

"Always looking on the bright side, eh, Dad?"

"You know me," I said, though I admitted I hadn't been that afternoon, and told her about Dirk red-tagging the furnace and paying him with a kited cheque from John's stash.

"Well, at least you got something out of him after all his nonsense," she kidded. She said she felt terrible and apologized profusely that she hadn't been over to the house to give me a hand with the packing yet. Between orchestra rehearsals, homework and assignments, and everything else pre-Christmas going on, there just hadn't been any time. But the good news, she said, was that she'd cleared her schedule; that *her* people, would get in touch with *my* people and, if it was all right, she'd come over after school the next day and put in a few hours. I told her I didn't know I had any "people" but said an after-school visit would be delightful, whether we ended up doing any packing or not. I said I only wanted her to do it if she had time, that there was nothing to worry about, everything on the moving front was rolling along just fine. "It's the least I can do," she said. "Don't worry about the time. I should have come over long before now."

I walked her up to the front steps at Julie's. We hugged and kissed cheeks. She looked me in the eye, said she could tell how tired and frustrated I was with the whole business and, trying to sound encouraging, reminded me that it would all be over with in a couple more days. "You can do it, Dad," she said. "That's what you used to always tell me when I needed perking up. 'Remember Hannah, life is ten percent what happens to us, and ninety percent how we react to it.'"

"Charles Swindoll."

Shivering because of the cold, she kissed me on the cheek again, ran up the steps and went to the front door, turning and flashing me a smile before she opened up. "Just hang in there, Daddio. I love you."

"I love you too, honey."

"See you tomorrow then!"

"I'll have the tape gun all warmed up and ready to go," I said.

It had been a long day and I was beat, too tired to even think about doing any more packing, so I headed back to Callum's. I found him lolling in the steaming hot tub on the deck in his backyard. His face in a blue, phosphorescent glow from the underwater lights, he was sitting back in the foaming tub, puffing a Cohiba cigar, nursing a nearly full glass of what looked like bourbon in his hand, a wide, slightly inebriated smile on his lips as he hoisted the glass and bellowed: "Grab a gar out of the humidor and a glass of this twenty-year-old Tennessee bourbon, Sledge, and get your fat butt into this hot tub right now!"

Though I don't go in for cigars or hot tubs as a rule, I made an exception that night. Poured myself some Tennessee bourbon in the kitchen, retrieved a Cuban cigar from the humidor then went outside, slipped into the warm, frothing water and made myself comfortable in front of one of the Jacuzzi jets.

Callum howled when I told him about the episode with Red-Tag Dirk; said he would have been happy to give me the $1,500 if I'd asked.

"I know you would have, Doctor, and I appreciate it. But it wouldn't have been half as much fun."

"I guess you picked up a few things from your shady brother after all," he said, passing me the lighter.

"I guess I did," I said, taking a sip of the vintage bourbon then firing up the Cohiba.

CHAPTER EIGHTEEN
MOVING DAY

After an eleventh-hour packing frenzy that wound down around 4 a.m., moving was about the last thing I was in the mood for when my cellphone alarm went off at seven o'clock Thursday morning. I was lying under the duvet in my own bed, having thrown caution to the wind and decided it would have been pointless to go back to Callum's when I had to be at the house again by 8 to meet Deshaun, defiant that I was going to spend the last night in the house I'd been living in for ten years lying between my own sheets, my head on my own pillows, my clock radio playing classical music while I drifted off to sleep.

I'd made myself a nice dinner early in the evening (a final barbecue on the 'Broil King' I'd won a number of years ago in Tim Hortons' Roll-Up-The-Rim-To-Win Contest), had a medium-rare beef tenderloin, Parisienne potatoes, asparagus, several glasses of Australian Cabernet with it, then met Nicky outside Julie's house about 10:30. Julie's dog Becca along with us, we walked over to the Rouge River and went down to the beach, had a heart-to-heart talk about the case, the upcoming move, marijuana, the police attitude toward it and, more frustrating, how ignorant so many people were about its benefits, Nicky declaring fervently at one point that, even though we'd been busted, he wasn't going to let it de-*tour* him from the cause. It was merely a roadblock that one day he'd figure out a way around, he knew he would . . . it was just a matter of time.

We stood there by the water in the freezing cold for a good hour, sharing the first joint either of us had smoked in five months, a strain called Sativa Spirit that he'd been working on at the time of the bust, several clones of which he'd given to a friend, who a couple of days ago had come across an ounce or two in the bottom of his freezer and wanted to make sure Nicky got some. A snap and sparkle in the frigid air, the moon shimmering on the water, Nicky talked about his plans for the future, the kinds of things about growing that he wanted to learn and get better at doing; maybe find a doctor who could sign the forms for a Health Canada licence so we could grow again, legally this time.

As rocky as things had been during the autumn, we decided it was good to be moving out of Friendship Avenue, away from people like Mary-Ellen and Wes, Nicky and I laughing as we envisioned appropriate revenge scenarios for what they'd done, schemes that were clever enough to prevent anyone from pinning the pranks on us, which would be our whole point, of course. It was the not knowing that would drive Mary-Ellen around the bend.

When it was time to go, Nicky took in a deep breath of air

and let it out luxuriously, said he had a feeling tomorrow was going to be a "really great day . . ." It was one that I certainly shared at the time, but it quickly became a distant memory the moment I slid out of my warm bed that morning, the cellphone alarm resuming its annoying warble as I went looking for my shoes and clothes amid the warren of packed and half-packed boxes cluttering the cold bedroom. I got dressed, brushed my teeth and, with a couple of Egg McMuffins and coffee at McDonald's in mind, went out to my car about 7:30, only to discover, as I was opening my door, that the front left tire was as flat as could be.

With Deshaun and his movers scheduled to arrive in about an hour, I hoped there was a chance he'd be late and put in a call to Dan at Sure-Stop Auto, one of the neighbourhood car-repair shops. Dan said he was just opening, he didn't have a portable "pig" air compressor at the moment, but that Gord Ralston who ran the auto repair-shop across the road did, and he'd probably let me borrow it if I asked him nicely.

I made it up to Gord's on foot in about twenty minutes, carried the "pig" back to the house and pumped up the tire. I drove up to Dan's and let him plug the leak, then stopped off at McDonald's, as originally planned, for the Egg McMuffins, a coffee for me and a large orange juice for Nicky, who was coming over to help with the move.

Though he had agreed to the plea bargain the Crown had offered, Nicky remained out on bail until it could be put before the court in January. He was still prohibited from being in the house. Julie had called me just as I was heading out to meet him at the beach the night before, telling me that, as his surety, she couldn't give her permission for him to help me with the move. I told her there was no possible way I could handle everything by myself, but that was fine. She and Lenny and the bank could do whatever they wanted with Friendship Avenue; I'd be long gone by morning.

His mother having decided I was serious, Nicky was waiting for me when I got back to the house at 9:15. There was no sign of Deshaun yet, so we slipped inside and had our Egg McMuffins at the kitchen table and went over escape routes that he could use if the police happened to show up, his only other option to say he worked with Deshaun, a good backup plan, or so we thought until the doorbell rang.

Nicky bolted out the sliding-glass doors, shot across the yard and flew over the back fence. I grabbed my paint can and brush by the coat closet and went to answer the door — but it was just Deshaun and his two helpers. The three of them in their late twenties, Deshaun had shoulder-length dreadlocks, while the other two sported Afros tucked under large green-and-yellow Jamaican toques. Deshaun was full of apology about the lateness, saying he'd had to get rid of some things that were in his truck on the way over.

Nicky came walking around the corner, a look of relief on his face, met Deshaun and his crew then showed them into the house so they could lay out their tarps and drop-sheets.

Deshaun's eyes bugged a bit when he saw how much packing still had to be done, but I told him it wasn't as bad as it looked. Everything he was moving to the storage unit was ready to go, labeled with neon yellow Post-It tabs. Purple tabs were on things that I was throwing away, green ones were on things that he was welcome to if he was interested; as to price, we could talk about that when he was done. That sounded good to Deshaun, so we got underway.

Stephen phoned at 10:30 to say the "excrement was

really hitting the whirling blade." The girls were losing it because they hadn't yet received a signed agreement, and were demanding one in the next few hours. Skolnik, the lawyer for Howie Gertz, had upped the amount owed to $93,000. "That's fifteen grand in the past fuckin' week," Stephen joked.

"Nice work if you can get it," I said.

Bill Summers called about half an hour later. Irked and on edge, he said he was extremely disconcerted about the way things were looking. Giving his sternest warning yet, he let me know that the deal was going to die on the table if I didn't resolve matters with Revenue Canada. I told him that's exactly what I'd been trying to do for a week now, but I'd only been given the phone number of the person who might actually be handling my file the previous afternoon, the first name I'd been given turning out to be someone who worked in Indian Affairs. I said I'd already left two messages for the gentleman this morning, but according to the phone greeting it might take up to twenty-four hours for him to return the call.

"We don't have twenty-four hours."

"I told him that in my message, Bill."

"Well, you'd better hope he calls you back."

"I'm hoping," I said, and after I got off the phone with him, put in another call to Mr. Archambault at Revenue Canada.

Lenny phoned just before noon for an update, telling me the buyers were in a panic. Their movers were going to be finished loading their truck by one, the deal on their house having closed about an hour ago. I told him the same thing I'd told Bill: I was waiting to hear back from the guy at Revenue Canada. "But things are going well over here," I said to console him. "I should have everything out and the place spic and span by six."

"They're pretty anxious to get in."

"Well I'm pretty anxious to get out," I said, and let him go.

With two full-load trips to the storage facility, Deshaun, through some kind of genius packing, managed to fit the entire contents of my house into the ten-by-twenty foot unit I'd rented, not an inch to spare when we lowered the door and slapped on the padlock. Back at the house by 1:30, he loaded up his truck with the lamps, chairs and couches he'd agreed to take off my hands. He said $1,050 would probably do it as far as payment went. I pointed out we'd agreed on $850 when we first talked. He said that's right, we did, but the extra two hundred was for the furniture he was taking, which he would resell cheap to people he knew.

"Sounds good to me," I said, too tired to argue, we shook hands and I counted out his cash, twenties and fifties — noticing, though, as Deshaun headed off and I turned to go back in the house, that ever-vigilant Mary-Ellen McCluskey had been peeking out her storm-door watching the whole transaction. I looked over, smiled and waved, but she quickly stepped back and closed the inside door. I suggested to Nicky that we might take a trip to McDonald's for half an hour or so, just in case Mary-Ellen got itchy fingers and, in another act of civic duty, decided to call and report us.

Staying on the safe side, Nicky slipped into the house through the back door when we got home half an hour later; started gathering the stuff together that we were throwing out, which his friend Chris was coming over later to take to the transfer station. A pleasant, ultra-polite and hard-working boy a year older than Nicky, Chris had a father who was in the junk removal business and was loaning Chris his truck and trailer with a hydraulic bed in it, something that would make it a breeze to offload things at the transfer station. My left arm barely functioning, my knees throbbing with all the heavy lifting, I gave Nicky as much of a hand as I could lugging boxes and garbage bags up from the basement, arranged them in piles in the now-empty living room and was standing in the front hall, catching my breath, when my cellphone rang, the caller ID showing "Revenue Canada."

It was Mr. Archambault returning my call. He verified my social insurance number, was quiet for a moment, presumably locating my file, then told me that before he could do anything about lifting the lien against me, I'd have to file my income tax return for the previous year, which he said I'd failed to do. He wondered if I was aware of an $18,800 amount owing from 2001. I explained this was the first I'd heard of it, asked him why the problem wouldn't have presented itself before this. "Well, Mr. Illidge," said Mr. Archambault, "that presents another problem I'm afraid. The tax department placed their lien a year ago, but you wouldn't have heard about it since you didn't file last year. I'm going to need that 2006 return before I can do anything."

"You're saying you want me to send in my last year's income-tax in the next hour?"

"That's the idea."

"But I'm right in the middle of moving, Mr. Archambault," I protested. "There's no way I can get access to my income tax materials right now. And the deal on my house is riding on you lifting the lien — you're going to get the $18,000, I don't see what the big deal is here."

"Without the 2006 return," he said flatly, "there's nothing I can do."

"I don't understand, Mr. Archambault! My house deal is —"

The phone blipped and the line cut out; my battery had died.

I ran inside to see about using Nicky's cell, but he said his battery was running low too and he didn't have his charger with him. It was 2:45, Bill Summers in his last phone call had told me that the Registry Office closed at 4:30; if he didn't have something from Revenue Canada by 3:30, at the latest — and even that was cutting it close because Julie and I still had to come in and sign the papers — he wasn't going to be able to proceed.

I rounded up all the change I could find, hopped in my car and drove up to the neighbourhood pub, the Black Dog, where I knew there was a payphone in the hall by the washrooms. Nobody using it, I dialed the toll-free number, punched in Mr. Archambault's extension and worked on keeping my composure while I waited to see if he was going to pick up.

He answered after five rings, heard it was me, took my social insurance number again, for security reasons, and we resumed our conversation where we'd left off, the matter of my 2006 tax return and when he could expect to receive it.

It was all I could do not to explode into the phone. However I put on the most obsequious voice I could muster, promised I'd send him a completed 2006 tax return by the following Thursday if he would just let the deal on my house close. I said there were children involved, and a divorce proceeding. I explained that I was up against the wall and begging him to please let the deal go through. "*Please*, Mr. Archambault."

"I'm sorry, Mr. Illidge, but we need your 2006 return."

"I'm begging you, Mr. Archambault! I'm down on my knees here and I'm *begging* you to please let the deal go through . . ."

At that moment I saw a man coming out of the washroom off to my right. I put the receiver against my chest and called over, asking him if he could do me a big favour.

"I'm *down on my knees*, Mr. Archambault!" I said into the phone with pointed emphasis and sank to my knees. "There's a man standing right here beside the phone. You can talk to him if you want to — he can tell you. *I'm down on my knees here!*" I said in desperation, pointed to the receiver and passed it to the man.

Clueing in to the the situation, the man held the phone up to his ear. "He's down on his knees all right," he said, handing the receiver back to me, still on my knees as I waited for Mr. Archambault's reply.

Silence for a moment, then for another, Archambault came back on the line and, after getting the names, addresses and phone numbers of two people he could contact in order to ensure that the matter was being taken care of — adding that he would be monitoring my file until he was in receipt of the 2006 return — agreed to send my lawyer Bill Summers a legal waiver by fax in the next half hour.

"Thank you!" I practically shouted into the phone, letting out an exhausted breath as I got to my feet and set the receiver back in its cradle.

"You better go in and have yourself a drink there," the man who'd spoken to Mr. Archambault said, an amused but sympathetic smile on his face.

"I think I'd better," I said, returning his smile, and after calling Summers, Stephen and Lenny with the news, joined him at the bar for a few minutes, picking up the tab for his next rye and ginger ale, the least I could do for his help with the intractable Mr. Archambault.

Back at the house by 3:15, Nicky's friend Chris and his girl-friend Melinda were running boxes, bins and green garbage bags out to Chris's truck, while Nicky was loading lamps, artwork, boxes in which I'd packed dictionaries, my writing materials, computer and personal items into his minivan to take over to Julie's. He'd commandeered the spare bedroom in her basement, which nobody ever used and which she never went into. And there was a lock on the door in case she wanted to go snooping, Nicky apparently the only one with a copy of the key.

I went inside, plugged in my phone to recharge and then brought the vacuum, the mop, and a bucket of cleaning supplies from the laundry room, set them in the alcove beside the stairs in the front hall and took a moment to plot my strategy. Nicky, passing by with the floor lamp from my office, suggested I start upstairs and work down, telling me not to worry about the basement, he'd been cleaning it up as he went along.

"So," I kidded him as he headed for the front door, "are you having a really great day?"

"The best!" he called back over his shoulder, and went outside.

When I hadn't heard from Bill Summers by 3:40, I decided I'd better get myself over to his office and find out if Mr. Archambault had come through with his waiver. He had, according to Bill's secretary, but when she took me into his office, Bill was fuming because he'd been trying to call me for the last twenty minutes and got no answer. The clock was ticking, he said gruffly, made me sit down at his desk, put a pen in my hand and had me sign a Change of Title document and a sheaf of various legal papers, talking fast and explaining their purpose as I signed away.

Since Julie had already been in to see him, he whisked the last page out from under my hand the moment I'd put the dot over the final "I" in my last name. He grabbed his suit-jacket off the back of his chair, mumbled irritably as he was putting it on and huffed, on his way out of the office, that there was no guarantee he'd make it to the Registry Office by 4:30 when it closed, but he'd give it a shot. He said, as we stepped outside and I walked with him to his car, that if he did, he would hold onto the money from the sale in trust for forty-five days; that if there was no agreement between Julie and me on how it was to be divided up, then the funds would be paid into court until such time as we had one. He opened his car door, threw his briefcase into the passenger seat and zoomed out of the parking lot at what, for someone like Bill, seemed an excessively high speed.

Too busy to worry about how things would turn out at the Registry Office, I went home and got started on the cleaning, did the whole upstairs in about an hour, then went to my office in the basement and made a final push to have my books packed and upstairs in the living room ready to go by six, the time by which I was to be out of the house.

A packing demon, feeling I was pretty much on target to meet the deadline, I was sliding a full box of books into the open area at the bottom of the basement stairs when Nicky appeared on the landing halfway up, a worried look on his face: the new owners and their father had just arrived and were waiting in the front hall.

"What time is it?" I asked him.

He checked his cellphone. "6:05."

"How do they seem?" I said, stepping around some boxes and moving for the stairs.

"Not happy," he said.

A couple in their mid-thirties, the woman petite and thin, with short blond hair, her husband dark-haired, a lanky six-foot-six I would say, she broke away from him and the elderly gentleman standing with them, came across the hall and introduced herself. Her name was Carina, she said, turning and introducing her husband, whose name was Joe, and her father-in-law, Hector.

"I guess everything went okay at the Registry Office," I said lightly.

"It was tense there for a while," Carina said, smiling a little uneasily.

"Sorry about that," I said. "My life's been pretty hectic over the last week. You know what it's like when you're moving."

Joe's father laughed and commented, in a strong Spanish accent, that everything was too much of a runaround these days. It wasn't good for us, in his opinion. "No good for the health!" he said waving his hand.

I apologized to Carina and Joe that I wasn't able to be out by six o'clock, and explained that it had just been my son and I and his friend, and we were working as fast as we could. I told them all the warranties, instruction booklets and repair bills were in labeled envelopes on the kitchen counter, gave them my cellphone number and said they could call me any time if there were problems. I said I could promise them I'd be gone by ten o'clock, however under the circumstances that was the best I could do, since there was still work to be done on the garage — I didn't want to leave a mess.

They were visibly disappointed, for which I didn't blame them, but seeing my disheveled look, the cleaning supplies,

Nicky, Chris and Melinda slugging boxes overflowing with books out the front door, I think they got the picture. Joe said that in the big scheme of things it was no problem, they'd just come back at ten. Carina said she was happy with that, so we shook hands all round and they went on their way.

With Chris and Melinda rolling along in the garage, Nicky and I took two van-loads of Staples boxes filled with books over to Julie's. The basement bedroom was already crammed full of other things and there was no space inside the garage, so the only alternative was to stack them against the outside wall, where they'd be sort of sheltered by the eaves.

When we were pulling away after delivering the second load, Nicky asked me whether it was realistic to think about hanging onto a thousand books, when the odds were I'd be living in an apartment, at least for the next little while. He said it was no problem to call up a couple of his friends to help him take them over to the recycling depot at the transfer station. He said he knew how hard it would be to see them thrown out, but he said he didn't know that there was any other option, really. Looking back at the forty or so boxes stacked against the garage wall, a light snow starting to fall, even though I knew it was going to come to this, the books simply had to go, the fact was they'd played such an important part in my life, it was hard for me to imagine not having them around anymore. I told Nicky to make the call to his friends, my only stipulation that I didn't have to go along and give them a hand. "Not an issue," he said. "Think of it this way, Dad. Maybe they'll come back as new books, maybe even some of your own."

"The great book-spirit lives on."

"They'll be *read*-incarnated," he joked, the two of us breaking up at such a novel idea.

By 9:30 everything was out of the house and I was beginning the final clean-up. Chris and Melinda were done in the garage and just sweeping up, chatting and laughing with Nicky while he loaded his electric tools, drills, saws, welding equipment and other "industrial paraphernalia" as he liked to call it, into his Voyager.

I did one last circuit of the house from top to bottom, turning lights off and closing doors behind me as I went. I put our coats and boots, a suitcase with some clothes I was taking back to Callum's, the last bag of garbage, the vacuum and all the cleaning supplies except for the bucket, the mop and the box of Spic and Span, outside on the front porch.

I sponge-mopped the kitchen floor, shut off the lights when I was done and backed my way down the hall; gave the laundry room a once-over then returned to the front hall where Nicky had rolled up the carpet inside the front door, and Melinda was crouched down holding the dustpan for Chris, who finished sweeping up the floor and stepped back onto the front porch. I cleaned the last section of the floor, passed the mop and bucket outside to Nicky and, reaching into the corner beside the door, picked up the can of paint, the painter's cap and the paintbrush and handed those out too. I stood in the door, one hand on the handle, the other on the light switch. I took a final look around, smiled and, as the cops in the raid had, shouted, "You'll never live in this house again!" turned off the hall lights and closed the door for the last time.

Chris's truck was parked on the street in front of the

house, the truck bed and the trailer he was towing packed to the limit. I thanked him and Melinda for coming to the rescue, said we couldn't have done it without them. I gave Chris $250, said it would have been more if I'd had it, but hoped that was okay. He was elated with the payment, saying he and Melinda were just glad they could be of help.

Nicky threw the last few things in his van, closed the hatchback and the side doors and came around the front of the car as I walked up the driveway.

"You saved my life, honey," I said to him as we hugged. "I owe you a big one."

"Didn't I tell you it was going to be a great day?"

"You did," I said. "Though I'm not exactly in a hurry to repeat it, if you know what I mean."

He laughed, said he knew exactly; asked me if I was sure I didn't want to go to Swiss Chalet. He was meeting Chris and Melinda there to have some dinner. Chris was buying. I said that was a tough one, but I was beat and would probably go back to Callum's and have a glass of his Tennessee bourbon, smoke another of his big Cuban cigars and steep my aching knees and back in the hot tub for an hour or so.

It was 9:50 by my dashboard clock when I got in the car. I'd hardly pulled out of the drive behind Nicky when I saw the headlights flip on in two cars parked a few houses down, on the other side of the street. They came past me and in my rearview mirror I saw that they'd turned into the driveway: the new owners.

I continued on down the street almost to the corner, pulled over to the curb and parked. Grabbing a small fare-well present I had in a plastic grocery bag on the passenger seat, I trotted back up the street to Mary-Ellen's house, the lights on upstairs, but the main floor dark, as it usually was by this time of night. I took the little Japanese Buddha from Nicky's growing unit out of the bag, having reattached the still-smiling head with some Krazy Glue. No one about in the street, I scooted in front of the McCluskey's garage, hustled up the walk, hopped onto the porch and set the statue down about three feet back from the door. I rang their bell three times, did it again, like it was urgent, then turned, jumped from the porch and beat it down the street.

I started up the car, pulled a quick U-turn and drove up the street, slowed down as I was passing by Mary-Ellen's house and looked over: the porch light on now, Mary-Ellen still inside at the storm door, Wes had come out, picked up the statue and was holding it up to the porch light so he could make out what was written on the neon yellow Post-It note I'd stuck to the Buddha's chest, a one-word message printed on it in bright blue letters: *PEACE!*

January 27, six months to the day after the raid, I made my final appearance in drug court at Old City Hall for Nicky's sentencing hearing, during which, if the judge agreed to Nicky's plea bargain, I was apparently to have all charges against me dismissed, my bail conditions finally lifted: I'd be free, in other words, to return to 122 Friendship Avenue, the court apparently unaware that I was no longer living there and, as Officer Val and her cargo shorts crew had been prescient enough to predict the night of the raid, never would be again.

Nicky's lawyer, Larry Heffernan, was third in line at the Crown Attorney's lectern, his cellphone in one hand, a sheaf of legal-sized file folders clutched in the other like he was one busy guy, chuckling as he chatted to the lawyer next to him. Carson's lawyer, Leslie, wasn't present that day since the charges against him had been dropped after he signed an affidavit agreeing not to testify in the event our case ever went to trial, which Carson's lawyer had assured him, as Malcolm had me, it never would.

Julie was sitting with Nicky about four rows back from the bar, while I, having arrived a few minutes later, had taken the end seat on the bench that ran along the back wall of the crowded courtroom — realizing, too late, that the police officer standing guard in the corner off to my left, was none other than my no-whistling nemesis, Officer Endicott. Still a few minutes before the judge would arrive, I considered having a little fun with him, for old time's sake; I pursed my lips like I was going to whistle, though didn't actually do so. I snuck a glance at Endicott when his eyes seemed to be on a man causing some commotion at the front of the room, but I wasn't putting anything past the crafty Endicott. He shifted his gaze, stared right at me with a "just try it" look in his eyes. I kept my lips together, waiting for his glare to stiffen in response to my defiance . . . at which point I gave him a thin smile, threw him a nonchalant wink and turned away, not wanting to press my luck. I smiled when I noticed that, unlike in Room 110, where my scheduling appearances had been held, in sentencing court there was no lopsided calendar duct-taped to the wall beside the clock; a sign, it seemed to me, that maybe proceedings of a more serious nature took place here.

Malcolm had told me that things could go either way at these sentencing hearings. Though Nicky had agreed to the Crown's plea bargain — a $3,000 fine to the government, $3,000 to a drug treatment charity of his choice and one year's probation — according to Malcolm it was up to the sentencing judge to accept or reject it; what the Crown had offered was only a recommendation, which the judge was at liberty to change according to his or her view of the particulars in the case.

Something else to understand, Malcolm explained that there were "hawks" and "doves" on the judicial panel. Hawks were hard-line conservatives who had never whiffed marijuana, let alone smoked it, while the doves tended to be more liberal in their judgements, more tuned-in to changing social norms and who probably had smoked pot at some point in their lives, or might, in some cases, even still be doing so.

A few minutes after 9, His Honour Judge Branco entered the court, all rising as a man who looked to be in his early sixties made his way to the bench, shot an unsmiling look at those of us standing in front of him and then sat down. He had broad shoulders, a thick head of black hair, a wide face and a prominent, slightly misshapen nose on which sat a pair of over-size, black-framed glasses. Along with the requisite white collar tabs and black court gown, he wore a crimson-red hood around his shoulders, designating some sort of higher judicial status, I guessed. A certain imperiousness in his bearing did not give me a good feeling, as it suggested Judge Branco might be hawkishly inclined when it came to drugs. He adjusted his glasses with his thumb and index finger and nodded down at the court clerk that he was ready to proceed.

The first case presented by the Crown was put over to another date, the accused ill and in the hospital, Nicky's was called next. This was the first time he'd been in court since the bail hearing, and I knew he was tense about how things would go, but in his white shirt, blue tie and dress pants he looked calm and composed as he walked up to the bar and joined Larry in front of the judge.

At her usual accelerated pace, the lawyer for the Crown

read out the case summary, explained that the accused, Nicholas Bennett Illidge, had pleaded guilty and agreed to a bargain, the terms of which were satisfactory to the Crown. But aggravated by something he'd heard in the case summary, Judge Branco was suddenly boiling mad, up on his feet and, the moment the Crown had finished talking, announcing in a booming voice that he was having *real* trouble understanding what we'd have been doing with over 200 plants in the backyard of a family home. "Where were they living, for crying out loud," I remember him asking, "on the Ponderosa?" The 200-plus figure given in the Crown's case summary was a number I'd never heard before, the backyard location of the plants even more baffling. I felt like getting up and shouting, "I'm having *real* trouble understanding that too, Your Honour. Someone must have mixed up the case files." But I knew Endicott would be on me the moment I opened my mouth, Judge Branco probably more than happy to cite me for contempt, trouble that Nicky didn't need at this point, so I bit my tongue over the erroneous information and let him press on with the perturbed rant he'd segued into: denouncing as deplorable any father who would subject his family to "something as egregious as this," and then have the gall to make one of his kids take the rap for him. His blustery pontificating done after a couple of minutes, he ran his eyes around the silent courtroom, sat down, a little out of breath, and picked up his pen.

Still having real trouble, by the looks of the bothered frown on his face, he leaned forward in his seat and studied the file, lifted his head after a minute and, still greatly disconcerted, directed an accusing glance around the courtroom until his eyes fell squarely on me, the only white adult male not affiliated with the court. He kept the stare going when the Crown approached the bench and said something to him that I wasn't able to hear, after which he threw me a last hot glare, shook his head in evident disagreement with the plea bargain but, after a reprimanding glance at the Crown, reluctantly signed it and told Nicky he was free to go.

I met him in the hall outside the courtroom, hugged him, told him I was proud of the way he'd conducted himself in front of the over-the-top judge, the two of us agreeing he was something you'd expect to see in a Cheech and Chong comedy — a nutjob right up there with old Officer Val.

Receiving pointed looks from his mother, Nicky said he'd talk to me later, and walked over to join her and Larry, who were conferring nearby. Larry noticed that I was looking in his direction. He kept talking to Julie but raised his voice loud enough so that I'd be sure to hear him tell her: "Like the judge said, it was a case of the son taking the rap for his father!" No doubt the defence Larry would use with Julie's family when the time came to explain why, for $15,000, they'd ended up with Nicky pleading guilty as charged, while the real culprit was walking away scot-free — instead of heading off to the penitentiary for several years, where they all felt I deserved to be.

I stared over, considered, as a retaliatory move, walking up to Larry and letting him know, in similarly loud and condemning tones, that I was onto his fake phone call scam, and had been all along. I decided, though, to stick to higher ground; gave him my best close-lipped grin, flashed him the peace-sign then turned and made my way down the hall toward the exit.

A frigid January day outside, the old tower clock chimed the hour above me as I paused for a moment at the top of the courthouse steps, hands in my coat pockets, my breath fogging in the chill air, thinking about the "rap" that Branco, and now Larry and Julie, were accusing me of having cravenly dodged. Here I'd had my home invaded by gun-toting police based on a snitch phone call from a busybody next-door neighbour. Along with my children, I'd been harassed, abused and traumatized in my own living room for two hours by an unhinged and possibly sociopathic police officer, while her equally vicious squad members vandalized my house searching for drugs that weren't there, Carson, Nicky and I aware, at every moment, that the slightest wrong move on our part could have resulted in our being shot: "resisting arrest" as the cops would have deemed it, justified in their use of "lethal force" because they'd have "feared for their lives."

If that wasn't enough, I'd been falsely accused of being a cocaine dealer, a marijuana trafficker and the leader of an organized gang; in their arrest report the police had lied about my home being riddled with toxic mould, merely to fuck me up a little more than they already had, then presented it to me as a fait accompli worth laughing about that the federal government would confiscate my house and have it torn down, leaving me liable, according to the cops, for so many lawsuits that I'd have them "coming out my ass for years."

I'd watched my son wrongly convicted of drug trafficking because of a fee-churning, incompetent lawyer, and had just been disparaged and publicly outed as a criminal by a loud-mouthed buffoon of a judge for, in his personal opinion, hanging my son out to dry by forcing him to "take the rap" for something that he'd decided was my fault.

I was without a home, and had been for six months, dead broke, getting by on handouts from my friends, living out of the trunk of my car, my place of work taken away from me, unemployed and, at fifty-six years of age, probably unemployable. All my possessions, with the exception of a bed, my computer, some books, some clothes, some dishes and pots and pans, had been thrown away, my children, if they weren't upset enough, forced to go and live with their mother and cope with the very issues that had brought them to my house in the first place.

None of this was the end of the world, of course, but what I wanted to know, as I headed down the courthouse steps to grab a coffee at the Tim Hortons across the street, was just how much more of this so-called "rap" people were expecting me to take?

Though I was scheduled to appear at another hearing three days later, at the Ontario Court of Justice, just across from City Hall on University Avenue, this time to sign away the proceeds of the sale of 122 Friendship to Skolnik, on behalf of Howie Gertz ($92,000); Julie and her eldest sister Carol ($80,000), and several other creditors who'd crawled out of the woodwork with judgements against me ($20,000), I decided that I'd had my fill of the justice system for now, and notified Julie's lawyer Victoria, that I wouldn't be in attendance at the hearing; asking her if she'd be good enough to let the other interested parties know on my behalf.

Julie's sister Carol had tried to lawyer me to death when Julie and I first separated; she'd never really liked me and, in truth, I'd never really liked her that much. It was Carol who'd been Julie's principal enabler over the years, something I still had difficulty forgiving her for. But she and her family had always been there for our children, and would continue to be, that went without saying. They'd also borne the brunt of the worst of Julie's illness, had managed to help her try cleaning up her act, get her life back in order and start down the road to recovery. I would always be thankful to them, and indeed, felt badly that they were getting about $50,000 less than they might otherwise have been entitled to.

No, it was the $92,000 being claimed by Howie Gertz that had me hesitating to sign any agreement. I'd been thinking over what my lawyer Stephen had said about walking away any time I wanted. If I refused to sign, the proceeds of the house sale were to be paid into court, and would remain there until such time as I did feel like signing. It was a "Catch-23" situation, as Stephen's bankruptcy expert Al had pointed out: "If you screw Howie, you end up screwing your wife and kids, metaphorically speaking of course."

Victoria got back to me right away about my upcoming absence from the hearing, in a panic that I was intending to let the $225,000 proceeds of the sale be paid into court, her client to receive no money. She asked what it would take for me to sign the agreement, adding that, considering I'd described my circumstances as destitute, they *might* be able to squeeze a little bit out to alleviate that, the emphasis on "little bit," of course. I suggested that $5,000 wouldn't go amiss, a figure Victoria confirmed, within a few minutes, that her client could live with.

Not having heard otherwise, my assumption that things had proceeded without a hitch at the settlement hearing, a judge's order dispersing my funds came in the mail three days later, a sixteen-page document with His Honour's messily handwritten *Nota Bene* part way down the last page, indicating that $1,000 was to be deducted from the $5,000 settlement for court costs. I wondered how he'd arrived at that particular amount as the penalty for not showing up to watch my money being given away, but considering I was down to the several dollars in loose change that I had in my pocket, four thousand wasn't too bad.

I duly headed off to the Attorney General's office the next morning to collect my windfall, the building near Yonge and Dundas in the heart of downtown. I parked illegally, ran two blocks to the office and, after a ten-minute wait before my number was called, presented myself at the cashier's wicket, handed over the judicial order and asked when a cheque would be ready. The clerk, a guy maybe in his early thirties, perused my document briefly then asked if he could see two pieces of photo ID. I had only one, my driver's licence.

"Unfortunately," the clerk said, "I'm required to ask for two. A valid passport would do, or an affidavit from a lawyer attesting to the fact you're who you say you are." He said he'd go ahead and put the cheque request through, but it wouldn't be released to me until they'd verified my identity with that second piece of ID.

I explained that I didn't have an up-to-date passport (it had gone missing in the raid), and lawyers charged $150 minimum for an affidavit, $150 that I didn't happen to have. "Unfortunately, sir," he said, "I can't do anything about it. These are the Attorney General's office protocols. Sorry."

I drove over to Malcolm's that night, had him do me up the required affidavit, and headed back down to the Attorney General's office first thing next morning. I turned off Dundas, three blocks west of the building, onto a street behind Old City Hall (I'd parked there whenever I came to court) and went on the prowl for a meter, four dollars or so in change in my pocket, the last of my money.

Moving slowly, the parking spaces all taken, no sign of

any drivers returning to their cars anytime soon, I was about halfway down the block when I noticed a woman in a stunning, calf-length black fur coat standing by the door of a white Cadillac Escalade that was parked at a meter across the street. She had her arm in the air and it looked like she was waving at me, calling out something that I couldn't hear.

"You want my space?" I heard her say when I lowered my window. "I've got two hours left!"

"Thanks!" I said, gave her a thumbs up, made a U-turn then slipped into the spot when she drove off.

It was -10°C, -17 with the wind-chill, according to the radio, the three-block jaunt along Dundas Street a cold one — even people who were well bundled-up looked anxious for the light to change at Bay Street. As I waited with them, I happened to see a homeless guy, maybe in his fifties, though he looked much older, sitting on the curb off to my left. Long-haired, bearded, a weather-beaten face with not much in the way of teeth, he was wearing a tattered brown overcoat, nothing on his head, no gloves and had only one leg, a grey wool sock on his good foot, but a hole through which the nail of his big toe was sticking.

He saw us waiting, put on his best smile and muttered something I couldn't hear because of the traffic noise. The light turned green, people started forward, and I stepped quickly over to the homeless guy, took out the two toonies that I'd saved on parking and put them in his one hand. With his other he grabbed me fiercely by the wrist, his fingers the coldest things I think I've ever felt. "Hey, buddy," he said in a gravelly voice, "thanks a lot, eh?"

"If I had more, I'd give it to you, buddy," I said, and withdrew my now freezing hand and hurried across the street.

"God bless and good luck to you, buddy!" I heard him call out behind me.

A young woman was working the cashier's wicket that day. I gave her my name, explained about the second piece of ID and passed her the affidavit from Malcolm. She had me sign my name in a few places, issued me a receipt and handed over my envelope. I took a moment, opened it up and looked to make sure everything was in order.

I guess in their scrupulous attention to "protocols," the Attorney General's office had overlooked the scribbled *Nota Bene* from the judge on the last page of his order, since the cheque was made out for the full $5,000.

Hustling back along Dundas Street, I made a point of crossing at the lights on the north side of Bay so I could share the news with the one-legged homeless guy. Still at his pan-handling post, I walked up to him, reached down and shook his hand.

"I just made a thousand bucks because of you!" I shouted over the street noise.

"You did?"

"I let you have those toonies, then an error in my favor gave me a thousand bucks more than I was supposed to get. Thanks!"

"Any time, buddy!" he said, cracking a toothless smile. "Any time . . ."

"What's your name?"

"Bill!"

"What's your last name?"

"Alldrich!"

"Bill Alldrich."

"That's it!"

"Good luck to you, Bill."

"I'll need it!" he said, laughing uproariously at his own grim joke until he started coughing, and I went on my way back to the car.

CHAPTER **TWENTY**
MRS. POLITYKA

With the police returning the $1,000 they'd taken from Nicky's safe the night of the raid (they'd called me to come and pick up the cash at the Evidence Centre, the money that had supposedly been the proceeds of his trafficking), as well as the $2,000 several friends were generous enough to lend me, I was able to rent a recently renovated basement apartment in a small bungalow not far from Julie's, where the kids were living. The house overlooked a ravine, was a fifteen-minute walk from the library, Mr. Beans' coffee shop and close to the beach, where, as it turned out, I ended up spending a fair bit of my time after determining that my landlords Jean and Andy, along with their daughter Lois, who lived with them, were serious alcoholics. They drank from the time they got up, usually around noon, until four or five in the morning, when they stopped shouting at one another, and either passed out on the living-room couch, or staggered down the hall and flopped into bed. They were large people, and sometimes, if they missed the bed, their bodies would hit the floor with such a horrendous thud (their bedrooms being right above mine) that I'd lie there praying the ceiling joists didn't give out from the weighty impact.

The three of them were also chain-smokers. Andy was the worst offender, according to Jean. She was always complaining about the new burn marks she was finding on the carpet and the couch where he'd been sitting, scolding him and giving him stern warnings that it was just a question of time before the whole place went up in flames.

Nights when heavier drinking was going on, I'd wait till they were asleep, take my flashlight, run upstairs and, the door to their apartment always open, pop into the living room and check for still-smoking butts, stub them out if I found them and return to my apartment, crossing my fingers that they hadn't taken any to the bedroom with them. All of them were usually so far gone at that point — Dante's inferno could have been raging around them, and I don't think they'd have lost a minute's sleep.

The fire, when it finally came, wasn't due to their cigarette smoking, however. It started in the electrical panel, located on the wall above and a few feet over from my bed, the original box that had been installed when the house was built forty or so years ago. It was the loud crackling that woke me up, a little before 5 a.m., sparks like fireworks flares shooting halfway across the room, the wires in flames in several places, more igniting every few seconds.

I happened to have a couple of boxes of baking-soda in the fridge that I used to kill the fire. When Jean and Andy came downstairs the next morning to find out why their power wasn't on, I told them that I was going to find somewhere else to live. Two days later I moved into an apartment that Nicky had rented on a quiet street about ten minutes west of Jean and Andy's.

His landlord was a retired electrician named Rick. Nicky's apartment was on the main floor in the front part of the house, Rick lived in the rear. Nicky was doing so well with the landscaping business he'd started that he found he could afford his own place. I gave him a hand with his lawn-cutting and landscaping, started work on what I thought would make an interesting novel, and often went for walks around the corner to the cemetery grounds behind the Anglican Church where, by a weird coincidence, my mother's parents were buried — Thomas James Shea and Viola Grace Robinson, both "At Rest" according to their gravestone.

While Thomas James had passed away when I was twelve, I'd never known Viola Grace. She died at the age of fifty, shortly after a two-year stay in a lunatic asylum, as they called them in those days, in Whitby, Ontario, just east of Toronto. My Aunt Mary had explained to me once that Vi, as she was known, never recovered from the effects of the shock therapy she'd received in the psychiatric hospital. Four months after she'd been released, the Bleaks were back as bad as ever. She suffered a fatal heart attack on September 3, 1950, a year to the day before I was born. My birthday coinciding with the anniversary of my grandmother's death, the weeks leading up to it were the bleakest of the year for my mother.

I did most of my thinking there beside Viola's gravestone. I felt a connection to her now that I knew, from firsthand experience, a little of what she must have gone through. One day I showed up and someone had left a lawn chair for me off to the side of the plot. I went to sit down on it, but saw that a four-leaf clover laminated in clear plastic had been left on one of the arms, further proof, if I needed any, that besides Grandma Vi, somebody else was watching over me too.

Nicky had sold his Plymouth Voyager for scrap — it had close to 400,000 km on it, and was in need of $2,500 worth of repairs — and was driving a new Ford Ranger truck. His Aunt Carol, impressed with his landscaping success, agreed to co-sign the car loan for him, but with only one parking space at Rick's and his mother no longer willing to have it sit in her driveway, Nicky had to do something about his 1995 Monte Carlo. It was his pride and joy, but to his disappointment it had never been quite the same after the night of the raid. It ran fine and the body was in good shape, but it needed some major work (transmission, cooling system, brake lines) to make it drivable, the cost of which was out of Nicky's range, as was the $500 in extra insurance that he'd have to pay if he did get "The Monty" back on the road again.

He'd brought it over from Julie's while Rick was in Panama over the winter, in hopes of having his mechanic certify it so he could put it up for sale.

I was out the afternoon he took it to his mechanic, Mike, whose shop was along the alley that ran behind the plaza at the bottom of our street. I got home a little after 5, was having a beer and thinking about what we'd do for dinner, when Nicky phoned. He'd just picked up the Monty and was making his way along the alley, filling me in on Mike's assessment that Nicky would end up spending far more money fixing the car than he'd ever get out of it, so his advice was to sell it for—

"Shit," Nicky said into the phone. "I'm just coming out

to the Swiss Chalet parking lot, and there's two cops with takeout heading back to their cruiser."

"Why don't you back down the alley to Mike's?"

"I think they might have seen me. It would look too obvious."

"But you'd still be on private property. They can't touch you till you hit the street."

"I'm not doing anything wrong. I'll just wait till they leave."

The parking lot was six houses down on the same side of the street as Rick's. I came out to the front porch and could see The Monty sitting at the end of the alleyway behind the restaurant, the cops approaching their cruiser with the Swiss Chalet takeout bags, the black cop slipping behind the wheel, his partner, a short white guy, taking the passenger seat.

"Okay, they're going," said Nicky, as the patrol car pulled out and turned for the exit. "Crap. The guy flashed his lights. He wants me to go first."

"Maybe I should come down, just in case."

"He flashed his lights again. I'll have to go."

"Keep your phone on."

The Monty moved forward slowly, the patrol car pulled up behind, waited for Nicky to turn onto the street then followed him — roof-lights flashing and alarm-buzzer sounding instantly, Nicky with no choice but to pull over to the curb.

On the sidewalk in front of Rick's now, I watched the black cop step out of the patrol car, hook his thumbs in his gun belt, walk up to the driver's-side door and knock on the window.

I heard the loud raps, the sound of the power window going down, told Nicky again to be sure and keep his phone on.

"You're a drug trafficker," I heard the black cop say.

"No, I'm not," Nicky said.

"You saying our computer's wrong?"

"No."

"Got any drugs with you in there today?"

"No I haven't, Officer."

"You sure, now?"

"Yes, I'm sure."

"Maybe we better see. Get out of the car."

He stepped back, thumbs hooked in his gun belt again. "Leave the phone inside," I heard him say as Nicky was getting out of The Monty. "Turn it off, too," he added.

As I watched from the porch, the black cop motioned Nicky back to the cruiser, had him put his hands on the front hood and spread his legs while the white cop patted him down for weapons.

Finding Nicky clean, the black cop had his partner start searching The Monty, pointing at Nicky like he was telling him to stay right where he was, and then returned to the cruiser, where he opened one of the takeout bags and began dipping into the French fries.

The white cop finished his search — no drugs after all — took a pen and a small black notepad in which he wrote some things down before pulling a ticket pad from inside his jacket, which he started filling out.

He handed the summons to Nicky when he was done, pointed back down the street to the Swiss Chalet parking lot. Nicky pointed up the street at Rick's house. The white cop shook his head, a cue for the black guy to get out of the cruiser and come forward, brushing salt from the French fries off his hands. He, too, pointed back to the restaurant parking lot.

Nicky hopped in The Monty, three houses down from

Rick's at this point. He started up, made a U-turn and, under the watchful eye of the two cops, returned to the Swiss Chalet lot and parked it.

The cops turned their roof-lights off, pulled a U-turn and went on their way.

Nicky walked up the street, the two of us standing on the sidewalk in front of Rick's. They'd charged him with operating a motor vehicle without insurance. A $5,000 fine upon conviction. There was a court date on the ticket if he wanted to fight it. Because The Monty was uninsured, they'd made him take it back to the Swiss Chalet. He was to call a tow truck to bring it home. If he had any thoughts about doing it himself, they warned him that they'd give him another $5,000 fine and have him arrested, telling him they monitored these things.

We waited about fifteen minutes, until we knew the cops would be tucking into their chicken dinners, then I walked down and brought The Monty back to Rick's. The two of us stunned more than anything by what had just gone on, while we were eating dinner, Nicky, with his innate optimism, said he wasn't going to let it de-tour him; he had his defence all worked out. He felt sure that once the judge heard he was driving a new, fully insured vehicle and had been for some time, understood that the Monte Carlo was being sold for scrap and there'd never been any intention of putting it on the road, the charges against him would be dropped. "I mean, how much sense does it make for me to pay a $5,000 fine on a car that doesn't exist anymore?" he wanted to know.

It didn't, as things turned out. The police lied, neglected to mention they'd been on dinner break in a restaurant parking lot, and that the black cop had profiled him as a drug trafficker based on the fact Nicky was driving a black Chevy

Monte Carlo with tinted windows. Nicky's defence was that the cops had basically entrapped him on private property. He told the judge he'd offered to take the cops down the alley for his mechanic to verify his story, but they wouldn't do it.

The judge wasn't buying it either, and referred to the police "disclosure of evidence" for the case. He held up a photocopy of a three-by-five-inch piece of notepaper (a copy of which had been handed to Nicky when he took the stand) that had six lines of hastily scrawled writing on it, the first four lines indecipherable, the last two reading:

"*Car insured.*"

"*No.*"

And announced he was imposing the full $5,000 fine.

"Will you be taking care of that today, Mr. Illidge?"

"No, Your Honour," Nicky said.

"Check with the cashier in the court clerk's office, then."

When his insurance company got wind of the conviction a few weeks later, they canceled the policy on his Ranger. If he was caught driving it now, the fine for a second offence was $10,000.

Nicky called various companies for quotes, the cheapest offering him coverage at $1,180 per month, first and last payments due on signing: $2,360 that Nicky didn't have — and wouldn't be able to come up with, without the use of his Ranger. By the time the no-insurance fine was paid, and the $1,180 per month in insurance was added in, Nicky calculated that in four years, when his truck was paid off, he'd have shelled out over $65,000 in insurance, enough to have bought himself five brand new Ford Rangers. How crazy was that?

Nicky gave Rick his notice, discouraged that, after a year of living on his own, he was headed back to his mother's, into a house she'd rented near Broadview and Danforth where she allowed him to park the Ranger until he could afford to insure it.

Without any income, his landscaping business impossible to operate without his truck, aside from the loss of independence, Nicky had no real regrets about leaving Rick's since, as well as a terrible landlord, he'd turned out to be quite the jerk, but it meant that I no longer had a place to live or work. The blunt reality was that I had no idea how I was going to make money doing anything other than writing. I'd be turning fifty-seven on my next birthday. Getting a conventional job of any kind was pretty much out of the question, as it had been in the eight years since I'd left teaching. The feedback I almost always received on any applications I submitted, was that I was overqualified, over-experienced and, though they weren't allowed to say so, over-aged.

I called up an old friend, Kelly Wansborough, for some advice. Wansie someone who never hesitated to call a spade a spade, he told me straight out that it was time to drop my high-minded scruples, let go of my vanity and pride and face up to the fact I was in desperate straits and should have no qualms about applying for welfare. "That's what it's there for, Paul," he said. "You've paid hundreds of thousands of dollars in taxes over the years, you have no liquid assets, no pension, no job — no likelihood of finding one anytime soon — and no place to live. Either that or book a cot at the Harbour Light Shelter, do up an 'in-need-of-spare-change' sign, and start hanging around with your homeless brethren panhandling outside Tim Hortons at Bloor and Yonge."

My scruples not quite as pronounced as Wansie had made them out to be, I looked up the phone number of the nearest "Ontario Works" office and made the call. Along with "social assistance," Ontario Works was the new term for welfare, this according to the businesslike but pleasant fellow who took my information. When he learned about my circumstances, he asked for authorization to conduct an "intake" interview on the spot: questions about basic identification, finances (none), assets (none), living arrangements ("the street"), employment status (none), at the conclusion of which he gave me an appointment to meet with "Number 208" two days later, a Friday, at a Toronto Social Services office in east Scarborough, about a fifteen-minute drive from Rick's, the address that I'd given as the last place I'd resided.

Assured by the intake worker that I'd be accepted into the welfare fold, I still needed to find somewhere to live. Friends that I'd known long enough to ask about letting me move in had told me that the drug bust *did* put "a bit of a taint" on things. They'd sort of assumed that it was drug-trafficking that had led me to this unfortunate impasse in my life, the thought of a marijuana dealer living under their roof not a very comfortable one. On top of which, as was pointed out to me, I didn't have a job, few prospects of obtaining one in the foreseeable future, people could be worried that once I was in, they'd never get me out, plus as one friend I ventured to ask for accommodation put it, "$350 to pay in rent?" (The maximum Ontario Works would allow.) "I wouldn't get your hopes up, Paul."

Adam Cromartie the only one of my friends I hadn't asked about moving in, I called him up and broached the idea. We'd been friends since junior high school. He'd been my screenwriting partner for ten years before I got married and was best man at my wedding. He'd sold his house and was in the process of moving into an apartment a few blocks away, a two-bedroom spot with a fireplace and a huge living room, in the basement of a large house that backed onto the Scarborough Bluffs. I was painting it for him and, in about two weeks, was planning to help him move in.

I briefed him on the upcoming welfare appointment, telling him that if things worked out, I could offer $350, even the full $570 of my cheque if necessary for rent. Food I would take care of, with money Nicky would be able to give me from time to time, now that he was making some again. He'd decided to pay the $1,180 a month car insurance, seeing it as an incentive for he and his partner, Chris, to keep "growing" the metal recycling business they'd started. I promised Cromartie I'd stay out of his way, said I'd be busy working on my book about the drug-squad raid and its aftermath (for which I'd picked up a contract with a Toronto publisher a few weeks earlier), and to top things off, told him I'd be more than happy to make dinner each night, since he was out on the road all day with his computer electronics business.

Knowing the jam I was in, that I wouldn't be asking him unless it was a last resort, Cromartie agreed to take me in — though only if the welfare money came through; things were tight for him financially too. Fair enough, I agreed, and armed with the name of his landlord and a copy of his rental agreement, I drove to the office in northeast Scarborough on the day of my appointment with #208.

Larger than I anticipated it would be, the waiting area in the Social Services office was a wide, low-ceilinged room with a row of grey, plastic backless seats fixed to the wall under the window, none of them occupied. There were several grey corridors angling off to doors that looked like they opened onto other corridors, and a glassed-in reception kiosk in the centre of the office where, after taking a numbered chit from the dispenser at the entrance, I waited my turn.

My number was called after about five minutes, the clock on the back wall of the reception kiosk showing 10:16 as I presented myself at the speaker built into the glass, leaned down, said my name into it and waited for one of the three women sitting at computers on the other side of the glass to stand up and come over to the microphone on their side of the glass. The one who did peered out at me for a moment then asked me to repeat my name. I did, she said it back to me, pronouncing it terribly. No stranger to such confusion, I slowly spelled it out for her, pronounced it the correct way, adding the helpful information that it started with an 'I.' She studied the computer screen for a few seconds, said she wasn't able to find it. She sighed in some frustration, scrolled up and down the screen again . . . and gave a wide-eyed start when it eventually popped into view.

Back at the microphone again, she told me to have a seat until Agent 208 was ready to see me. Whether it was the dead-serious way she'd said it or because the woman seemed to be about my age, I couldn't resist quipping into the speaker that it was too bad it wasn't Agent 99 I was waiting to see (the svelte brunette actress Barbara Feldon in the 1960s TV sitcom *Get Smart*). The woman either found the humour stupid (which it probably was), in poor taste, or had no idea what I was talking about. She gave me a prim, pursed-lip frown, told me tersely to take a seat then turned away and went back to her desk, the two other women staring over from theirs, disapproving frowns on their faces as well.

To my surprise (considering I'd appeared to offend her),

the woman to whom I'd made the *Get Smart* crack was on her feet, back at the mike and calling my name in a matter of minutes, instructing me to proceed to door number four, which I did, the electric lock buzzing for a second as I approached. When the grey steel door opened, I headed straight ahead down a grey, fluorescent-lit corridor past a series of numbered doors with small viewing-windows in them. Room 109, where I'd been told I was to meet #208, was on my left about halfway down the hall.

I opened the door and stepped into what I thought would be an office of some sort but, except for the fact it didn't have a bed, a toilet or a surveillance camera recording things (at least that I could tell), had the look of a jail cell about it — better painted but with the same low-wattage light behind a wire screen on the ceiling. The bare walls were an almond-beige colour, there were two black metal frame and fabric chairs in front of a chocolate-brown melamine counter, secured to the walls on both sides, a small space on the other side where there was a black swivel office chair in front of a computer, whose base, I noticed, was locked to an eyebolt on the desk unit. About three feet beyond it there was a brown door with a small viewing-window in it that looked out to a larger, brightly lit yellow corridor — from which a blond-haired woman in arty, large-frame glasses was peeking in at me, unlocking and opening the door after completing her brief visual inspection. Slipping into the room, she introduced herself, somewhat stiffly, as #208; adding, much less formally as she took her seat, that I could also refer to her as "Mrs. Polityka" if I wanted to.

"That's an interesting last-name," I said after we shook hands and I'd sat down. "Politica."

"The second "I" is a "Y," she smiled. "And the C is actually a K. People often make that mistake."

"Polityka. Just something about those second 'I's', isn't there? They can throw people off."

She glanced down at the file folder she had with her.

"I see what you mean. 'Illyich . . .'"

"Illidge," I said, correcting her.

"Sounds Russian."

"I'm told it was at one time. Peter *Illyich* Tchaikovsky? Vladimir *Illyich* Ulyanov?"

"Who?" Mrs. Polityka asked.

"Lenin? The leader of the Russian Revolution?"

"Well," she said, impressed. "Isn't that interesting."

"I've always thought so," I said. "Though it's not exactly something you can put on a job résumé."

She laughed at the joke, took off her glasses and set them on the desk, crossed her arms, sat back in the chair and asked me to tell her how I happened to find myself here at Ontario Works applying for social assistance.

I gave her a précis version of what had happened to me in the last two years, explained that I had no money, no assets, no place to live as of the end of the month, and no identification except my driver's licence. When she asked if I was currently employed, I said I wasn't, in a technical sense, but as a writer and ghostwriter I was always working at something, the only problem that the work didn't pay much, and rarely on a regular basis.

Mrs. Polityka said she'd never heard of someone being a ghostwriter before; asked me what that was. My friend Dean Tansey having recently sent a published copy of the book that I'd written for a judge on the history of the criminal insanity defence, I took it out of my writing bag and showed it to her, along with copies of some of my Shakespeare novels, and several other titles of which I was the author that I'd brought with me just in case. I pointed out my name, a glowing reference, in the Acknowledgements section at the back of the book I'd written for the judge, explaining to Mrs. Polityka that I'd done the actual writing of the manuscript, based on his notes and research, though it was published under his name. "I was the ghost," I said. "Something else that's a little hard to put down on your résumé." She chuckled, returned the book and we got down to business.

Over the next fifteen minutes she gave me a certified cheque for $35 to get a replacement birth certificate, authorized me to receive my two blood pressure prescriptions every month from Ontario Works, along with $570, the standard single-person supplement, adding that she'd also give me $250 toward the cost of moving into my friend's apartment, $820 in total that she said would be deposited in my bank account within forty-eight hours.

I thanked her for all her help; told her she'd just saved my life and it was nice to know "the system" was actually working. She said they tried to do their best for clients, though it wasn't always that easy, letting me know that since my new address at Adam Cromartie's was in the Central, rather than the Eastern service area (she wasn't sure why they'd even sent me to this office in the first place), my file would likely be transferred to another worker within a month or two, from whom I'd be hearing as soon as that happened. We shook hands; she smiled and wished me good luck with the ghostwriting then left the room, the lock clicking in the door behind her.

Walking through the waiting area on my way out, the woman I'd checked in with when I arrived was standing at the microphone having just called someone's name. She followed me with her eyes, suspicious for a moment until she recognized who it was. A hint of a smile spreading across her face as I sauntered past, maybe she'd got the Agent 99 joke after all.

As good as her word, the $820 from Mrs. Polityka appeared in my bank account three days later. It seemed almost too good to be true, but I'd averted disaster, Nicky, Hannah and Carson were more than a little relieved, Adam was happy for the company and the extra money that would be coming in, and I was living on a quiet, well-treed street in a house on the Scarborough Bluffs overlooking Lake Ontario, my writing desk set up across from my bed, my room the one I'd just painted for Adam a month earlier. Things, as they say, were starting to look up.

CHAPTER **TWENTY-ONE**
MR. JOHN

I lived at Cromartie's until after Christmas, then arranged, in January 2010, to fly to Nova Scotia to live with Don Beamish in East Margaree, a small fishing village on the northwest coast of Cape Breton Island. We'd talked about the idea when he was in town for the One of a Kind Craft Show at the end of November, my third annual appearance as smooth-talking cutting board salesman "Larch Wood." Don would be travelling to trade shows in the United States all of February and the first part of March. His place would be empty and I could stay there rent-free if I'd look after his golden retriever Lily for him. Don thought it would be an ideal place for me to start working on my book.

The flight to Halifax was with Porter Airlines, which operates out of the Toronto Island Airport. The terminal was only a ten-minute drive from where, as far as I knew, my brother John was still living, so I called him up to see if, rather than come all the way in from Cromartie's by 5:30 a.m., I could spend the night at his place and have him drop me off at the Porter terminal the morning of my flight.

He called me back several days later and left directions to an Italian restaurant on Queen Street East called "Adriano's," where I was to meet him at 6:30 the night before my flight. Nicky drove me to the restaurant and we transferred the overweight, packed-within-an-inch-of-their-lives suitcases to the back seat of John's Mercedes E-220, Nicky and I agreeing, when we were done, that it was going to be weird being separated after seeing each other every day for almost two years.

Nicky said he would mail me two or three hundred dollars in cash and my blood-pressure pills every month; maybe include a little bit of vacuum-sealed "toodle" material as well. There was email, of course, plus we could talk on the phone every few weeks and keep each other posted on developments. Nicky was determined to find a decent apartment for us by the time I came home from Nova Scotia in the spring. His and Chris's metal-recycling business was really starting to pick up, their sales to various metal companies were on the rise, and it was still only January, a sign of how much growth there could be by March, when spring cleaning season began. Nicky was "unde*toured*," confident that by then his share of the revenue would be more than enough to cover the rent on a new place for us to live.

In the meantime, he was prepared to make the best of it at his mother's, who was away for a little while. We had a good chuckle about John's top-of-the-line Mercedes. Glossy black and gleaming under the parking lot's lights, it was by far the most expensive vehicle in the lot — the E-220 a $90,000 job Nicky was sure. "I guess the bankruptcy business is really booming," he said as he locked the car and handed me the keys; pointing out, just in case I hadn't noticed, John's personalized licence plate: "RSKY BZNS." He always liked to have it on at least one of the luxury cars he drove.

Adriano's was a small place, with dark Italian décor, red globe candles burning on the mostly unoccupied tables, red cloth-shades on the lights hanging above them, John was having a glass of white wine and nibbling on his perennial appetizer: garlic bread topped with a slice of tomato, fresh basil and bocconcini cheese. He offered me a piece as I was sliding into the banquette, "The best you'll ever have," he said, and set the platter on the table in front of me. "So how's Nick?" he said.

"Good," I said lightly. "He's just taking your car for a little spin around the block."

John's eyebrows shot up in alarm, and he stopped chewing his tomato bocconcini mid-bite.

"Just kidding," I said, throwing him a smile, laid his car keys on the table and reached for a piece of the tomato bocconcini.

A short, heavy-set gentleman with neatly combed, white hair shuffled quickly up to the table, set a glass of white wine in front of me and, after John introduced him as Adriano and we shook hands, said, in Italian-accented English, that he was delighted, though a little bit surprised, to meet me. All these years he'd been coming to "Adriano's" and he and his wife, Rosalina, had no idea that Mr. John even *had* a brother.

Not wanting to complicate things unnecessarily, I held back from telling Adriano he had two, actually. I almost quipped that there were probably quite a few other things about "Mr. John" they didn't know either, but said instead, giving him a conspiratorial wink, "I try to keep a low profile, Adriano. You know what I mean?"

"But of course!" he winked back, laughing. "So *this* is your little brother!" he said to John as he continued wringing my hand and, before I had a chance to correct him on the fact that I was actually the older brother, added that he could definitely see the resemblance between the two of us. "Mind you," he mugged, throwing me another wink, "it's no secret as to who got the good looks!"

The old chestnut cracked the two of them up. I would have laughed, too, except the fingers on my right hand were beginning to lose feeling with the vigorous workout they were getting from Adriano as he continued laughing at the joke.

I finally wrested them free, picked up the menu and ordered the veal shanks on Adriano's recommendation, John not only endorsing my choice, but assuring me that, as with the tomato bocconcini, it would be the best I'd ever had.

In a cream-white, button-down shirt and blue sports-jacket, his wavy, short black hair recently cut and showing few, if any, traces of grey (dyed or not, he'd never tell), John adjusted his rimless glasses with his thumb and index finger every few minutes while he talked (a longtime habit, as was clearing his throat, sometimes noisily, every five minutes or so), updating me on what his three daughters were up to: Jennifer, the eldest, married to Tom Patchell the Crown Attorney, had a three-year-old boy named Aiden; Megan and her boyfriend Colin were living in London, England, and thinking of getting married over there. Emily, his youngest, was engaged to an "older man" (one with a lot of money, he quickly added) and was living at his horse farm these days in the Caledon Hills northwest of Toronto.

They were more or less estranged from their father, even before his bankruptcy misdoings in 2001 (the last straw for his daughter Megan, who changed her surname to her mother's maiden name because she was so angry), but to hear John tell it everything was absolutely hunky-dory between the four of them these days, he and the girls, and their partners, one big happy family, everyone getting along "swimmingly" — even better, according to him, now that he was a grandfather.

Family matters over with, as per our regular routine, he brought up the names of a number of mutual friends from high school, several whose obituaries he'd noticed in the paper recently, others he'd bumped into around town the last little while, then several more people that he'd heard one thing or another about through the gossip grapevine; John taking pleasure, as he always did, in being the first one to pass on a piece of breaking news. Next came the sports roundup: the latest NHL hockey standings, the upcoming Super Bowl, the Vancouver Olympics, after which he made a brief foray into politics, telling me that he'd just learned that Barack Obama only made $450,000 a year as president of the United States. He wondered why anyone in their right mind would even want the job with a pittance of a salary like that. I explained that the $10 million dollar book deal and $100,000-an-appearance speaking fee he'd receive once he left office, would probably keep him off the welfare rolls, for a little while anyway. As for our Prime Minister Stephen Harper shutting down Parliament as he'd done two weeks before rather than risk a no-confidence motion from the opposition parties, John expostulated for a few moments on why it was the right thing for him to have done, when the "left-wing" Liberal party of Michael Ignatieff was planning a coalition with the separatist Bloc Québécois and their not-to-be-trusted leader, Gilles Duceppe. He didn't know how anyone in their right mind could see *that* as a good thing for the country, not with the post-2008 economy in the shitter as it was.

He then segued onto the topic of Bernie Madoff, providing me with the latest details about the king of the Ponzi schemers, currently doing 550 years in prison for his $55 billion fraud — John reminding me twice, during the conversation, that he had predicted what was going to befall Madoff before anyone else. Reminding me, as well, that Madoff had been an idiot, left a paper trail a mile wide behind him and basically got nailed because he was too greedy. What did he think was going to happen? John wanted to know, rhetorically I supposed, so I let the question go unanswered.

As was always the case when he got to discussing high-profile fraud cases — the way an enthusiastic sports fan might talk about great plays and players of the past, there was never a word spoken about, nor even the slightest allusion to, his own fraudulent activities.

Not that it was taboo for me to question him about them; I'd done so quite a few times: asked him things like why he'd done what he did; where he'd "squirreled" away the $70 million dollars; how and when, or if ever, he was planning to get his hands on the money, and what he was going to do with it in the event that he did. Every inquiry, however, was met with a stony silence, John quickly looking away and staring into space as if he hadn't heard the question, and so I just stopped asking. I accepted the fact that even if he'd broken down and, in an apparent fit of conscience, decided to come clean about his exploits, whether it was in front of a judge or on the *Jerry Springer Show*, knowing him the way I did, any resemblance between my brother's version of events and the truth would have been, as they say, purely coincidental.

The fraud update concluding, he finally got around to asking how my own "kiddies" were — this the term he still used to describe Carson, Nicky and Hannah. It was one that used to drive Julie crazy, as did his habit of addressing his wife Nancy as "Mother," and all the other women and girls in the extended family as "Dear." Though not nearly to the same extent as it did Julie, it bothered me too, I think because John assumed he was being cordial, affectionate and endearing, when in fact he came across as cold, supercilious and patronizing, anyone listening easily able to detect, in his breezy aloofness, a not-too-thinly-disguised disdain for women — something that also didn't sit right with me. I wasn't aware of, and had no recollection of, any of the males on either side of my mother's or my father's families ever using those particular terms in that way. I mentioned it to John one time; asked him if he knew where they might have come from. Stumped at first, it crossed his mind, after thinking about it, that he'd probably picked up the habit from Nancy's father, Ed Fawcett, who used to do the same thing with her mother and the other women in her family; John said he'd never really noticed it.

Homemade Italian tiramisu for dessert (another endorsement from John that it was "the best you'll ever have"), he thought we should pass on coffee, since we had to be up at five the next morning. He told Adriano to go ahead and make up the bill and, with a distracted look on his face (some uneasy glances over at the front door, and out the window across from our banquette) listened rather disinterestedly while I continued my brief rundown on what the "kiddies" were doing — interrupting me, at one point, to ask how old they were now. Information I'd just given him a few moments earlier, he was amazed all over again when I told him, and laughed when he thought back to some of the times he'd had with them when he was "laying low" at our house in 2001–2002 — "going to the mattresses" what he liked to call it, a line from *The Godfather*, one of his all-time favourite movies.

No telling when I'd be seeing him again, probably not before my book was published, I explained what it would be dealing with, that it was non-fiction, a true story, and he was in it, warts and all, and waited for his reaction. The news not appearing to register with him one way or the other, I told him that writing it in Toronto just wasn't going to be feasible, the environment at Cromartie's not really conducive, so Don had invited me to try my luck "down east."

John wanted to know what the hell Don was doing manufacturing cutting boards in a place like Cape Breton; said he couldn't imagine how he was able to make money doing something like that, let alone in rural Nova Scotia. I explained that Don just managed the company for a wealthy young guy, originally from Toronto, and mentioned his name, a moneyed Old Toronto family, about whom John immediately started to talk, telling me who was related to whom in the family, how they'd made their money, what they were currently worth. He said he'd done deals with them here and there, lunched with them at the Albany or the National clubs, flown them in one of his airplanes, even taken the scion of the family out in his antique motorboat, *Blackie II*, which, now that we were talking about it, John reminded me he'd bought for just under $100,000 but had managed to sell for more than twice that much at auction. This triggered further reminiscences of other deals that he'd put together at different times; the personalities, the players, the under-the-table details, though never too many of course.

That was the fascinating thing about listening to my brother talk: he provided you with a minimum of information, but a maximum amount of entertaining enthusiasm, along with the quick, self-deprecating humour of the born raconteur; convinced, as he had been ever since he was a boy, that if he believed hard enough that what he was telling you was the truth, you would believe it, too. Indeed, in talking to different people over the years who had lost money to my brother, I found that, in not a few cases, the victims readily admitted that if he'd come strolling into the room just then and asked for money, they'd probably have ended up giving him some: "He's one of the most gifted self-promoters I've ever run into," said one gentleman who had invested several million with John's company, never to see it again. He would have invested more, he said, if he'd had it, because John could persuade you that you didn't have a thing to worry about, he was going to look after it all and make you rich. Another commented, "Your brother always looked like a million bucks. Top-of-the-line luxury cars, Porsches, Mercedes, BMWs; the Rolex watch, the Armani suits and Gucci loafers — the wad of cash you'd sometimes see him carrying around, four, five thousand dollars. Why wouldn't you think he was going to make you a lot of money?"

The cash wad very much on display when, at a signal from my brother, Adriano's wife, Rosalina, a plump, black-haired woman in her early sixties with lively blue eyes behind fifties-era teardrop glasses, brought the check over to our table, the smile that lit up her face, when she saw the two crisp $100 bills he'd peeled off and set on the change-tray (our tab was about $70) telling me all I needed to know about her and Adriano's exuberant affection for "Mr. John."

CHAPTER **TWENTY-TWO**
WINNER'S CIRCLE

As it was only a little after 8:30 when we left the restaurant, I had John stop at a Dunkin' Donuts near his house so that I could pick up a coffee; regular-strength, rather than decaf, as my nerves needed steadying after two hours at close-quarters with my brother, his consuming narcissism entertaining up to a point, but after that it became too exhausting providing him with the oohs and aahs of approval for which he'd always had such a desperate need.

We drove into his subdivision (built on the site of the former Greenwood Raceway), turned onto his street, Winner's Circle and, pointing out his place as we passed by — a three-storey, Cape Cod–style townhouse — he explained that parking was in the rear. He drove to the end of the block then turned into a lane that led down a row of double garages, John hitting the remote door opener when we came to his. He backed the Mercedes in beside his "other car," a new-looking white Ford

Explorer. "Deluxe Edition," John let me know as we got out of the car.

I managed, after some strenuous tugging, to wrangle my suitcase from the back seat of the Mercedes, the door only opening halfway in the narrow gap between the two cars. John watched with an amused smile on his face as I strained to hoist the seventy-pound suitcase over my head and squeeze myself, sideways, up to the door. "You look like Mr. Bean," he said, holding it open for me.

"Thanks," I said, out-of-breath and not so amused, setting the suitcase down as I stepped into the tiny backyard and followed him into the townhouse, one of the original ones in the development, John said, built in the early 2000s after the old racetrack closed down.

We stayed in the high-ceilinged, designer kitchen while I drank my coffee and he had a cigarette, something he said he'd taken to doing now and then. He stood at the stove and turned the vent-fan on while he was smoking. The room was spotlessly clean, the black-marble counters were bare and, as I discovered when I went hunting for some sugar to add to my coffee, the custom-built oak cupboards were too. The only evidence that someone was even living there, as far as I could see, was the Bell Canada bill and a payment envelope that John had set — very precisely, by the looks of it — in the centre of a mahogany secretary that he was using as a phone table.

After my comment that he was running a pretty lean domestic operation, John chuckled and, strangely for him, opened up about his personal life, explaining that with his second wife Mandy out of the picture now ("I'm gonna hit her for spousal support, though," he quickly added), he'd been spending most of his time lately at his new girlfriend's place, a woman named Connie who was fifty-three, two years younger than John, and, according to him, had a $175,000-a-year job as comptroller for the City of Brampton. She was living in a large house in Mississauga, which she'd got as part of her divorce settlement a few years ago. Her son and his girlfriend were residing there too, both in their late twenties, with good jobs and ostensibly saving to buy their own place. Connie was trying her hardest (with his encouragement, John said) to get rid of them, as they seemed to be doing a lot of other things with their money besides saving for a house. Naturally, John said, she wasn't having much luck persuading them it was time to move on. His feeling was that she should just sell the house out from under them — she'd get seven or eight hundred thousand for it — the kid and his girlfriend could fend for themselves, and Connie and John could buy a spot of their own. He said the $2,500 rent on this place was killing him in the meantime; he didn't know why he was even hanging onto it, except the owner was a business associate of his who'd fallen on hard times and needed the money.

How much of the story was true, I couldn't have said. There were enough elements that had the ring of truth to them to be plausible, though as I thought about it while John was enumerating the pros and cons of moving in with Connie, it struck me that the modus operandi was an eerily familiar one: a middle-aged woman with a high-paying job, a house worth half a million dollars or more, smitten by his charms and swept off her feet in the rapture of new romance; John wining and dining her till he'd persuaded her that she'd be smart to let him turn that several hundred thousand into a few million for her . . . a proposal which I had no doubt he'd made, or would soon be making, to the unwitting Comptroller Connie.

John lit up another cigarette — only pretending to inhale, I now noticed, exactly the way he used to when we were twelve and puffing a Rothmans that we'd pilfered from my father's pack — and, as he had at dinner, began reminiscing about the past, this time about some of the characters we'd known and the experiences we'd had when we were teenagers working at Eunice Denby Flowers Ltd., the tony Forest Hill flower shop that was owned by our parents' friends, Eunice and Jack Bennett. John and I worked there on Saturdays during high school, as well as before all the big days like Christmas, Easter, Valentine's, Mother's Day. John was a runner in the delivery trucks, while I manned the packing counter along with a crew of firemen friends and old war buddies of Jack's, who came in on their "lieu days" to help out, along with the ever-changing assortment of full-time packers that Jack hired through classified ads. Derelict types, heavy drinkers all, they weren't averse to passing John and me the mickey bottles of Seagram's V.O. (everyone's drink of choice, apparently) whenever they went around.

The chief instigator of these little nipping sessions was a short, elfin-featured Irishman in his mid-sixties named Sean Flanagan, in charge of the packing room, deliveries and dispatching. With his light-red hair, his impish smile, his loose-fitting false teeth, thick-lens glasses, a gimpy leg and a wall eye, I once kidded him that he was a dead-ringer for the philosopher Jean-Paul Sartre, of whom Sean claimed to have heard . . . but with whom, he added, a twinkle in his eye, he *completely* disagreed.

Not that he would have known, but it was Sean who provided John with what I afterwards came to regard as the "Great Gatsby" moment of his life, the moment he had his first glimpse of what life could be like if you had money. It was a Saturday afternoon, the spring of 1969, and the Eunice Denby delivery van was set to leave on the last run of the day: a large order of centrepiece arrangements in Greek urns and tall, expensive crystal vases that was going to a house in Toronto's wealthiest enclave, the Bridle Path. Sean had been planning to deliver the flowers himself, but had been nipping at the bottle a little too heavily during the afternoon and was in no condition to drive, let alone carry a couple of thousand dollars' worth of elaborate floral arrangements into an important customer's house — in this case the Black family on Park Lane Circle, the residence of George Black, father of Montegu and Conrad, friend and associate of Canada's wealthiest man, E.P. Taylor, and a multimillionaire in his own right as head of the Argus Corporation.

Drunk and a little wobbly on his feet, Sean grabbed John anyway, and told him to come along to the Blacks as his runner. They went out to the garage, where I was already in position. As Sean moved to climb behind the wheel of the delivery van, I caught him by the arm, grabbed the keys to the van and tossed them to John, then told Sean that Jack wanted to have a word with him, and he didn't look happy.

In a panic because he'd been caught drinking on the job several times before, he asked me, near tears, what he was going to do: Jack would probably can him if he found out. And what about the order for the Blacks? It should have gone out earlier — Al wouldn't be back with the other truck till after five.

I told him John was taking care of the Blacks; that Jack didn't want to see him after all, but I suggested that if Sean were smart, he'd make himself scarce until John returned; and that he'd also give me the bottle of Seagram's V.O. hidden in the inside pocket of his jacket which, after a meek protest, he handed over.

Shortly before 5, Jack got wind of what was going on and came downstairs from the business office to wait in the packing room with Sean, whom he'd rounded up and whom he'd forgiven for the drinking, but was furious with because he'd let a sixteen-year-old boy, who'd only had his driver's licence for three months, deliver a $2,000 order to one of his best customers and, even worse, all by himself.

The designers who'd done up the Black's arrangements waited in anticipation, too, bickering away at each other in French, swearing in English, blaming everything on Sean, who stood between the two of them wringing his hands with a mixture of worry and despair, throwing me urgent, pleading looks, like he wanted me to be a good kid and just give him his bottle of whisky back.

Jack stood by the order desk puffing away on the last of his cigar, glancing nervously at the clock above the packing counter every few minutes. Shaking his head disconsolately when it got to be 5:45 and there was still no sign of my brother, he mentioned to Al, his most stalwart driver, that maybe it was time he headed over to the Blacks to check on the situation.

But Al was just trotting up the steps to the garage when the double doors leading into the packing room swung open and there was John, with the widest smile I'd ever seen on his face. He stayed up on the landing while the rest of us gathered down below at the bottom of the steps.

"Well?" Jack asked him.

"Piece of cake," John said nonchalantly. "And they gave

me a tip for bringing everything in by myself. Forty bucks!"
He beamed, pulling two twenty-dollar bills out of his pocket
and holding them up: quite a sum of money, in those days,
when you were only making $3.50 an hour.

On the bus ride home that night, John couldn't stop talking
about the Black's house: it was huge, an estate, the lawns like
you'd see on a golf course; huge rooms, artwork, fireplaces,
an indoor swimming pool, limousines and expensive cars
in the driveway, all of them black, something that, with his
love of cars, I could tell John found especially impressive. He
declared that he was going to live in a house like that himself
some day; and all the cars *he* ever owned were going to be
black, too. The vow about his house one that he managed
to keep, albeit on a slightly smaller scale with the homes he
eventually owned, aside from the white Ford Explorer sitting
outside in his garage, in the forty or so years since he'd made
it, I'd never known him to break the one about black cars
either. As Nicky joked about it one day while John was living
with us, "What other colour car are you going to drive, Dad,
when your licence plate is 'RSKY BZNS'?"

"We better get to bed if we want to be at the terminal by
5:30," said John, finishing the last cigarette in his pack and,
as he had with the previous ones, putting it out under the tap
and setting it down with the other butts in a neat row beside
the sink. "Probably only take us ten minutes to get there at
that time of the morning," he said à propos of the drive,
walking over to the table, picking up the Bell Canada bill and
standing with his hand on the light switch till I'd brought my
suitcase from the back door, at which point he flicked it off
and we headed upstairs.

He showed me to a guest bedroom on the second floor,

pointed out the bathroom to my left, on the other side of the stairs, the master bedroom further along, at the end of the hall, the door open a crack, a table lamp on inside. John asked me if I had everything, said he'd left towels and a face-cloth in the bathroom for me; that he'd set the alarm for five so I could grab a quick shower before we left.

I told him I was good to go, that he might have to come in and shake me in the morning, though, because with the packing I hadn't slept much the night before. Not a problem, he said, bade me goodnight and started up the stairs to the third floor, where there was a large, wood-paneled den with a fireplace that doubled as John's "business office."

The two of us had sat up there when I came over to see him in November 2007, just after I found out Howie Gertz was intending to extort $92,000 from Julie and me. I explained to John that she was going to lose a good chunk of what she was hoping to receive from the house sale because of it, and I was looking at being left bankrupt and homeless. I asked him if there was any way he could convince Howie to do the right thing and reduce the amount he was asking for or back off entirely, since the judgement, as we all knew, was based on bogus evidence. Unfortunately, John said, that was something he couldn't do. Howie monitored all his transactions like a hawk, so loaning me money wasn't going to be an option. He did, however, have a new scheme on the go that he thought might work. He and a lawyer named Pete Anselmo had a company that backdated promissory notes. According to John, all I needed to do was write up one from my publishing company, dated some time in 2000 when business was at its peak, acknowledging a loan from a shell firm of his and Pete's for the total equity Julie and I were expecting to get from the house, plus a hundred grand on top, about $330,000 he figured when he did the math. His company would present the note to my real estate lawyer, tell him that I must have forgotten about the earlier business loan but say they were willing to negotiate a settlement, going as low as $200,000, which, or so John said, he'd have to accept in order to close the sale. Anselmo and he would take their $50,000 fee on the way through, and the kiddies and I would net $150,000, thirty-grand more than I would have received if Howie hadn't stuck his nose in. It was as convoluted a pitch as I'd ever heard, even from him. I was so confused by the numbers he was throwing around, I couldn't have told you who was to receive what from whom, or why. I was put off, as well, by his blasé attitude toward what I knew were serious illegalities; I questioned whether everything could be as cut and dried as he was indicating and asked him how, to begin with, I was supposed to go about getting a promissory note from seven years ago authenticated, a worry John blithely brushed off: apparently a promissory note only requires a signature, a date and an amount, and it takes precedence over all other creditor claims. "It just needs to say 'Promissory Note' at the top. That's it." I said I'd have to think it over. I didn't know if I had the nerves to pull off something as dicey as that. "It's just business, Paul," he said with a dismissive shrug. "It's a totally foolproof scheme. Anselmo and I are doing really well with it. It's worth a try. All they can say is no."

"Or haul me off to jail for fraud," I said.

"Nah," John came back, at which point he got up from his chair, said he felt like a glass of wine and headed downstairs, leaving me to think over what I'm sure he felt was a too-good-to-be-true proposal.

Figuring I had what I needed, and that the conversation would shift to less consequential matters, I took out the microcassette tape recorder that I'd had running in my shirt pocket, pressed the Eject button and slipped the tape into my pants pocket. Maybe it was some hard evidence of the type that Al had said I'd need in order to fight Howie's judgement, maybe it wasn't, however it was good material to add to my dossier on the sometimes fascinating, sometimes repugnant and more often than not criminal exploits of John James Illidge, on which, after twenty or so years of studying them, I had become somewhat of an expert. When he returned with a bottle of wine and two glasses, I told him that the back-dated promissory note idea just wasn't going to work for me, thanks just the same. "Just let me know if you change your mind," he said, and poured me a glass of wine.

I'd had the tape running off and on at Adriano's earlier in the evening, and again when John and I were talking in the kitchen. It was a habit that I'd picked up when he was living with me and that I continued afterwards on the rare occasions when we met up. I never knew what was going to pop out of my brother's mouth, but it was usually out-landish, often compelling and always difficult to disbelieve. I was planning to use the microcassette again when we were driving to the airport in the morning; see if I could find out more about his girlfriend Connie (if that was her real name) so that I could contact her, maybe through the comptroller's office in Brampton. Warn her about striking up any kind of serious relationship with John: tell her that I was his older brother; that John was a con artist extraordinaire who was only interested in putting his hands on as much of her money as he possibly could.

Whether she'd believe me or not was another question; Connie wouldn't know me from Adam, of course, and might already have taken a bite of the forbidden apple, so to speak, in which case she'd be on her own, learning for herself — as who knows how many others had before her — that the Eden she thought John was taking her to with his big-spender ways wasn't quite the paradise it seemed; that as Nancy, his first wife, who knew him better than anyone else, aptly used to say: "There's a lot of glitter in John's world, which is what all the women fall for; unfortunately, in the end, very little of it turns out to be gold."

I put the tape recorder in my suitcase, got undressed down to my T-shirt and underwear and removed the frilly cushions, neatly folded comforters, teddy bears and stuffed animals from the bed (left behind, or so I assumed, after his wife Mandy moved out), switched off the bedside lamp, slipped under the covers and must have drifted pretty quickly off to sleep. I was dead to the world for what must have been a few hours . . . until the bedroom door burst open and John — the hall light on behind him, standing in silhouette in the doorway — asked, with concern and apprehension in his voice, if something was wrong. He said I'd started yelling; that he'd heard me from upstairs and the cries had woken him up. Confused, disoriented, barely awake, I mumbled that everything was fine; said I must have been talking in my sleep.

Still in the doorway, his face in shadow, John said okay, no problem, apologized for waking me then closed the door behind him as he went out, turned off the hall light and, from the sounds of it, headed back upstairs to the den.

Things were far from fine, though. I was scared, had been having the worst sort of dream, one in which I was in a dark place, suffocating and about to take my last breath. I sat there in the darkness for a few minutes thinking about it. I could make out the sound of the television upstairs in the den, John moving around, unable to get to sleep, the two of us alone together at three o'clock in the morning for the first time since we'd been boys, in our childhood home at 327 Scarborough Road in the Beach, the beginning of September 1960, three days after my ninth birthday. John was seven at the time, our younger brother Peter was five, in a bedroom of his own along the hall, our sister Frances not yet born. And just as he had been only a few moments ago, in my mind he was standing in silhouette at the door of our bedroom that night nearly fifty years ago, the light on in the hall behind him, pleading with me, on the verge of tears and in a panicked voice, to wake up. "Something's wrong, Paul! Hurry up and get out of bed!"

Hand in hand, we stepped out into the hall, John pointing to his right, toward the bathroom. The door was open, the light on, nobody in the room . . . but the mirror over the sink, the walls around the bathtub and beside the toilet, were splashed and streaked with blood, several of my father's Wilkinson Sword razor-blades and their paper wrappers lying on the floor in a pool of blood beneath the sink.

Unable to look anywhere else, I left John at the door and, avoiding the blood, walked quickly into the room, head down, looking at nothing except one unwrapped razor-blade with some drops of blood on it that was sitting on the edge of the sink. No idea why I did so, I snatched it up and brought it with me when I went back to the hall.

John pointed to the right, the stairwell, where there were more bloody handprints on the wall leading downstairs, along with a trail of blood on the carpet runners on the stairs.

The light was already on in the dining room as we passed through, as it was in the kitchen, too, where the trail turned left to the basement door, John standing back, telling me to go first.

The trail turned left at the bottom of the stairs, ran along the hall past the furnace room, the recreation room and into the corner at the back of the basement, where the washer and dryer were kept: my mother in her pink, but now bloody nightgown, lying on her side on the floor, in a fetal position, her wrists and neck slashed and bleeding badly, a stream of blood trickling toward the drain about a foot away from her hands, no expression on her face, her eyes closed.

Feeling sick to my stomach at the sight of the blood, I ran upstairs behind John, told him to go wake up Dad then sat down at the kitchen table.

I heard my father stumbling on the stairs he was running so fast. He rushed into the kitchen, turned down the basement stairs and nearly tumbled again. John joined me at the table, staring at the bandage on his left hand, the two of us sitting in silence until the wail of agony my father let out, a few seconds later, told us he'd found the body.

Within seconds he was back in the kitchen. He grabbed the phone receiver off the wall and dialed, shouting into it, "I need to report a suicide!"

He told John and I to go up to our room and stay there. Our younger brother Peter, who was awake now, came in to sit with us. He wondered what was going on (we told him Mommy had had an accident), and was soon complaining that he really had to pee. You'll just have to hold it, I said. I don't think I can. All right, I said, took him downstairs, out the front door and let him go beside the front garden. John came, too. He said there was no way he was going to stay up there all by himself.

In maybe ten minutes, I don't think it could have been more, Mrs. Comars, our neighbour from two doors down, was bringing John, Peter and me, in our slippers and housecoats, along the sidewalk to her house. A warm, kindly woman who sometimes went to our church, she gave us hot chocolate in the kitchen and told us everything was going to be all right. John could sleep in Michael's room (they were in the same class at school), Peter could go in with Christopher and I could stay with Billy, who was in my class at school. She woke the boys up after we'd finished the hot chocolate, explained that the three of us would be living with them for the next little while, and sent the six of us on our way.

Billy asked if I wanted to talk about anything, or whether I'd mind if he went back to sleep. I said I was feeling wide awake, would probably stay up for a little while, so he should go ahead. After exchanging goodnights with him, I went to stand at the window (Billy's room was at the front of the house), and watched what was happening up the street at ours: an ambulance had pulled up, a police car, too, neither of them with their lights flashing.

After what was probably only a few minutes, though at the time seemed like forever, I noticed two attendants wheeling a stretcher down our front walk, my mother lying on her back under a blanket that went up to her chin, my father following behind, hopping in the back of the ambulance once the stretcher was in. I watched it move up the street until the red tail lights were out of sight, my right hand in the pocket of my housecoat, clutching the Wilkinson Sword blade.

We lived with Mr. and Mrs. Comars for six days (Mr.

Comars as light-hearted, friendly and kind as his wife), no one expressly telling us we couldn't go back to our own house, yet it was something John and I had no interest in doing, at least until the mess had been cleaned up, something we decided our father was doing since his car was always in the driveway when we walked past. Mrs. Comars retrieved our clothes and anything else we needed. We went to school every day, played with our friends, did our homework after dinner in our rooms and, when it was completed to Mrs. Comars' satisfaction, were allowed to watch television for an hour or so, and given hot chocolate each night before going to bed, the others at nine o'clock while Billy and I, as the eldest, were permitted to keep our light on until 9:30.

When we did go home, the house was spic and span, everything freshly painted, new broadloom on the hall stairs and the bathroom completely renovated. My father's mother, our Grandma Illidge, moved in to look after us. She was seventy-six at the time, a tall, large-framed and bosomy woman with wavy silver hair, twinkling blue eyes, a ready smile and who, when she spoke, never pronounced her H's, a product of growing up in a working-class section of London, England, I later found out. She had a full store of adages, maxims, old sayings and philosophical tidbits that she was more than 'appy to dispense in her robust, Cockney voice whenever such advice seemed warranted. She had a great liking (somewhat obscurely, I always thought, since she only had an elementary school education) for the works of the seventeenth-century English poet John Milton, after whom my father had been named, and whom my grandmother would quote from memory after a few glasses of sherry.

Her passion, though, was bingo, which she played several

nights a week with her "friend from the Old Country," Mrs. Choate, at a big hall near Queen Street and Logan Avenue. She would have her winnings proudly on display at breakfast the next morning — not always, but often enough for Peter, John and I to know that she must have been good at it, if she could make so much money. There'd be five-, ten- and twenty-dollar bills arranged like a fan beside the platter with our eggs, bacon, and butter-lathered toast after she'd had a big night. Sixty or seventy dollars, four or five hundred at today's rates. She taught us how to play, happily supervised our pretend games which had John, his own winning touch already on display, calling out "Bingo!" way more often than Peter and I ever did.

Whether it was because it wasn't a subject you talked about in those days, or because they assumed, despite our young age, we'd have been able to figure out for ourselves what had happened from what we'd witnessed, no one, not even our father, said a word about our mother — not even whether she was dead or alive — until one Saturday, several weeks later, Grandfather Shea, my mother's father, drove Peter, John and I to Niagara Falls for a day of sightseeing: a ride on the *Maid of the Mist* up the river to within twenty yards of the Falls, followed by a visit to the observation deck in the electrical station underneath them.

The excursion on the *Maid* would have been more exciting if the boat hadn't bobbed from side to side so much in the waves, a few times like it was perilously close to capsizing. The trip beneath the Falls would have been more enjoyable, too, if my grandfather hadn't taken John and me aside, suited up in our rubber boots, raincoats and sou'westers, the wall of thundering water maybe fifteen feet away from where we were standing, and started shouting at us over the noise, in a scolding voice, that we'd been "bad boys" and had "made our mother sick." In rubber boots, a raincoat and sou'wester too, he told us that from now on he expected us to behave ourselves, there was to be no more trouble for our mother when she eventually came home, or there'd be consequences, my grandfather asking John and me in a stern voice when he was done if he'd made himself clear.

Afraid to do anything else, I remember nodding, I think John did, too, and we went back to looking out at the cascading tons of water. I'm not sure how much of the scolding my brother took to heart, since he was used to receiving them almost daily from my mother, but I remember feeling humiliated, ashamed and then extremely angry with him by the time he was finished talking, because I knew very well, even if I *was* just nine, that what he'd said to us about being bad boys wasn't true at all. While she might have been sick in some way that I didn't know about, or wouldn't have understood, I knew in my heart it was wrong for him to be blaming my brother and me. I couldn't see why my grandfather would even have mentioned it, when we knew full well it was the bandage John was still wearing on his left hand, and nothing else, that had caused her to try and kill herself.

She'd been in the kitchen, three days before the suicide attempt, icing the cake she'd made for my birthday, listening in while I practised the piano, shouting at me when she thought I'd made a mistake; ordering me, as she regularly did, to play the passage over again, this time with no mistakes. Her voice was louder than usual that day, her mood more agitated and distressed than it usually was leading up to my birthday — because, as I later learned, this was the tenth anniversary of her own mother's death.

She screamed suddenly, a shriek that I could hear over the sound of the piano, and went storming downstairs. Knowing something was wrong — there was something different, more fiercely angry about this particular cry — I stopped playing, got up from the bench, hurried through the dining room and stood at the top of the basement stairs listening to my mother scream at John, slapping him in the face, punching him too, it sounded like, as she dragged him crying and protesting up the stairs, screaming and thrashing in her grip as she yanked him over to the stove and held his left hand down on the already glowing front element for a second. "That'll teach you to play with matches!" she shouted at him, threw down his hand and, spotting me standing there, snapped: "Put some butter on it," then stormed through the dining room and went upstairs to her bedroom, slamming the door shut behind her.

Our father drove us downtown for a short visit with her the following spring, ten minutes together on a bench in the walled grounds of 999 Queen Street, nobody saying very much at first, John, Peter and I trying our hardest not to look at the white gauze bandages wrapped around her neck and wrists which, even though she'd obviously tried to hide them by wearing long sleeves, were still quite conspicuous. My father sat on the bench beside her. A nurse in uniform stood off a little ways, minding the wheelchair in which my mother had been brought out. She sobbed quite a bit, whimpered when she talked, her voice hoarse and weak when she attempted to ask us questions about school, whether or not we were behaving for Grandma Illidge: badly embarrassed on each occasion that the words weren't coming out clearly, or so she thought, asking the questions over again, getting more riled and frustrated with herself — to the point that she broke down in tears because of her seeming inability to talk properly. The nurse suggested that she'd probably had enough for now; bringing over the wheelchair, she and my father helped my mother into it. "Goodbye, boys," she said, her voice wavering, and the nurse wheeled her down the gravel path toward the gloomy, soot-covered building. I learned a number of years later that she'd been "put back together" by the plastic surgeon for the Toronto Maple Leafs; that the electroshock treatments she'd received during her time in 999 Queen had erased both her memory of the breakdown, and the depression that had preceded it, the event, as a result of the therapy, one that she would never recall having ever taken place.

As for the Wilkinson Sword blade that I'd salvaged from "the scene of the crime" as I came to call it, the day we moved back from the Comars' house, I hid it in a place where I was sure nobody would ever find it: in *Bleak House*, one of a set of six novels by Charles Dickens that Grandma Illidge had just given me for my birthday.

I rummaged through the drawers of my mother's dressing table and found a jewelry box just slightly larger than the razor blade. It was cream-coloured, about an inch-and-a-half-by-an-inch-and-a-half square and about an inch deep, the name "Donadio of Venice" engraved in royal-blue letters on the lid, along with an address, a five-digit phone number, and the words "Since 1882" printed just below.

I took the blade out of the wrapper, opened *Bleak House*, a big book at nearly 900 pages, to page 218, Chapter 16 — "Tom-all-Alone's" — set the jewelry box, lid-side down, in the centre of the page, ran the blade along all four sides and removed the small square of paper. I repeated the operation on the page underneath, using the edges of the first square to guide the razor; after which I turned the page and cut out a similar-sized square in the centre of the next one. I worked on the page-cutting in my spare time over the next few days, until I'd hollowed out down to page 758, Chapter 56, "Pursuit": a hidey-hole into which the Donadio of Venice box, with the Wilkinson Sword inside, fit perfectly. I closed the book, ran it upstairs to my bedroom, and placed it back on the bookshelf over my bed, and though I've never read the novel, never even opened it again, it's the one possession of mine that I've never felt I could let go.

I had it with me that night at John's, wrapped in a green plastic garbage bag and two dark-coloured towels and buried at the bottom of my suitcase, a precaution I thought I should take, even if I was overdoing it. I didn't want the alarm sounding when I went through the airport metal-detector. If it did for some reason, and they questioned me about it, I was planning to keep my cool and explain that the blade was just something I'd put there close to fifty years ago and forgotten all about; a lie, of course, but then, who was going to believe me if I told them the real story?

CHAPTER **TWENTY-THREE**
319

Around East Margaree, a small fishing village on the Gulf of St. Lawrence side of the island about thirty minutes south of the Cape Breton Highlands, the friendly local residents knew me as Paul the Writer, down from Toronto working on a book, an old friend of Don Beamish.

Off to a good start on my book, I wrote for eight or nine hours a day, sometimes more, seven days a week during February and early March when Don was away doing his U.S. trade shows. I took breaks, of course; went for long, picturesque walks through the Margaree River valley; wandered by the ocean; went into Margaree to shop and got to know a cast of friendly, entertaining local characters. There were spirited discussions and stimulating conversations with some of Don's fellow Buddhists, who welcomed me into their *sangha* (congregation); I had full-night sleeps, read a dozen or so books, ate seafood, listened to live fiddle music, watched movies, went to several amateur theatre productions and even had the opportunity to hear a talk at the Gampo Abbey Buddhist monastery on "Finding Joy in Everyday Life" by the revered teacher and author Pema Chodron, who graciously signed my beaten-up, elastic-bound paperback copy of her book *When Things Fall Apart*, of which I'd been reading a page or two just about every morning since I first picked it up three years earlier: a fitting irony that the book was in such poor condition, it seemed to me, since the more I used it, and the more it fell apart, the more "back-together" I found myself becoming.

Which is how, when he was dropping me off at the Halifax Airport at the end of April, I told Don I felt about my months "on the island": that after my great fall as it were, the relaxed atmosphere, the simpler and slower way of life, and the good-natured, fun-loving folks I'd got to know had helped clear my head of a lot of things that had been bothering me. Work on the book was going well; writing about the raid and its effects had turned out to be extremely therapeutic. All in all, I'd had one of the best times of my life.

"That'd be yer Cape Breton rehab," said Don, grinning as he handed me my ticket. "Come back anytime, b'y — we'll take care of you!"

I flew home to Toronto and, after two weeks at a friend's at Yonge and Eglinton, moved into a house owned by one of Nicky's landscaping clients, a single guy in his early forties who did electrical work of some kind in the oil sands out in Fort McMurray, Alberta. His previous tenant had taken off unexpectedly, so Neil was looking for someone reliable to rent his house while he was away; he thought Nicky and I would fit the bill perfectly.

The house a four-bedroom, two-storey place on a cul-de-sac at the end of a quiet, well-treed street, it was close to our old West Rouge neighbourhood (only five blocks west of Friendship Avenue), closer to the lake, the library, the local shopping plaza and Mr. Beans than Jean and Andy's had been and, best of all, our landlord lived 2,500 miles away: finally we had a place that we could call our own.

My friend Cromartie brought my computer over (in Cape Breton I'd worked on a semi-functional Dell laptop Don had loaned me), as well as my clothes, books, kitchenware and artwork that I'd left at his place while I was gone, along with a piece of mail that had just come for me from the City of Toronto, Department of Social Services, the first communication I'd received from them since my meeting with Mrs. Polityka, eight months ago.

The letter informed me that my Ontario Works file had now been transferred from Scarborough East, to the West Office, but went on to say that I'd been placed "on suspension," and wouldn't receive my next $570 cheque or medical benefits, until I'd had a "status review meeting" with my new caseworker, #319.

News that I can't say I was thrilled to receive (though the timing was certainly good: I don't know what I'd have done if I'd been suspended while in Cape Breton), I called the Scarborough West office right away; left my name, phone number and, at the prompt, a voicemail for "319," feeling a little odd, as I did so, having never left a message for a number rather than a person before.

Even odder, or so I thought, was the callback from 319 the next day: a man, as it turned out, who, while he seemed polite enough when he was setting up our appointment for later that week, at no point bothered to give me his name; let me address him as "319" during our entire conversation and, in answer to my question as to whom I should ask for at reception when I came in, said in a snippy, indignant tone: "319, of course."

"Of course," I said apologetically, as if it should have been perfectly obvious. Keen to stay on his good side, however, I was about to add that I was looking forward to meeting him — but 319 had already ended the call.

As Nicky was using his truck the afternoon of the appointment, I took the bus over to the Scarborough West office at Lawrence and Kennedy Road, walked north for several blocks past the strip malls and plazas, stores advertising discount furniture, lighting products, carpets, electronics and appliances, until I saw what I guessed was the Scarborough West Ontario Works office, a five-storey main building with smaller, two-storey wings on each side set back from the street across a large parking lot.

The setup inside was as it had been at the Scarborough East office, the only other person in the waiting room besides me was a woman in her early twenties, sitting on a bench by the windows with a baby carriage in front of her, the infant wrapped in a blanket, cradled on her shoulder. I walked straight ahead to the glassed-in reception counter where four women were on duty, three of them sitting at their desks in front of computers, one standing at a microphone on the other side of the glass. She listened to the speaker on her side of the counter as I leaned down to the one on mine, gave her my name and said I was meeting with 319.

"Three-ninety?" the woman's voice came back over the speaker.

"No," I said. "Three-nine*teen*."

"There's no three-ninety at this office, sir."

"Maybe not," I said into the mike, and enunciated more clearly. "But I'm looking for *three . . . nine . . . teen.*"

"Three-nineteen?"

"That's correct."

"All right," she said. "Have a seat and we'll call you when 319's available." I went over and sat down near the window, watched as she crossed her arms and, peering out from behind the glass at the now empty waiting room, lingered at the microphone for several minutes before she returned to her desk and sat down.

A different woman got up from her desk about five minutes later, went to the microphone and called my name, pronouncing it correctly, to my surprise and, after I showed her a piece of photo ID, informed me I was to proceed to the door off to my left and wait. My meeting with 319 would take place in Room 117.

Reaching below the counter, she hit a switch that activated the electronic lock on the door. It started to buzz, and continued to until it closed behind me. Only one way to go, I headed down the narrow hall, checking the numbers on doors till I found 117 and went in. It was a small room with a fluorescent light overhead, the beige walls bare. There was a dark-brown melamine desk running the width of the room, an extension perpendicular to it against the wall on the other side, a computer screen bolted and cable-locked to the desk, a door with a small viewing window a few feet behind it, through which I could see a brightly-lit yellow hall. I sat down at the desk, set my work bag on my lap — had hardly done so when the door behind the desk opened partway, and a man poked his head into the room. "Paul?"

"319?"

In his early forties, wearing round, tortoise-shell glasses, a short-sleeved floral-pattern Hawaiian shirt and blue jeans, his long brown hair gathered behind in a braided ponytail that reached down to his waist, he nodded and, without opening the door much more, slipped into the room with a legal-size file folder under his arm, sat down at the workstation, put his hand to the side of the computer screen and turned it on.

We started by reviewing my case file, 319 looking at his computer-screen and typing while we talked, telling me that the information I'd provided 208 during my "intake" meeting had been misplaced somewhere between her office and his. He was going to start a new file and have me sign a new Participation Agreement and new Employment Counselling and Placement forms as well. Though I had no idea what he was referring to (Mrs. Polityka hadn't mentioned any such documents), I almost asked him how my file could have just disappeared for eight months, but I went with the flow, said that that sounded good to me, and off we went: 319 in his chair facing the computer screen, his back almost to me, his fingers tapping rapidly away on the keyboard as he talked. Other than an occasional scolding glance after something I'd said, it seemed to me I was having more of a conversation with his three-foot ponytail than I was with 319.

Eyes intent on his computer screen, a firm, legal tone in his voice, he read out the list of responsibilities that I'd have to accept as an Ontario Works client, outlined the conditions that I had to abide by in my participation activities, as well as the terms according to which I was required to report on them, the main thrust of this more-than-a-little-tedious recitation of detail that he *"really* needed to see me hunting for a job." On which point he turned to me abruptly. "Have you been out there applying for any in the last eight months?" I said I had been, both out, and in: emailing applications to internet postings (I'd sent several dozen while I was in Cape Breton), but also responding to newspaper ads if they seemed to have possibilities, and to Help Wanted signs displayed in store windows if I happened to notice them ("the kind of shit they want to hear," according to a friend of mine's son who'd been on welfare for several years).

"Unfortunately, though," I said to 319, "despite the odd interview here and there, job offers haven't exactly been pouring in."

"How many positions would you say you've applied for?"

"Maybe forty or fifty since January."

"That's not a lot, Paul," said 319. "Some people are putting out that many every week."

"Really?"

Eyes back on the screen, his fingers making up for lost time, he nodded.

"I find it saps my motivation when everyone tells me the same thing, that's all."

"Which is?" he asked, stopped typing and glanced over.

"I'm overqualified, over-experienced and, though they can't say it, over-age. Which I can understand," I quickly added. "I'm not pissed off because of it or anything. People tell me those are just the realities of the job market these days. And the last thing I want to do is take a job away from a young person."

"Well," 319 said somewhat stiffly, though not looking

away from his screen, "one of the conditions of income support is that you're supposed to be working toward getting a job, hopefully one that will allow you to get *off* support."

"I understand that, 319. I'm just saying, it feels like I'm wasting my time."

"That's why it's called Ontario *Works*, Paul. It's not welfare anymore. *Your* job is to *get* a job. *That's* what you're being paid $570 a month for."

"I'm trying to do that, believe me," I said, and felt it was an appropriate time to add that I actually *did* have a job, that I was an author.

"That's not really a job," 319 said, squinting at something on his computer screen.

"I'm not sure what you mean."

"A steady-paying job, with a paycheque to put in the bank every few weeks. That's what you're supposed to be looking for."

My sense of things that there was no point tangling with the man over the fact there are all kinds of jobs that don't provide a paycheque every few weeks, I told him that, as an author, I *did* get paid, just not on a regular basis. "The more time I spend writing, the better work I do. The more money I might be able to make with it down the line."

"But you can't expect the government to support you doing that."

"Why can't I? I've probably paid $800,000 in income tax over the years. You're saying the government begrudges giving me $500 a month back so I can keep myself alive?"

"Let me spell it out for you, Paul," he said, his eyes shifting more quickly between the computer screen and the keyboard now. "You have to be actively seeking a *paying* job. That's what you signed on for with your Participation Agreement in September '09."

"I don't remember Mrs. Polityka having me sign any Participation Agreement."

"Be that as it may," 319 came back, "you can't just sit in front of your computer all day when you're with Ontario Works."

"Well, what are you and billions of other people doing every day?" I said, smiling to cover my sarcasm, aware that with but a few frosty strokes of the keyboard, my $570 a month could be history.

He stopped typing, turned in his chair and, crossing his arms, gave me the anticipated chilly look. "Have you got a decent résumé?"

"I think so," I said. "I have six or seven actually." I opened my work bag, pulled out the file folder with copies of my Writer, Teacher, Publisher, Musician, Landscaper and Sales Associate résumés in it, and passed it across the desk.

He opened the folder, spent a couple of seconds perusing each of the résumés, then closed it and turned back to his computer screen. "What's your instrument?" he asked as he resumed typing.

"Keyboard. Piano, organ, and I know my way around an accordion in a pinch. Though there's not a lot of work in polka parties any more," I said.

A sense of humour after all, 319 chuckled at the quip and said that he was a musician, too. He played bass guitar in a band with a few of his friends; it was a garage band for now, but everybody had day jobs, so it was kind of hard to get out there on the circuit.

Not sure what "circuit" he was referring to, I watched

him as he performed a final flourish of fast typing, cued his computer to "Print" then promptly punched "Enter" with his index finger, shot to his feet, said he'd be right back and left the room.

I folded my hands on the desk, looked around the tiny office and found myself, for no particular reason, whistling "You Can't Always Get What You Want" under my breath, then Gerry and the Pacemakers' "Ferry Cross the Mersey," until 319 reappeared, about five minutes later, with a hefty stack of documents, fifty or sixty pieces of legal-sized photocopies in his hands, the pages collated, stapled and ready to go: one copy of each of the four agreements for me, one copy for my case file, one copy for office records, one copy for 319.

He loaned me his pen, telling me to review the documents — not to hurry, he said, but his next appointment *was* waiting — and when I'd done so, had me sign in several places a "Participation Agreement," a "Structured Job Search Agreement" and an "Independent Job Search Agreement," as well as an enrolment confirmation in the "Employment Placement Program," my first meeting with a counsellor to go over my "employability skills" scheduled for three days later, there at Scarborough West, in Meeting Room A, from 1:30 to 3:30 p.m. According to 319, the counsellor would check out my various résumés, give me formatting tips, introduce me to the latest job-search techniques, provide information about more specialized resources that I might need, and direct me to programs catered to the jobs that I was looking for.

This was quite a lot to swallow. Plus the idea of listening to a colleague of 319's spout more bureaucratese at me for two hours was one that I looked forward to about as much as a root canal. I would have tried to worm my way out of the session right then, but I knew he was in a hurry to get out of there. As well, while browsing through my copies of the various agreements, something that seemed more worth mentioning caught my eye: according to the "Structured Job Search," I was not only committing myself to 125 hours a month looking for a job online, in the newspaper and store-front windows, I was also supposed to spend 100 on my "Independent Job Search."

"That's 225 hours," I pointed out to 319. "Fifty hours a week, seven hours a day, including Saturdays and Sundays."

"The two are considered to be taking place concurrently," 319 clarified.

"It's *still* 125 hours. That's a lot of time to be searching —"

"Which is what it *takes*," he said impatiently, "if you're truly serious about landing anything in today's job market."

"I'm serious enough," I said, "but it sounds a little unreasonable to me, and I'm not too clear what the difference is between an independent search and a structured one, to be honest." I knew that he was dying to wrap things up, that this wasn't a good time to be quibbling over a detail in the five dozen or so pages he'd given me, so I shut up, went ahead and signed the agreements officially binding me, for the next three months, to spend most of my waking hours in pursuit of gainful employment.

Nothing more from 319 once I'd endorsed each document in three places, he quickly passed me back the folder with my résumés in it; said again that the employment counsellor would be happy to go through everything with me. He reached behind the computer, turned off the screen and stood up. "Make sure you attend that counselling session," he warned me, "or there's no payment next month." Warning he'd be checking the attendance list to make sure my name was on it, he stepped away from his chair, opened the door and, his ponytail swinging wildly behind him, left the room before I had a chance to ask him what his name was.

The employment counsellor Bhupinder Manjoub had no such reservations about giving his, however. He'd written it on the blackboard in Meeting Room A prior to the start of my counselling session at Scarborough West social services later in the week — or, more correctly, at the start of *our* job-counselling session, since there were about twenty-five other people in attendance besides me, fellow Ontario Works miscreants, or so I assumed, complying with case-worker-imposed suspensions as I was. Four rows of chairs, ten to a row, were arranged in the classroom-style room, a desk at the front with a screen pulled down behind it, in readiness for a PowerPoint presentation by the looks of the projector set up on a small table in the centre of the room and the remote Bhupinder was twirling excitedly in his right hand. A man in his late forties, he was thin, close to six feet in height, had short, neatly parted black hair and wore glasses, grey dress pants, a short-sleeved white shirt and a light-red tie.

Punctuality a big point with Bhupinder — the number one requirement of employers today, according to him — he turned around to look at the clock above the blackboard, waited a moment till the hands showed exactly 1:30, then as he said he liked to do, began the session by telling us a little about himself. You could hear, by the passion in his cheery, East Indian voice when he spoke, that it was a story he was proud to relate: how he'd immigrated to Canada, done an assortment of odd jobs for the first little while, and then was lucky enough to land a position with the City of Toronto Social Services Department, one that he'd held for almost fifteen years now. He loved his work, was devoted to it, really, and, if he did say so himself, had been very successful at it. And, he said, waxing even more enthusiastic, now that he had put his eldest child through university, like father, like son, the boy was hoping to get on with the City of Toronto, too. Whether that would prove to be the case would remain to be seen, Bhupinder chuckled, and after giving us a chance to ask any questions we might have had up to that point (there were none) segued into an explanation of what employment counselling at Ontario Works was all about, and what it might be able to do for us.

It seemed to me, as I took a gander around the room, that my eyes weren't the only ones glazing over at the anticipated dullness of the topic. My elbow propped on my desk, my chin resting in my hand, I faded in and out of a light sleep during his lecture extolling the notable benefits of the City of Toronto's Employment Placement Program. I don't think it even occurred to him that we were an indifferent audience, that we were present for no other reason than we had to be in order to qualify for next month's welfare cheque. Nobody was listening to a word he was saying.

Yawns in abundance, smiles in short supply, people were bored stiff, nodding off or already asleep as he continued his paean to the Employment Placement Program . . . wrapping up his spiel by suddenly dropping his hitherto jolly manner, putting on a belligerent frown and warning us, in a reprimanding voice, that we "weren't going to be any more successful at getting a job in the future than we had been in the past." His frown deepening, he paused and looked around the room to see how the insult had registered. "Can someone tell me *why* I would make such a statement as that?"

No one could, so Bhupinder, his frown shifting into a knowing smile, directed our attention to the front of the room, where he clicked his PowerPoint remote and the projector blinked on. "I can *say* that," he explained emphatically, "because, like so many other people looking for jobs these days, *none* of you have access to the . . ."

He took a few steps back, so we could all see, and directed our attention to the words that had just appeared on the screen: HIDDEN JOB MARKET. "And *without* that access," Bhupinder added dramatically, "do you know what your chances will be of finding a paying job?"

No one with any apparent interest in answering the question, I didn't want to see Bhupinder left hanging (I'd found myself in the same situation from time to time as a teacher) so I ventured a guess and blurted out, "None?"

"Very good!" he said, greeting my response with a pleased smile, elaborating for several minutes to clarify what the "Hidden Job Market" actually was, how it worked and, more important for us, how the Employment Placement Program could be an invaluable asset in our "job-search toolbox." And to explain just *how* invaluable, he began asking employment- and job-related questions that, though some of us tried, we couldn't seem to answer to his satisfaction.

He'd wait for ten or fifteen seconds after posing each one, until it was clear, from the silence pervading the room that we were in need of his help, at which point he'd patiently direct our attention to the front of the room, where he revealed the correct answers on his PowerPoint slides. No charts, scales, graphs or diagrams, the slides consisted of single words, or numbers, again in the centre of the screen: things like "15" for the number of seconds employers devote to reading a job-application résumé; "NO" the answer to the question "Do you telephone an employer to ask about your application?"; ".02%" — the number of internet applications that resulted in someone being hired for a job; "Between 21 and 46" — the average percent of applications that resulted in employment for those who had participated in the Ontario Works Employment Placement Program; fairly exact numbers, it seemed to me, a percentage range that, as far as I knew, didn't technically qualify as an average, so I spoke up and asked Bhupinder if those percentages applied to jobs in all fields, or just some.

"It does," he answered quickly. "All jobs across the spectrum."

"Is there any way you can tell us which jobs fall into the forty-six percent category?" I asked, only half-kidding. "I mean, if we're going to be spending our time in a program for jobs that have a lower placement rate . . . you know what I mean?"

"I do," Bhupinder said, giving me a sly smile. "But I can't give you *that* kind of information, of course. It's part of accessing the hidden job market."

"So there's no way you could be a nice guy and give us a hint?" I said.

"Unfortunately not," he replied with a frown, and carried on with his presentation: blanket statements, sweeping generalizations, implausible comparisons, simplistic analogies and some pretty pompous pronouncements about us not understanding the realities of the employment market today.

Bhupinder seemed to be doing his utmost to make us feel

like we were incompetent, lazy boobs, flashing his single-word, single-number PowerPoint slides at us every few minutes and reading out the answers in a loud, clear voice like maybe we were not just unemployed, but deaf and illiterate, too.

The slide that broke the camel's back, so to speak, was the one he showed us last: "32." He explained, when the number appeared onscreen, that the EPP course ran for twenty-six weeks, in the Etobicoke Resource Centre, in the west end of Toronto, from 8:30 to 4:30 p.m. Monday to Friday; literacy and communication skills, computer basics, résumé writing, job-search strategies, and, of course, access to the Hidden Job Market.

The woman beside me, in some agitation by this point, spoke up. "I live at Morningside and Sheppard in the northeast part of Scarborough. For me to make it to Etobicoke by 8:30 in the morning, I'd have to leave my house at 6 a.m., and I wouldn't be home till close to 7:30 at night. You want me to do that for thirty-two weeks, just to qualify for $570 a month?"

A few others spoke up in complaint as well.

"Yeah!"

"Totally!"

"Right on, lady."

"It's *not* thirty-two weeks," Bhupinder corrected her, missing the point. "It's twenty-*six* weeks."

"Well, why does your slide say thirty-two?"

"It *used* to be thirty-two. We recently reduced it to twenty-six."

"So why the thirty-two? Why doesn't it say twenty-six?"

"Is it thirty-two or twenty-six?" someone else piped up.

"It's *twenty-six*!" Bhupinder said, clearly uneasy with this line of questioning.

"Maybe it's time to change your slide," the woman beside me said, shaking her head, a smirk on her face as she lowered her sunglasses, dialed a number on her cellphone and put it up to her ear.

Rattled by the insurrection he had on his hands, Bhupinder hastily switched off the projector, raised the screen and, noting that it was nearly 2:30 and time to be moving on, announced that there would be no break; that in the second hour, he was going to take us through exactly what *would* happen to our monthly payments in the event we *did* acquire one of the jobs that he'd spent the first part of the session persuading us we could never get.

As numbingly boring a topic as I could imagine, on top of the dressing-down 319 had seen fit to give me a few days earlier, I felt I'd had enough interaction with the Department of Social Services for one week, and slipped out quietly while Bhupinder was writing something on the board. If my staying for only half the session meant I'd only receive half my payment next month, so be it. I'd just start half-searching for a job; that way, or so I reasoned as I made my way along the hall toward the exit doors, if nothing materialized, I'd only be half-disappointed.

CHAPTER **TWENTY-FOUR**
DR. T

No further word from 319 about skipping out on the counselling session, my \$570 a month continued to come in, the metal recycling business Nicky and his friend Chris had started in the spring was flourishing, and my book was moving forward at a reasonably steady pace, a result, I'm sure, of the fact that Neil's house was by far the best living arrangement we'd had since Friendship Avenue. It helped, too, that a friend of Nicky's named Patrick Brody moved into our spare bedroom toward the end of the summer. Twenty-three at the time and in the landscaping business, Patrick was finding it impossible living with his parents and wanted to be out on his own. It was Patrick who'd loaned Nicky the \$3,000 to pay off his drug fine. He was a hard-working, high-energy, get-the-most-out-of-life guy and, like everyone else in Nicky's circle of friends, enjoyed having a joint now and then.

Nicky's and Patrick's friends became mine too. In their

early twenties now, I'd known many of them when they were in high school. Some had jobs, a number were taking university or college courses, all were still living at home with their parents. They reveled in the opportunity to hang out at Tudor Glen, a parent-free zone where they could chill with friends, have a beer and smoke a joint without being hassled. Most Saturday nights there was a potluck dinner. Twenty-five to thirty people were usually in attendance, everybody bringing food, drink and musical instruments. After dinner and a few puffs of whatever herbal product was going around, Nicky's friend Chris, who moonlighted as a DJ, would set up his turntable, sound and light system in the recreation room and spin dance-mix hits for a couple of hours, until Carson, Nicky and their band Out Go The Lights took the stage and dug into some classic rock favourites, and the dance-party continued. Neil Young tunes always prominent in their sets, they made "Like A Hurricane" their closing number that summer, the third anniversary of the raid.

Things were sailing along nicely at Neil's. Life was good. We were working hard, getting along well with each other (this was Patrick's first time living on his own) and having a lot of fun, in spite of the fact that Neil himself turned out to be another in our growing list of flaky landlords. Nothing to do when he had time off in Fort McMurray, he'd breeze into town every ten weeks or so and live with Nicky, Patrick and me at Tudor Glen. He justified the intrusions as his right as our landlord, an opportunity to see how we were "treating the place." He'd be up showering by six, go out for an hour, presumably for breakfast (his bedroom door padlocked in his absence), hole up in his bedroom most of the day, walk five blocks to the neighbourhood pub every night and stumble in the door at two or three in the morning, pouring out a slurred, ashamed-of-himself confession to us if we happened to be up, the same one every time: he was an alcoholic and just couldn't help himself when it came to booze.

On Friday nights around dinnertime he'd bring home a voluptuous, heavily made-up woman wearing flashy jewelry, a sexy, tight-fitting outfit and high-heels, he and his escort (a different one each time) chatting with us for a bit then disappearing upstairs for a few minutes, Neil bringing a large suitcase down with him when they returned to the living room. With his shaved-bald head, still dressed in his customary camouflage-pattern pants, black lug sole boots, white T-shirt and green army jacket — apparently oblivious to the incongruity of his wardrobe choices — he'd announce that they were off to spend the weekend at one of the big downtown hotels. Three days in the lap of luxury was how Neil described the junkets, assuming, in his naiveté I suppose, that Nicky, Patrick and I wouldn't recognize a high-priced booty call when we saw one.

These vacation stays were especially irritating because, as we came to learn, Neil had a slew of quirks that would drive even the most accommodating tenant around the bend. He demanded that we keep doors to the outside locked at all times, even if we were home. He was always checking the deadbolts, knobs and latches to make sure we were complying with his edict, scolding us roundly when he discovered we weren't, ultra-paranoid about someone breaking in and robbing him, even though the most novice of vandals could have told you at a glance there was absolutely nothing in the place worth taking. He insisted on using plug-in air-fresheners, "Tropical Bouquet" his scent of choice, an acridly sweet aroma that the three of us found toxic to breathe. Nicky having to stay outside because of his allergies, Patrick and I would remove the fresheners from the wall sockets around the house at our first opportunity (there were eleven in total) and chuck them in the garbage, only to find, within a few hours, that Neil had gone right out and bought a dozen new ones. He would have a tantrum if we left anything on a chair or a couch on which he wanted to sit down. He would let us know how upset he was was by taking his Gibson guitar, standing in front of Nicky and me (he was afraid of Patrick, who was about eight inches taller), and belting out tunes as loud as he could in his high-pitched, whiny voice. Shouting rather than singing the words, he'd beat down on the strings with his pick as he hurled boiling-mad renditions of songs by the Rolling Stones, The Animals, Johnny Cash or Neil Young at us. His voice straining, he'd play the whole song through with his eyes closed, then blink them open as he strummed the final chord, looking over at us with a stricken expression on his face like he might be about to cry; waiting for either Nicky or me to turn to him and say, "Yes, Neil? What did you have on your mind?"

He told Nicky, after his fourth holiday sojourn, that he wanted Patrick out before he came home next time. As Neil saw it, he was renting to Nicky and me; having Patrick there wasn't part of the deal. Among other things, it meant that he was forced to park his car on the street when he was at the house. Patrick's truck took up the second space. Neil said he couldn't have that when we were only paying for one.

The three of us decided we couldn't have that either, that Neil was not only one weird hombre, his controlling and self-serving approach to landlord–tenant relations wasn't something we were prepared to put up with. Though the rent was a relatively low $1,300 a month, which included utilities, Neil was the kind of guy who would have been a pain in the ass even if he were letting you have his house for free.

We started hunting for a new place and saw our hopes dashed pretty quickly by the sky-high prices people were asking for houses that, to us, barely qualified as dumps. Visions of Jean, Andy and Rick were never far from mind when we were talking to potential landlords, none of the dozen or so we met striking us as particularly tenant-friendly. With no success and Neil expected back in two weeks, we offered the place to a female friend of Nicky's and Patrick's. Angie and a friend of hers would rent Tudor Glen so Neil wouldn't be left with an empty house. Nicky would move back to his mother's, Patrick would go to his parents'. I wasn't sure what I'd do, though Angie said it would be no problem for me to stay and keep working on my book. But Neil went berserk when Nicky called him to propose the new arrangement. He wasn't going to rent to girls. He couldn't believe Nicky would betray him like this. Said he was just like all the other tenants he'd rented his house to. Everybody was just out to fuck him.

We hadn't been, of course, though that's what ended up happening. Patrick got the good news that an inheritance from his grandmother, which had been in the works for some time, had finally come through. He'd have enough money to buy his own house if he wanted to. He asked if we'd be interested in moving in with him, an offer to which we said yes immediately. Though we told him it came with one proviso: that there be no Febreze air fresheners allowed within 500 metres of the house. "Not even to remind us of what we're missing?" Patrick joked.

"Not even," Nicky said, unamused.

Since Patrick had no experience with real estate, an agent friend of mine took him under his wing. Within a week he'd found Patrick a cute, ten-year-old, three-bedroom house on a quiet street in one of the best areas of Whitby, Ontario, a commuter-suburb twenty miles east of Toronto. It was about half a block from the lake, a conservation area and bird sanctuary to the right at the bottom of the street, the fifteen-acre park and grounds of the Whitby Psychiatric hospital to the left. He moved in December 1, and Nicky and I joined him in January.

It was by far the most normal living arrangement I'd had since leaving Friendship Avenue: I had my own bedroom, there was a shopping plaza close by, a Tim Hortons coffee shop, a drug store, a Metro grocery store and a little diner where I sometimes had the $3.99 breakfast. Patrick was out all day at his landscaping job, and Nicky was off doing his scrap-metal recycling with Chris, which left me eight or nine hours of peace and quiet to work on the memoir. My desk and computer were set up against the window in the small living room just inside the front door; my piano, which Patrick had paid to have moved from Neil's, against the wall to my right. I could wheel my chair over to the keyboard anytime I felt like it and play some tunes. If I wanted fresh air, I could walk to the bottom of the street and stroll the grounds of the psychiatric hospital — the third new building on the property, as I later learned, but the same institution in which my Grandma Vi had been a patient from 1948 to 1950. Nicky's apartment at Rick's had been around the corner from where she was buried; now here I was living a couple of hundred yards from where she'd spent the last two years of her life. What were the odds?

Sometimes I'd walk to the east side of the hospital grounds and head up Gordon Street to the Tim Hortons. Occasionally there were groups of psychiatric patients and a supervisor walking up the street along with me. Harmless, hapless, medicated to the hilt I'm sure, a sad, silent lot that you couldn't help but feel sorry for, three of the more lively ones I came to call "the Babblers" because they talked to themselves non-stop as they shuffled along behind their supervisor. Two of the Babblers were women, the third a sturdily built man in his mid-forties who, whatever the weather, wore a Hunter green baseball cap on his head. Mumbling and muttering to himself about who knows what, he would break away from the group the moment he noticed me. Apparently unable to recall any of our previous conversations (I bumped into him two or three times a week), he'd sidle up and start walking beside me. "Bet you can't guess what my name is?" he'd say after a couple of minutes. "No, I can't," I'd reply, playing along. He'd stop, put his hands on my shoulders, turn me so I was facing him, then with a sly smile on his face, point his finger at the bright red letters stitched above the bill of his green cap. "Call Me Steve," it read. So I always did, though I noticed that his supervisor, when she called over to tell Steve it was time to fall back in with the group, addressed him as Howard, something I could never bring myself to do, however, as Steve seemed to be having so much fun with his delusion.

We'd been living at Patrick's for about three months when Nicky received a letter from the Ministry of Transportation informing him that as there was still $4,100 remaining on his driving-without-insurance fine, his licence had been suspended. As well, since he had yet to qualify for his G licence (the final upgrade in the government's graduated program) within the five years since he'd obtained his G1, his licence had been cancelled as well; he'd have to apply for a new one, and begin the graduated program from the start as though he was a new driver.

A second letter, this one from the company handling his auto insurance informed him that they'd been alerted to the no-insurance fine and his licence cancellation, on which basis they were withdrawing their insurance coverage, reminding him, in the notice's final sentence, that he "continued to be responsible for paying his $1,180 monthly premium until his policy was restored."

Without a licence and an insured truck, he couldn't do his metal recycling with Chris. Revenue plummeted to next to nothing, and their dreams and hard work would be down the drain until Nicky completed the re-licencing process and put some money toward his insurance fine. It was an impossible situation, really, since even when he was good to go with his licence, he'd need to pay at least $1,000 off the fine and upwards of $1,500 a month for car insurance, an amount that would mean that after he paid it, his rent and his $300 car loan, plus his share of the $3,000 for printing and distributing metal-recycling flyers, no matter how many hours he worked he'd still be losing money and falling further into debt.

The only solution, or so it was explained to us at the licence bureau, was for Nicky to transfer ownership of his Ford Ranger to me.

Through an agent at State Farm, a woman who'd been one of Nicky's lawn-clients, I managed to take out a policy on the truck: two hundred dollars a month, renewable every six months, no credit check necessary. Nicky's Aunt Carol bought him four new tires as a birthday present and the vehicle passed its emissions and safety checks with no problem. We went back to the licencing bureau (I drove, while Nicky kept an eye out for the cops, since all we needed was to be nailed for having no insurance, a $10,000 fine for a second offence). When it was our turn we presented our filled-out paperwork, the licencing fee and the State Farm insurance certificate to a woman perhaps in her early thirties — a cheery, encouraging smile on her face while she was serving us, like she somehow *knew* that, for us, this was no ordinary transaction.

A new set of licence plates, a sworn affidavit of transfer, my signature in half a dozen places and everything else appearing to be "hunky-dory" according to Elyse . . . she was handing me the ownership package, I was just putting my fingers around it —when to my horror she withdrew it, saying she remembered there was one other thing she was supposed to check.

No idea what it could be, I noticed her jaw dropping and her eyes going wide as she stared in some disbelief at the screen. "You'd better have a look at this yourself," she said, angling it so I could see:

Paul Illidge
122 Friendship Avenue
407 Toll-Road Charges: $4,972

"*FUCK!*" I shouted, backing away from the counter. Turned to see more than a few eyes in the waiting-area looking over at me in alarm. "407!" I said by way of explanation, people relaxing when they heard, several nodding in sympathy, a few shaking their heads, a brawny guy with a moustache, tattoos on his forearms wearing a Pittsburg Steelers ball cap, calling out, "How much?"

"Five grand."

"Fucking pricks," he said.

"It's twenty-seven-and-a-half percent, daily interest," Elyse pointed out as I returned to the counter. "If I were you, I'd take care of it as soon as I could."

"I haven't owned a car since 2007," I told her. "I last drove the 407 in 2001. I've licenced four cars since then, how could it be a problem now?"

Elyse didn't know, said she was sorry, but had to get on with her other customers.

Then, as Nicky and I walked out to the car, it hit me. My brother John had got me to lease a Honda CRV for him when he came to live with me after his bankruptcy in 2001. For his girlfriend Mandy, he said, who drove in from Ottawa every weekend to see him, and up to his farm in Collingwood, two hours northwest of the city. She would have used the 407 regularly. As she'd skipped out on the CRV payments after a year (Honda repossessing the car, which was in my name), she'd probably stopped paying her toll-road charges too. Even if it had only been a few hundred dollars at the time, as Elyse warned, with a 27½% daily interest rate, the bill could add up pretty fast.

With a potential $10,000 fine for a second driving-without-insurance conviction, Nicky had no choice but to drop out of the metal business. As it was our main source of income, my $570 a month was all we had to live on now. Chris, hoping to keep recycling metal on his own, was giving Nicky $3,000 for withdrawing from the partnership (all the cash he could borrow from his dad), but that would be gone within a few months.

Patrick was sympathetic, of course, and commiserated. But he said the costs of home-ownership had turned out to be more than he'd bargained for, he was strapped for cash and it was stressing him out. He needed to have paying tenants in the house to help pay the mortgage and taxes. What made the decision so tough, he said, was that the three of us had become good friends in the last year; he hated to think he was throwing us out, but he just didn't know what else he could do.

Nicky would move back into his mother's apartment, which came with a parking spot where he could leave his truck until something could be worked out in the way of insurance. With the chances of finding a job slim to none, he thought he might go back to school; maybe study to become a chef. That way he could qualify for student welfare, $570, the same as me, $200 of which he could give to his mom for the rent she was asking, then put the other $300 toward his monthly car-loan payment.

Coming up with a place for me to live was a little more complicated. I'd put out feelers to friends and acquaintances who I guessed might have space and be of "charitable spirit" toward a starving-artist writer, one who was neat and tidy, willing to sleep anywhere and wouldn't disrupt their normal routines in any way, not when I'd be spending ten to twelve hours a day in front of my computer. "Why, you'll hardly even know I'm there," I said in my email pitch.

No takers, one friend leveled with me and explained that $350 just didn't cut it in today's rental market. Another joked, only half-kidding, that he was worried if he let me in he'd never get rid of me. One said it was terrible that my life had "gotten to such a low point." The other ten or so never bothered to reply.

None of them cold-hearted misers, all longtime supporters of my writing, I wasn't so much bothered by the rejection from a friendship point of view, as from a professional one. This would be my fifth move in the last two years. As I said to Malcolm, who was sympathetic and had offered his cabin near Minden, Ontario, if nothing else panned out, not a lot of writing gets done when you're living on the run. He said he could see that, but suggested people's reticence stemmed from the fact that what had happened to me was their idea of an urban nightmare: finding themselves with no money and no place to live. "Your situation reminds them of their worst fears, Paul. That's all it is."

With four days to go before Patrick's new tenants moved in, Malcolm's northern cabin looking like it would be my abode for the winter, Nicky returned from the local grower's supply store early one afternoon with the news that he'd been talking to his friend Glenn, the owner, about doing some consulting work Glenn was lining up: helping people who'd obtained permission from Health Canada to grow their own marijuana, but had no idea how to go about doing so. Oddly enough, it wasn't a required qualification for obtaining a licence; Nicky would simply be acting in an advisory capacity, providing expertise and tips on the growing process; there was nothing illegal about doing that, at least according to Glenn, because everyone was participating in the government's medicinal program.

An excited smile on his face as the two of us walked into the kitchen, he plucked the portable phone from its stand and had me follow him into the living room. He sat me down in one of the armchairs then pulled a yellow Post-It note out of his pocket and handed it to me. "Dr. T" was written in blue pen, a long-distance area code and phone number below.

This Dr. T was apparently open to signing Health Canada grow-licences and, according to Glenn, I could make an appointment and he'd see me within two weeks. He'd just signed Glenn's application form, he was a good guy, up-to-speed about Health Canada marijuana regulations, Glenn sure that he'd sign one for me if I applied. The fee was $250, and the licence would be granted and mailed out in eight to ten weeks if everything was in order.

A marijuana grow-licence was something I'd been wanting to have since the night of the raid. I couldn't see why, in a country with a much-boasted-about Charter of Rights and Freedoms like Canada's, one of those rights wouldn't be that an individual can "make" marijuana in one's home if he or she wants to, the same way people make their own wine or beer. I wasn't dangerous, I wouldn't be hurting anyone, and I had no interest whatsoever in trafficking; as far as I was concerned, what I did in the privacy of my home was nobody's business but my own. I was a responsible, intelligent, law-abiding citizen, less a threat to public safety (or so, from experience, it seemed to me), than those bent on enforcing out-of-date laws and doing all they can to demonize marijuana offenders with the hokey myths they subscribed to. The propaganda they promulgated in the process was as inaccurate, misleading and alarmist as it had been during the "reefer madness" of the 1950s. We were in the second decade of the 21st century, for heaven's sake. What was the big deal, really?

Nothing ventured, nothing gained, Nicky and I agreed, after talking about it, that I should take the last $250 of his settlement money from Chris and put it toward the Health Canada licence. Why not? My Ontario Works cheque would be coming through in about two weeks; Nicky would be moving back to Julie's, one way or another I'd find someplace to live and work on my book. We'd been waiting for this opportunity for so long, how could we afford *not* to go and see what Dr. T had to say?

I called the number Glenn had given Nicky and talked to his nurse, who booked an appointment for me the following week. I printed up and filled out the nine-page Health Canada application (basic information, an outline of what "security measures" would be used for the dried marijuana, one of the most straightforward pieces of government paperwork that I think I'd ever filled out), had a passport photo taken, and a little before eight o'clock one morning headed west on Highway 401 in the uninsured Ranger to make my 9:30 appointment with the doctor.

Nicky kept his eyes peeled for cops while I drove, just in case they decided to run the plates, which were still in his name, his drug-trafficking conviction the first thing that would pop up, as it had with the cops outside Swiss Chalet. It would be just what we needed, to get pulled over on our way to apply for a marijuana grow-licence.

Numerous slowdowns and frequent stoppages because of the rush hour, we arrived at the west-end hotel not far from the airport where the clinic was taking place with about five minutes to spare. We parked the Ranger and entered the front lobby, the concierge sizing us up and pointing to a hall off to her left, Dr. T's clinic being held in Conference Room D. Nicky wished me good luck, said, "May the Grow-Force be with you," and took a seat on a chair in the lobby, while I hustled down the hall, 9:29 by the clock at the front desk, right on time.

The conference room having been set up like a medical office, a woman in light-blue hospital scrubs with a stethoscope around her neck greeted me with a welcoming smile when I walked in. She verified my appointment on a clipboard she had with her then passed me off to a woman in regular clothes who brought me over to a long table across the room, and had me take a seat in front of one of three women, also in regular clothes, who were there to "advise and assist" in the application process.

The woman assigned to me went over my application with me, made sure everything was in order and that I understood its terms, conditions and various legalities, then had me print my name in capital letters at the bottom of every page, a little trick, she said, that they found expedited the processing of the licencing forms. "Good luck," she said after I'd handed her my $250, directing me further down the room to a desk that was set up in front of a grey, cloth-covered divider, where a nurse in plum-coloured scrubs and white running-shoes, also with a stethoscope around her neck, was sitting awaiting my arrival.

Over the next ten minutes she took a quick but what seemed like a thorough enough medical history, after which she inquired about my current physical health, tested my blood pressure, noted the two medications I was using (both compatible with cannabis use, so she said) then asked me to follow her around the divider to meet Dr. T.

A man about my age, well over six feet tall, with a tanned face, deep-brown eyes and long grey hair that fell halfway down his back, in his faded blue-jean shirt, similarly faded and patched blue jeans and red Converse low-cut running shoes he looked like someone who might have just got back from Woodstock. We shook hands, sat down on either side of a work table and discussed my application.

After perusing it, Dr. T said he noticed that I'd checked "Anxiety and Depression" as well as "Arthritis" as my reason for wanting medicinal marijuana. On the anxiety and depression, I described the raid and told him my doctor felt I was suffering post-traumatic stress. My symptoms included insomnia, nightmares, flashbacks, panic attacks, paranoia, agoraphobia, and a pronounced tremor in both my hands that disappeared completely when I used marijuana. My fear was that Health Canada might be leery of a self-diagnosis as a basis for approval, and so I'd checked off arthritis on my application too. I told him that I did indeed suffer from it in my knees, wrists and fingers, pointing out to him that, as I made my living as a writer, I felt its effects every day when I sat down to work.

Originally from Savannah, Georgia, as I later found out, Dr. T explained, in his slow, southern drawl, that there was no real way of X-raying for arthritis; that as for my anxiety and depression, it sounded, from the symptoms I'd described, that I *was* suffering post-traumatic stress. And while it seemed to him that it was worthy of consideration, he said I was right in my assumption. The government would reject it unless I had an extensive mental-illness paper trail.

He crumpled up the medical practitioner's form I'd filled out, tossed it in the wastebasket under the table then reached over to a series of different-coloured file folders he had with him, took out a fresh one, checked 'Arthritis' as the health condition for which I required treatment, and signed his name at the bottom: his prescription calling for 14 grams (half an ounce) of cannabis per day; the higher amount required, as I'd explained to him, since I ingested rather than inhaled most of my marijuana, several ounces at a time required for a batch of canna-butter cookies, and three or four carrot cakes.

"Well, you're good to go now," Dr. T said with a smile and stood up. "Happy baking."

"What would you say the chances are of my application going through?"

"Haven't been turned down yet," he smiled as we shook hands. He gave me my completed application and escorted me back around the divider, at which point the nurse who'd greeted me when I arrived materialized and walked me over to the door. "It'll be eight to ten weeks before the licence is issued," she let me know, "but Health Canada's usually pretty good with Dr. T's patients, so there's a good chance it might come earlier. Make a photocopy of the application before you send it off. It's your licence in the meantime. The police can't touch you. Good luck!"

CHAPTER **TWENTY-FIVE**
LET IT GO

Thoughtful as it was of Malcolm to let me have his log cabin for the winter, my friend Russ Tamblyn, who had seen the place and knew the area, felt it was a terrible idea. It was three miles from the nearest town, I wouldn't have a car, the snow was five or six feet deep during winter, there were power outages once or twice a week, there was no insulation, only an ancient space heater and a fireplace with a draft problem, and once I brought in food, the place would be overrun with mice. Russ said Stephen King's *The Shining* came to mind, and as I knew how things turned out for the writer in King's story, he said he couldn't in good conscience let me do that to myself. He had a better idea.

The morning I was to be out of Patrick's, Nicky drove out to Whitby, helped me load my clothes, my desk, my computer and a few books into the Ranger and we headed — via the back roads, of course — to Aurora, Ontario, twenty-five miles north of Toronto, where Russ lived. Friends since the late 1970s when we taught together, Russ had a furnished apartment in the basement of his house (renovated bathroom, stove and fridge, gas fireplace, door out to the backyard) that he sometimes rented out to community college students. As no one was there now, he'd let me have it for $300 a month, on account, kidding me that I could pay him back from the millions I made on my book.

Six weeks later, not the eight that I'd been expecting, Nicky picked me up at Russ's and we drove to the Purolator courier depot near Patrick's where I signed for a delivery from Health Canada: the envelope containing my suitable-for-framing marijuana grow-licence. We were elated of course, but at the same time bowled over at seeing the numbers actually in print, an official government seal, and the signature of the Minister of Health authorizing me "to store for personal use up to 3,150 grams (7 pounds) of marijuana at any time; have up to 420 grams (15 ounces) of marijuana on my person at any time; and have sixty-nine plants in production in my place of residence at any time."

"Uncanny," I said to Nicky, "that they'd have arrived at the number 69, when it was '69 PLANTS' Val's crew etched in black magic-marker on the wall of my office during the raid. How ironic is that?"

"We should mail it to Officer Val," Nicky said.

"Slip it in with a copy of the book."

"Better black out the address, though. Just in case," he said, smirking.

My six-month stint at Russ Tamblyn's coming to an end because he'd arranged to rent his apartment to a community college student for the summer (it had been a prolific stay;

since Russ was seldom home, knowing not a soul in Aurora and too low on cash to travel to Toronto, I just sat at my computer and wrote all day), Nicky arrived with the Ranger on the first of May, packed me up (he had his routine pretty much down to a science now) and drove me an hour and a half west to Peterborough, Ontario, to a house owned by a friend of his, Brent Murray.

Brent had worked at a construction job in northern Ontario after high school and managed to make a good chunk of money, what with overtime and isolation pay, but he'd quit the job a year ago to return to school, taking business studies at the community college that was just ten minutes up the road from the house he was able to buy with his construction money. It was a little bungalow in a new subdivision on Peterborough's western boundary, farm fields at the end of the street, cows grazing, a large pond, and a windmill beside the barn.

Though four guys had been living in the house with Brent during the school year, two of them had moved out, which freed up one of the two bedrooms on the main floor at the front of the house, or one in the basement, which was completely soundproof, according to Brent, as Ryan, the previous occupant, who'd moved to the bedroom upstairs, had done all the sound mixing for his DJ business here. With the door closed, Brent said he could guarantee that I wouldn't hear a peep. He offered to do a quick sound check, but I told him that wasn't necessary, I'd be happy to take the room.

My routines much like they had been at Russ's, I woke early, wrote, with a minimal number of breaks, for twelve hours a day, with time off for walks around town, to the library and a nearby Tim Hortons, dictating notes and reminders into my tape-recorder along the way. Dinner at about 8, usually a can of sardines or tuna, celery, some cookies and yogurt for dessert, I'd read for a few hours afterwards, have a bowl of Cheerios at my desk (the only table in the room) around 10:30, and be in bed by 11, my nighttime reading consisting of books that I knew would keep my mind off my own. Tolstoy's *Anna Karenina*, then *War and Peace*; *Vanity Fair* by William Thackeray; *Lonesome Dove* by Larry McMurtry, *The Liar's Club* by Mary Karr; and Bob Dylan's autobiography, *Chronicles*, which I read twice, I liked it so much. In fact, by the time I was finished with it, I'd underlined words and sometimes whole sentences on about every fifth page. Dylan's grandmother telling him that "Happiness isn't on the road to anything, happiness *is* the road," and "Everyone you'll ever meet in this life is fighting a hard battle so remember to be kind" were two phrases that I liked in particular.

Nicky and I were still living on my monthly welfare cheque (he had no other income, and his mother wasn't in a position to help him out beyond giving him free room and board), and I'd been transferred to the City of Peterborough's social services department, my new case-worker, Lorraine, cut from the same cloth as 319 as it turned out. On pain of having my benefits suspended, I had to show up for a meeting with Lorraine every three weeks or so and give her a complete job-search report, thirty-minute sessions similar to those I'd had with 319.

Like 319, too, Lorraine would sit sideways to me and type everything I said into her computer, her eyes on the screen the majority of the time, keeping up a steady stream of comments, criticisms and what I felt was an intrusive number of interrogation-style questions about why I wasn't finding work if I was doing everything I said I was. She glanced over at me occasionally, but never really looked at me until, when my time was up, she'd press the print button, jump up from her chair and dash out the door into the case workers' area, returning with thirty or forty photocopied pages, copies of my various Agreements (they weren't transferrable between offices for some reason), and a full transcript of our conversation.

Several times I showed up for meetings only to be told that Lorraine was on vacation, that I should have been notified about it when in each case I hadn't. Twice she was fifteen to twenty minutes late for the meeting (my appointments were usually right after lunch), going on the offensive to cover her tardiness the moment she sat down, her comments negative, suspicious and sometimes blatantly accusatory. Her purpose, as far as I could gather, was to discern whether I was legitimately on welfare, or operating some sort of scam and up to no good.

She reminded me regularly of the prevalence of welfare fraud in Peterborough these days as, according to her, eighty percent of the population was living on one form of social assistance or another. She was always letting me know that there was a twenty-four-hour snitch-line people could call to report cheats — and the callers didn't have to leave their names or phone numbers. She let me know, more than a few times, that she found it hard to believe someone of my age, experience and qualifications, would come to a place like Peterborough expecting to find a job, made a point of telling me one day that she'd called up Brent, my landlord, and he didn't seem to know the first thing about me, not even my last name.

And if I wasn't shaking in my boots at this, and a few

other surveillance tactics her department used, she pointed out in one of our meetings that she could demand a year's worth of bank statements from me at any time, just to see that nothing "untoward" was going on with my account; $20 a page it would cost me, she said, $240 that would come out of my cheque for that month.

"But, Lorraine, why would you even do something like that?" I asked her, trying not to laugh. "Why are you making me out to be the mastermind of some fraud scheme, for a whole $570 a month? I've been with Ontario Works for three years. You think I'm stashing the loot in the Cayman Islands?"

"We do things differently here in Peterborough," she said with a defensively straight face, turned back to her computer, assumed her stenographic pose, and off we went with my latest report.

Lorraine might have had her redeeming features, but if so, they sure weren't on display with me. She seemed to have a permanently hostile attitude toward me, was patronizing, demeaning and so confrontational about anything I said that after four months of this treatment, I looked up the number for the twenty-four-hour snitch line, went to the payphone in the parking lot beside Tim Hortons that I walked to every morning, and reported *her* as the real welfare bum. Although I wasn't compelled to, I left my name, my nine-digit case-number, and a brief message that I asked to be conveyed to Lorraine: "I quit."

The situation was deteriorating at Brent's around that time, too: his tenant Ryan (the DJ, living in the front bedroom upstairs) was behind $2,500 in rent, and his girlfriend, Dana, banned from the house until he'd paid some of it off. But whenever Brent wasn't around (he was in Toronto at his parents' or at his girlfriend's three or four days a week), whom did Ryan quietly sneak into the house but good old Dana.

An airhead, in everyone's opinion, with big boobs and a nice body, she and Ryan regularly mooched other people's food and booze, never cleaned up after themselves and, if they weren't lolling on the living-room couch watching TV while making out and groping one another, were off in Ryan's room having sex. The upstairs bedroom, however, wasn't soundproofed to the extent that the one in the basement had been. Though Ryan kept the club music pumping good and loud, Dana was a screamer, so every cry, wail, panted request or shriek of pleasure came through to the rest of us more graphically than we'd have preferred.

The Ryan and Dana Show continued off and on over the summer, a distraction I didn't need when I was trying to make as much headway with the book as I could, since I had nowhere else to go if I moved out of Brent's. I determined to make the best of a less-than-ideal situation and decided I'd stay on, burying myself in my book so that with the door closed in my soundproof basement bedroom I began to feel like a Trappist monk, my days spent alone and in silence — no TV, no newspapers, no phone or internet. Brent and the two other guys who lived in the house were back at college as of September so they were never around. I wrote, read, slept and wrote some more, ate little, walked as much as I could, and every night made a point of strolling to the farm field at the end of the street to watch the cows while I smoked a joint and thought about my writing for the next day. Making hay while the sun shines, as I thought of it. I was out of money now, and didn't know how much longer Brent was going to let me stay. He was a good guy, but I didn't want to turn into another Ryan the Sponge on him.

Nicky phoned the second week of October, excited to tell me that he'd left his mother's apartment and moved back in with Patrick in Whitby. His two tenants had vacated, my old bedroom was free again and I could have it back whenever I wanted. More good news in his call, he said that Patrick wanted him to set up a unit in his basement and start growing. Patrick had assembled X-rays and MRIs of his back, which he'd injured at his landscaping job a couple of years ago. The pain had become chronic now; left him lying on the living-room floor after work every day, too sore to move. He had Dr. T's number and was going to ask him to sign his licence.

In the meantime, he was hoping it would be all right with me to use mine, so things would be underway by the time his came through. He was buying pot now from a website called BudMail, an online store out of British Columbia, but the prices were way too high for the amount Patrick needed for it to do his back any good.

Nicky had Glenn, his grow-store friend, fix him up with several new strains whose genetics were excellent for pain relief. They weren't widely available — these were not commercial strains that produced quantity, but instead were bred for premium quality by growers that supplied the various compassion societies around Toronto.

Patrick springing for the cost of the equipment, Nicky working his cloning magic, we posted my framed licence at the top of the basement stairs (as we were required to do), and in a few months our first crop of plants was thriving peacefully under several 1,000 watt, Hortilux high-pressure sodium lights. We stuck to the terms laid out in the licence, followed through on our "projected security plan" (this the biggest section of the application form) and made a point of keeping the doors to the house and the basement locked at all times. The door to the room where the plants were growing had a key-lock on it, as did the freezer where the dried marijuana was to be stored. With an industrial-sized charcoal filter cleaning the air twenty-four-hours a day, unless one of us had tipped you off beforehand, you'd never have guessed, when you first walked in the house, that we had thirty-eight pungently-scented marijuana plants growing in the basement.

As grow-licences had to be renewed every year, with Health Canada asking Patrick's doctor to provide them with additional medical information and only three months remaining on mine, Nicky took me over to see Glenn, who gave me the name and phone number of the doctor who'd just signed his renewal. Dr. T had run into some legal trouble, apparently, but according to Glenn, this new physician, Dr. O, was a great guy, sympathetic to "the cause," and well informed about the Health Canada program.

Dr. O's office was about thirty minutes from Toronto, on the second floor of an office building that served as the hub of a busy plaza. Nicky came along for the appointment. We were surprised when we walked into his office and found about two dozen people waiting to see Dr. O (or two other family physicians whose names we'd noticed on the door). There were several mothers-to-be, mothers with babies, an elderly couple, a woman in a dress-suit, three or four teenage girls, a boy of about ten with his father, and a man in his late thirties supervising some toddlers in the play area. As normal a doctor's office as you're likely to find.

I checked in at reception, paid the $250 Medicinal

Marijuana Program fee, gave Dr. O's nurse my health card number and, after about a ten-minute wait (Nicky and I managed to grab the last available seats), my name was called by Dr. O, who was standing looking over the waiting room with a file folder in his hand.

A man in his early forties with sandy-blond hair, a blue button-down shirt, thin tie and khaki pants under his white lab-coat, he introduced himself as we started along the hall toward the examining rooms. He paused to shake my hand then stepped back and pointed me into the next room on my left.

We spent about ten minutes going through my application, Dr. O asking me more or less the same questions Dr. T had, to which my answers were more or less the same. Everything checking out, he signed for a new "prescription": 48 plants this time, instead of 69, with the licence good until the spring of 2014 when, he was sorry to say, the government was apparently changing the regulations and ending the program, replacing it with something new. Details were sketchy, according to Dr. O, but in his opinion it was disappointing. Rather than medical considerations, politics and tax-generation were the government's new priorities.

And sure enough, shortly after my new licence arrived, Prime Minister Harper announced how his government's re-designed marijuana program would work: people wanting to purchase marijuana could do so, legally, through registered government growers in different parts of the country. A doctor's signature was required to obtain a possession licence. Orders were to be placed over the internet, there would be three strains of marijuana available, at "market prices" set by the growers, on which there would be GST. The Conservative government was accepting applications from private business groups interested in the $2 billion in sales medicinal marijuana was expected to generate annually.

There were to be harsher, mandatory minimum sentences for people caught growing their own pot: anything more than five plants under cultivation would result in six months in prison (as compared, interestingly, with a term of forty-five days for "sexually touching a person under the age of sixteen"). If I held on to my forty-eight plants after the deadline for switching over to the new system and was busted, I'd be looking at a mandatory five years in prison: one day a guy just legally growing his plants, twenty-four hours later a felon facing a stint of hard time, in one of the new billion-dollar super-jails the government was building as a result of what the Prime Minister's spokesman, Minister of Asian Pacific Affairs Stockwell Day, explained as "the shocking rise in unreported crimes."

The media had a field day with the notion, no one quite sure how the government had gone about determining statistics on crimes that "may or may not have taken place." It was a bit of a joke, too, legal analysts pointed out, since these harsher "mandatory minimums" were to be applied only on conviction. The first thing defence lawyers were bound to have their clients do was demand a trial, maybe even a trial by jury. The court system couldn't handle the number of cases it had now; hence the prevalence (ninety-seven percent) of them ending in plea bargains. Were there enough Officer Val's out there, enough dedicated drug-busting crusaders to keep up with the thousands of people who "might or might not be growing?"

The way the police delayed and obfuscated in criminal

cases as it was, how long would it take to select twelve-person juries? Schedule judges, Crown Attorneys, find defence lawyers and mobilize court staff, just for the trial of someone on a charge of having eight or nine marijuana plants in his or her basement? And what right-minded, even slightly compassionate judge was going to confine someone to a prison cell for five or six years, simply because they were growing their own pot rather than buying it from the high-priced, government-appointed dealers?

Why was the government even thinking about "getting tough" on something they ultimately wouldn't be able to do anything to curtail, much less stop? Millions of Canadians were using cannabis regularly, thousands growing it, more turning to it medicinally, as well as recreationally, all the time. Even the leader of the Liberal Party of Canada, Justin Trudeau, announced publicly that, not only did he use marijuana from time to time; he'd done so as a sitting member of Parliament.

The news coming as a shocking revelation to no one except Prime Minister Harper that a man in his forties with a high-profile job, an accomplished wife, and three young children might want to have himself a puff of pot now and again, I was prompted by his scoffing condemnation of Trudeau's "use of drugs" to write an op ed on the need for the Conservative government to get with the times. Even President Obama's attorney general had conceded the War on Drugs had failed. Why was Canada still fighting it?

As for cancelling the medicinal marijuana program, I suggested that the government's new policy of making only three strains of marijuana available to medicinal users was like liquor stores stocking only three kinds of booze, one brand of beer, one of liquor, and one of wine — red or white since you couldn't have both. I wrote that I thought it was wrong for the government to turn a perfectly good medicinal program over to for-profit interests, a move that only guaranteed black market dealers higher prices for lower quality marijuana and brought criminal elements out of the woodwork and allowed them to thrive in ways they hadn't since the government medicinal program started in 2001.

"Canadians," I continued, "are legally allowed to possess quite an array of rifles, shotguns, various semi-automatic handguns, and all the ammunition they want. If the government is okay with some two million people keeping over eight million potentially lethal weapons in their homes (a CBC statistic), why is it so bent on prosecuting those who choose to grow a few non-lethal marijuana plants in theirs?

"As to Justin Trudeau's honest admission that he's smoked the vile weed, surely the government remembers it was his father, Pierre, who in 1967, as federal justice minister, was responsible for striking down the laws that made homosexuality illegal in Canada, declaring that 'the state has no business in the bedrooms of the nation.' Wouldn't it be ironic," I wrote in closing, "if it was his son who ended up adding, fifty or so years later, that it has no business in any other room of the house either?"

Patrick, Nicky and I were happy to continue growing in the meantime, careful to keep the number of plants we had under cultivation well below what we were legally allowed, focusing on quality over quantity, the three of us in agreement, come harvest time, that the results were "just what the doctor ordered."

All seemed to be going well on other fronts as well. I was starting in on the final section of my book, had been off welfare for a year, was eating properly again, sleeping well, living on an Ontario Arts Council grant my publisher had recommended me for, and the arrival of a surprise bonanza: a $3,000 cheque from my book distributor for the remaindered copies of my *Shakespeare Novels*.

So I was in a rather celebratory mood on Easter Sunday morning in 2013, when I set out for the Whitby GO station to take the train downtown to meet Carson, Nicky and Hannah for lunch at a restaurant we sometimes went to called Allen's. As Nicky was already in the city with his truck, I left the house a little after 10 and walked at a faster-than-usual pace over to the station so as not to miss the train.

Though I thought I'd been making good time, as I was crossing the parking lot, maybe a hundred feet from the entrance, I saw the westbound train arriving. My only chance of making it was to pass on buying a ticket and hightail it as fast as I could through the lot, into the station, along the tunnel downstairs and up to the track before it departed.

The train waited a few extra minutes, so I raced to the top of the stairs, tore across the platform and leapt into the closest set of doors, just before they closed. I slid panting onto the first seat I came to, gasping for breath after the hundred-metre dash. My face and upper body pouring with sweat, my heart pounding like it was headed into cardiac arrest at any moment, the next thing I knew, there was a GO Transit Special Constable standing over me, an older man, maybe in his late-fifties, a fringe of short grey hair under his dark-blue cap and a stern look on his face as he asked to see my ticket.

I admitted straight out that I hadn't bought one, but explained that I'd had to run to make the train and felt I was in heart-attack territory, which I assumed should have been obvious from the way I was perspiring and gasping for breath.

Readying a digital device in his hand, he asked for some identification. Not having any (at least that's what I told him, annoyed that he was actually going to write me up for a fine over my lack of an $8 ticket on Easter morning), the constable asked for my name, address and phone number, reminding me that if I gave him false information I was committing "transportation fraud."

Irritated that he was overdoing things, I gave my name as David Illidge (my second name) along with Patrick's address and what I thought was his correct home phone number. He punched the info into his device, studied it for a moment, took a hard look at me then grabbed the radio off his hip and called for back-up. I asked him what he was doing, why he was escalating the situation like this. It was me who was escalating the situation, he said, his temper rising. Providing false information to a transit officer, transportation fraud, he reminded me again, a fine of $360 on top of the $110 I'd pay for not having a ticket.

Back-up turned out to be a young, fresh-faced transit officer who looked to be about the same age as Nicky. He watched me while the older officer dashed up to the second-level of the car — where I could still see him — and dialed a number on his cellphone, Patrick's I had no doubt.

Meanwhile the young officer asked if I had the money to actually purchase a ticket; whether I'd be paying for it with cash or credit card if I did. I said I actually did and that I'd be using, cash. "Well," he said, as though that settled the matter, "you'll be put off at the next station, have to buy a ticket and catch a later train."

"Not quite," the older officer piped up, returning from making his phone call. "There's nobody by that name at the number you gave me."

"Who did you talk to?" I asked, knowing there was nobody home at Patrick's.

"Doesn't matter who I talked to. What matters is you're committing transportation fraud."

Not wanting to tangle with him any more than I had to, I said that I'd only been living at this place for a few months and never made phone calls; maybe I'd given him the wrong number. I told him I was going downtown to meet my kids for Easter lunch at 12:30; that if I had to wait an hour for the next train I'd be two hours late. I asked if he couldn't cut me some slack, it was Easter Sunday for Pete's sake.

"Neither here nor there. You supplied false information."

"Mistaken information. Why don't you let me see if you've got the right number."

"I've *got* your number. It's transportation fraud, Mister."

"So you're saying that the only thought on my mind as I was racing to catch the train was how I could get away with not buying a ticket?"

"You're not doing yourself any favours here, Mister."

"I just don't know why you're trying so hard to escalate the situation, sir."

"*I'm* not the one escalating the situation!" he shot back. "*You* are, Mister!"

"Look," I said, "just write me out the ticket. I don't care what it's for. But I'd really appreciate it if you wouldn't throw me off the train — on Easter Sunday," I repeated, hoping it might spark a little compassion.

"Too late for that now," he said, and scurried down the

aisle behind me, leaving the young officer in charge of me until, a few minutes later, we arrived at the next station. The older guy showed up just as we were pulling in, took one of my arms and instructed the young guy to get the other. When we came to a stop, the two of them escorted me off the train, waited till the doors closed and it departed, then walked me across the platform over to the chain-link fence beside the parking lot.

Five minutes and $470 later, the older officer finishing up with my tickets ($110 for not paying my fare, $360 for providing false information), the young guy began lecturing me: he was surprised that someone my age would try to pull something like this. It was the kind of behaviour they expected from teenagers, not older —

"I think you should shut your mouth right now, Junior," I said, cutting him off. "Giving me a ticket doesn't mean you have the right to insult me."

"I was just saying —"

The old guy muttering something, the young guy threw me a look but backed off, his partner passing me my tickets. I asked him if I could have his name so I could request him to be present in court at my trial. He said nothing, only pointed to the number "87" above the breast-pocket of his uniform.

"What about you?" I said, turning to the young guy. Nervous about the question, looking to his older partner first to make sure it was okay (the older guy nodded), he pointed to the number "76" on his chest. And the two of them sauntered down the platform into the station building. The kids were still at Allen's when I finally arrived at 2:15. They'd had some wine while they were waiting. I got the story of my escapade with 87 and 76 out of the way quickly, and we ended up having an enjoyable Easter lunch after all.

Six weeks later, the day of my trial, I arrived at the courtroom a few minutes late, proceedings already underway. The Crown Attorney was back and forth between her table and the bar, running through guilty pleas for GO Transit offences like parking outside designated spots or in handicapped areas, not having valid tickets, most of the fines in the $110 to $250 dollar range, which on the Crown Attorney's recommendation, the presiding justice of the peace was reducing to $20, $30 or $40, depending on the severity of the offence.

She'd noticed me when I came in and took a seat in one of the pews three rows from the bar. The justice of the peace did too, broke away from the Crown Attorney and, with a perturbed frown on his face, addressed me: "You there, in the third row, in the Hawaiian shirt. No gum chewing in court," and waited until I'd removed the half piece of Trident "Tropical Fruit" gum from my mouth before proceeding.

Things off to a rather shaky start with His Honour, they got worse when the Crown requested a few moments with me outside the courtroom. She sat me down, glanced at her BlackBerry (I think this was why she actually wanted a break) and let me know that all she had to do was prove that I hadn't bought a ticket and I'd have to pay the fine.

I explained that that wasn't the reason I wanted a trial. Officers 87 and 76 had abused and harassed me and, if nothing else, I wanted the opportunity to present my side of the story to a judge in hopes that he'd see that justice wasn't served, and acquit me. I said I was prepared to go ahead with a trial, which the court-clerk's office had notified me was to take place today. I'd requested Constable 76 to appear in court as well, but I'd noticed on the way out only 87 was present; hence my need for an adjournment.

The Crown constantly checked her BlackBerry while I was talking, like she was awaiting an urgent message; she asked to have a look at my two tickets. I handed them over, she gave them a cursory glance then told me that when I went before the JP, I was to ask for an adjournment — adding that a trial couldn't be held today, anyway. This was "plea court." Nobody ever requested a trial for transit offences. The fines were always substantially reduced.

I asked how substantially mine would be, if I pleaded guilty.

"I could probably go as low as $250 for the pair," she said.

"Still too much for me. I'm a writer. I have no money to pay a fine whatever the amount."

"Well," she said, giving me a sympathetic look as she stood up, "you'll just have to hope the JP grants you an adjournment so you can prepare for trial. It would have to be," she consulted her BlackBerry, "July 19th. Could you do that?"

"I could," I said, and we headed into the courtroom, the Crown pausing as I held the door open for her to check her BlackBerry one last time.

I had just sat down when the Crown waved at me urgently to come forward and take the stand. She explained to the justice of the peace that I wanted an adjournment; he turned to me, not pleased, and asked on what grounds.

"There were two constables involved in my arrest, Your Honour, number 87 and number 76. I see Number 87 is here, but number 76 is not present in the courtroom."

"You're supposed to be prepared for a trial today."

"I *am* prepared for a trial today, Your Honour, but with number 76 not in court, I don't find it possible to proceed. Hence my request for an adjournment."

"And this number 76 was involved, you say."

"Fully, Your Honour."

He mulled this over for a moment, as if it was a point of jurisprudence he'd never come across before.

"There are no fine reductions if you lose at trial."

"I realize that, Your Honour."

"As there's normally only one officer of record in cases like this, I'm going to deny your request for the adjournment."

"Whatever you say, Your Honour," I said. "But since I don't stand a chance of getting a fair trial without testimony from Number 76, I'll just go ahead and plead guilty right now."

Caught off guard by the sudden plea, the Crown looked over at me in wide-eyed surprise. She recovered quickly and said something to the judge I couldn't quite hear. The judge looking annoyed, whatever it was, he turned to me and announced that at the request of the Crown, the charges against me had been dropped. I was free to go.

I'd been listening to what people were saying when they made their guilty pleas, and the first and most important of the three questions put to them by the judge was whether they were making this guilty plea of their own free will. Since I would have had to answer No to the question, the case would have to go to trial and my adjournment request would have to have been allowed — and all this because I'd failed to buy a $7.95 train ticket on Easter morning.

Court-business proceeding, I stepped down from the stand and headed for the doors; spotted Number 87 sitting on the bench at the back of the room with about a dozen other transit cops. I caught his eye, flashed him a smile and a Peace sign, and went out. I glanced back into the courtroom while holding the door for a woman exiting behind me, and noticed the judge with his eyes on me and an irascible scowl on his face, as if he were saying to himself: "Gum chewers . . ."

I sent Malcolm an email later that day to let him know about my successful appearance at court. He wrote back congratulating me; said I'd obviously acquitted myself with aplomb and maybe had a second career ahead of me as a defence lawyer, adding that of course there wasn't much money in it these days, though he said it did pay better than writing.

He said he didn't want to dampen the victory celebration, but he'd heard the other day that my good brother John had been charged with possession of stolen goods — an Audi convertible he gave to this woman he's been living with, Connie Something, a town-planner in Brampton, apparently. He'd leased the car from a dealer in Newmarket but, surprise surprise, hadn't bothered making the payments and now the dealership wanted its car back. Plus it came to light, in the police spot-check, that he had several counts of forging and uttering hanging over him in Toronto court, $20,000 in cheques that he'd signed in someone else's name. It was this Connie woman who had called him up, Malcolm said. John, behind bars in the Brampton jail, wanting her to ask if he could retain him for his defence. 'With what?' Malcolm apparently asked her, telling her it wouldn't be the first time John had bilked him for his services. Connie said she couldn't blame Malcolm in the least; John was into her for about $200,000. She'd been thinking of booting him out anyway, since he was starting to cadge money from her neighbours, twenty or thirty dollars here and there, for booze she guessed. With the bottles she'd found hidden around the house, she said she was convinced the guy was a full-blown alcoholic now. The straw that broke the camel's back, Malcolm said, was that while Connie had been at work during the day, John had begun an affair with a female real-estate agent who was selling a house down the street from Connie's. She and Malcolm agreed that he'd just have to represent himself — at least until he found a lawyer who didn't mind accepting bum cheques!

Maybe it was my brush with the law over the train ticket, the harried, let's-make-a-deal Crown attorney and the tetchy justice of the peace, but it was about this time I began having real fears about the book being published. I was airing intimate and shocking family history, whistle-blowing on the justice system, the police and the civil service. Even riskier, I was coming clean with my admissions about marijuana and my attitudes toward it. Pot has been so demonized and criminalized, and the paranoia around all things cannabis has become so heightened these days, that most people lower their voices when speaking the word, can't bring themselves to say it on the phone or in email, and resort to code language and other forms of subterfuge if they do talk about it at all. Yet here I was standing up and publicly proclaiming that not only did I use marijuana on a somewhat regular basis, I grew my own plants, and did so in my own house. Would the police come looking for me? I wondered. The courts? The Social Services departments I'd been affiliated with? Would people who I'd mentioned in the book sue me for libel? Would there be repercussions for my children that I wasn't able to foresee? Above all, would anyone out there actually understand my story and appreciate the things I was trying to say?

Dread, guilt and increasingly severe panic attacks chipped away at my confidence. It took days before I could accept that a paragraph was as good as it should be. Then it was sentences that I felt I could never get "just so." When it came to the point that I was spending several hours on a single word, back and forth between dictionary and thesaurus but never happy with the results, the message sank in. I decided enough was enough; that for the sake of basic personal stability I simply had to abandon the book. I shut my computer down and wouldn't go near it. Moped around the house feeling sorry for myself, bemoaned my feeble literary talent, berated myself for having failed to meet my own expectations. That I might have set them too high in the first place never occurred to me. I was too steeped in feelings of self-reproach, shame and inadequacy to think straight or see things clearly. All the sacrifices I'd made, the thousands of hours of work I'd put in over the last three years or so, and what did I have to show for it?

Then, after an agonizing six days, I received an email from my writer-friend Dave Kingsmill, who had been reading sections of the book as I went along. He said he hadn't heard from me recently, and was wondering how things were going. I wrote back that I'd run out of steam, that I'd quit writing the memoir and this time it was for good. "I've lost my way, Dave. I'm getting nowhere, and the frustration and doubt are killing me." With replies like "You can't!" "Don't be an idiot!" and "I'm getting in my car right now to come over there and slap some sense into you!" it was Dave, despite a complicated situation of his own (he'd survived a liver transplant three years ago and his ninety-three-year-old, Alzheimer's-ridden mother was living with him and his wife), who managed to pry me out of my funk and inspire me to get working again. "It's shitty at times," he agreed. "But nobody said it was going to be easy. Fuck 'em if they don't understand. That's their problem, not yours. You have a good book on your hands here, Paul. Just *write* it."

Easier said than done, but I knew Dave was right. I put a new work routine together for myself and didn't waver in sticking to it. I stayed away from television, newspapers and the internet the way I had at Russ's. I got into the habit of drinking more Lapsang Souchong tea and less Tim Hortons coffee, with the exception of a medium decaf that I'd pick up at about 6:30 and take with me on my early morning stroll through the hospital grounds. I'd sit in the gazebo overlooking the lake for ten or fifteen minutes, then cut across the beach over to Whitby harbour and walk out to the lighthouse at the end of the pier, where I'd read a passage from my Pema Chodron book, *When Things Fall Apart*, passages that had always cheered me up in the past, and which did so again. "Relax and lighten up," and "Go toward the things that scare you," two of her more important pieces of advice, that's exactly what I tried to do.

I worked through the summer's three major heat waves, and despite having only one fan available and our air conditioner on the fritz, I managed to keep my cool whenever the power went off (always during thunderstorms, frequently on hotter days) and I lost material before I'd had a chance to save it. Money was tight, so Nicky and I went back to eating our $15-a-night dinners — spaghetti and salad, the occasional shepherd's pie or sometimes homemade macaroni and cheese — bumping the budget to $20 if Patrick was going to be eating with us. I took five days off in early August to sell Larch Wood cutting boards with Don at a trade show out by the airport, but got back on track with no problem (the $800 he paid me doing wonders for my motivation) and stayed at the computer with only a few breaks from dawn to dusk for the next two weeks, weary, worn down and worried that I was simply going to run out of energy one day, still with the rumblings of wanting to quit, but keeping them at bay more easily now that I was heading into the home stretch.

Finally, after almost four years of long days and more sleepless nights than I care to remember, living in eight different houses, working on five borrowed but not so great computers, thirty pounds lighter than I'd been when I began the book, "good fighting weight" my friend Dave kidded me, I typed the period on the memoir's final sentence at 1:52 a.m. according to my clock radio, September 3, my sixty-second birthday.

I pressed "Save" for the last time, closed the file on the final chapter, shut down my computer and sat there for several minutes staring at the dark screen, letting the feeling sink in that I was actually done. No trumpet fanfares, no kettledrum crescendos or jubilant cymbal bursts, just a moment of calm after what had seemed an awfully long storm.

Wide awake, not sleepy at all, I set the alarm on my clock radio, washed my face, brushed my teeth then got into bed and started a new chapter in a biography of William Faulkner that I was reading, this one — appropriately, it seemed to me — about the writing of the book for which he'd won the Nobel Prize, *Light in August*.

I dozed and read about Faulkner off and on through the night, until I found myself sitting on the edge of the bed, still wide awake when the radio came on at 5:45, a Mumford & Sons tune playing in the darkness while I got dressed.

Ready to do what I'd promised myself I would when the manuscript was completed, I grabbed the knapsack I'd packed before I went to bed, took my compass out of my shaving kit and slipped it into one of the pockets and went downstairs. I groped around on the kitchen counter looking for the car keys (Patrick was sleeping on the living-room couch so I didn't want to turn on the lights), found them and slipped quietly out the front door.

Fog enveloping the neighbourhood, the streetlights still on, I went to the backyard, took Patrick's yellow fibreglass canoe down from its fence-rack, centre-flipped it onto my shoulders and carried it out to the Ranger; strapped it on the truck bed, tossed in the paddle and drove down to the hospital grounds. I parked in the east lot, slung the knapsack over my shoulders, unstrapped the canoe, flipped it up and portaged it the hundred or so yards down to the beach that abuts the east side of the hospital grounds.

The fog was even heavier over the water. I shoved off and jumped in the canoe, sat in the bow seat facing the stern; let myself glide while I got out the compass, took a bearing for south-southeast (straight out into the lake) and started paddling through the fog, my eyes on the compass, which I had sitting on the floor of the canoe in front of me.

I continued paddling for about ten minutes, until I figured I was about half a mile from shore, at which point I stopped, put the paddle down, opened the knapsack and took out the brown-leather copy of *Bleak House* my Grandma Illidge had given me for my birthday fifty-three years ago. With two flat rocks duct-taped to the covers now so it would be sure to sink, I leaned over the side of the canoe, set it in the water and, as I wouldn't be needing it anymore, let it go.

This book is dedicated to my parents:

Beverley Elizabeth Shea
(1923–2005)

John Milton Illidge
(1923–1994)

To my son Nicholas, without whose courage
and un-detoured spirit this book wouldn't
have been written.

To David Kingsmill, FRPI, whose friendship,
discerning eye and ready humour helped me
keep things in perspective.

To the friends who believed in what I was
doing and generously provided me with
places to live and work. I thank you all.